So Good...
Make You Slap
Your Mama!

II

Enjoy!
Marlyn Monette

by Marlyn Monette

For more articles and recipes by Marlyn Monette, see her column in
The Times. To subscribe call (318) 459-3322,
1-(800) 525-4335 or visit www.shreveporttimes.com.

The Times
shreveporttimes.com

222 Lake Street
Shreveport, LA 71101

ISBN 0-9673339-1-1

Copyright 2005
By Marlyn Monette (318-868-5804)

First Printing
5,000 copies printed — November 2005

Testimonials:

"So Good...Make You Slap Your Mama! Cookbook author, Marlyn Monette took Historic Jackson, Louisiana by storm. Milbank Historic House and Bed & Breakfast played host at a book-signing event where Marlyn's charm, wit, unique literary style and delightful culinary concoctions kept guests enthralled for the better part of the day -- in other words, a good time was had by all. We await her newest publication with great anticipation and look forward to more stories about "Mama" and taste testing family treasures."

        Marjorie Collamer, Manager
        Pat Tolle
        Milbank Historic House
        Jackson, Louisiana

"Every so often, God puts certain people in your life for a reason. My time with Mama, aka Marlyn Monette, was one of the best times of my life! We shared several years in the kitchen at Occasions Catering during the development of *So Good..Make You Slap Your Mama."* The laughter and tears were unrivaled. We both were in need of "Depends" a few times. The cookbook is truly a reflection of her soul. Her love of family, her humor and her fabulous recipes are packed into that extraordinary book. I cannot wait to see what she has brewed up in this new *"Slap Your Mama*...Volume II."

        Susan B. Nance
        Fredericksburg, Texas

"We have thoroughly enjoyed using Marlyn's *So Good..Make You Slap Your Mama!* cookbook in our restaurant—all the way from her Banana Pudding to the Carolina Shrimp Grits! Her flavoring fits our customers' pallets perfectly. We specialize in catering meals to-go, and her dishes are just what our busy customers need. This amazing collection of recipes is a must have for any kitchen!"

        Elizabeth Hennigan, Owner
        Bon Appetit-Shreveport, Louisiana

Testimonials

"I was born and raised in South Louisiana (Lafayette). Imagine my excitement to find a kindred spirit upon moving to Shreveport/Bossier. Throughout my years of ownership in my own Cajun specialty meat market, Marlyn was an invaluable resource and a great friend to me. Her down home style of cooking and "joie de vivre" (joy of life) are contagious. The Slap Your Mama cookbook was hard to keep on the shelves, and this book is sure to be an even greater success. I can't wait to get my copy! Laissez les bon temps rouler, baby!"

Tommy Meaux
The French Market, former owner

"Marlyn, we both love the cookbook... we have talked it up quite a bit at the Inn and, of course, your article has been shown to everyone!! The best thing about your cookbook besides the recipes, of course, was getting to know you and your family. We almost feel like we could come to family dinner and know you all! We have made several recipes for our families, as well as the Inn, and get absolutely rave reviews every time! We cannot wait to read the next one... and actually we look forward to your next visit more than anything. Marlyn, you are an inspiration! Come back down and see us soon!"

Liz Wilkerson, Manager and Chef
Deb Phillips, Chef
Inn on the Creek and Absolute Charm Properties
Fredericksburg, TX

"Marlyn's recipes are best described as yummy efforts seasoned with wit and cooked up in a pot of simplicity. She's fun to read, and her creations will have you clamoring for more."

Vic Parker, Editor
Jefferson Jimplecute
Jefferson, Texas

"So Good..Make You Slap Your Mama! I say, *So Good...Make Me Slap...OFFICIAL* Cookbook of The Pulpwood Queens Book Clubs. That is, until we write one of our own! Anybody who can cook like Marlyn and then give us those recipes—you would be a complete fool to not walk, but run to your nearest bookstore to buy a copy!"

Kathy L. Patrick, Founder
The Pulpwood Queens Book Clubs
Jefferson, Texas

"Many adventures, most associated with good eats and hilarity, have come from our 20-year friendship with Marlyn and Ed Monette. Marlyn's sharp wit, culinary skills, and love for people come forth in her fine cookbooks (her "babies"). We wish her much love and success."

Linda and John Endicott
The Design Center
Marshall, Texas

$\mathcal{D}edication\ldots$

This cookbook is lovingly dedicated to my ninety-nine-year-old mother, Mildred Jumel White—the treasure of our family.

To my mother, every person she met was buried treasure to be discovered and enjoyed. Differences were a source of delight. Judgments and makeovers have never been her thing. We were nurtured—Dad, children, grandchildren, great-grandchildren—with an unconditional love that was gentle and simple, yet powerful.

Mom came from an old South Louisiana family with a rich history. When we were small, my Mom regaled my brother Scotty and me with tales of her family, the Jumels. She brought to life these proud ancestors who helped shape Louisiana's history.

A graduate of the class of 1923, Mom is the oldest living alumni of Baton Rouge High School. After attaining a two-year accounting degree at L.S.U., she was bookkeeper for Union Federal Savings and Loan for six years until she started her family. She excelled at everything she did, but her best achievement was wife and mother.

I have many wonderful memories of Mom and her influence on my life. Mom loved the movies, and every Saturday she took me downtown to a matinee. When the movie ended, we enjoyed a lovely lunch, followed by an afternoon of shopping and browsing. She was my beacon of sunshine—it was no wonder all my friends wanted her for their own!

Mom has lived at the Glen since it opened in 1986. Several months ago, I dropped in about 8:00 one evening and saw Mom going down the hall in her wheelchair. She was stopping at the door of each resident's room. Curious, I followed her. This wonderful person was peeking in each room, blowing a kiss and saying, "Goodnight, I love you."

My story—the cooking, the entertaining, the food writing—are all wrapped around my mama. When it came to making a house a home, she was the best. Mom was always prepared for unexpected guests—and there were plenty of those! A familiar scene was her huge black iron pot bubbling on the stove—full of gumbo, shrimp Creole , étouffée, or fish courtbouillon. I can still smell the aroma of her luscious devil's food cakes baking in the oven. My brother and I wouldn't even give her time to ice them—we would cut a slab and I'd pour Hershey's syrup on mine, while Scotty smeared his with marshmallow crème. Nothing has ever tasted that good—then or now!

These days, I hug and kiss Mom a lot! There's something I need and will never stop needing and that is my mama. And, although her mind has dimmed, and she's getting a little tired, to all the folks who stop to visit with her, she says, "I love you." And, I'm happy to say her wit is still there. Recently, I said, "Mom, you look ravishing today." Her reply was, "Do I? I didn't know I still had it in me!"

 My mother never wrote a cookbook, but she did write the story of her family's lives. It is written in her children's happiness and their feelings of self-worth and acceptance. It's written in the knowledge that they are loved. The story she has written is one that will be with us always.

Thomas Wolfe said, "You can't go home again." I disagree…you can always go home in the memories you carry in your heart.

Acknowledgments . . .

It is through the editorial effort of my friend, Beverly Pierce, that *So Good..Make You Slap Your Mama! Volume II* came into print. Her vast help with proof reading, editing, organizing, and recipe testing was ongoing until its completion. I am forever grateful for her insistence on excellence, and for her "prodding and pushing." Thank you, dear Bev!

For the final book proofing, I thank my friend, Rivers Wallace. Rivers is a retired English teacher, as well as a gourmet cook. She was forewarned that some of my colloquialisms would most likely cause her hair to stand on end. She took on the job with her usual gusto! Thanks, Rivers!

My computer advisors were my special "kids," Shelley Braswell and Tom Chavanne. They were there to help with each crisis. My daughter Debbie, set up the format and chapters for the book. Granddaughter Sara Grace diligently reviewed pictures with me for hours in the beginning phases of the book, then daughter Donna and granddaughter Jill were here to help with the final picture set up. My son Danny checked out each change as I emailed what was to be "the final chapter." They all lent much moral support.

Then, there's my best friend, my supportive husband Ed who ate leftovers for three months, pitched in with household chores and did most of the grocery shopping. His patience and support were always there for me. How blessed I am to have this wonderful man in my life.

Table of Contents

Introduction...

Six years ago, I wrote my first cookbook—*So Good..Make You Slap Your Mama!* It was written as a tribute to my mother, Mildred Jumel White, my children, Debbie, Donna, and Danny, and to my husband Ed. My treasured recipes went into the pages of that cookbook and, to my delight, six years later, almost eleven thousand copies have been sold.

When I began working on Volume II, I had no idea what a challenge it would be. After all, I had one cookbook under my belt and surely a second would be like "rolling off a log". As it turned out, the writing of that second cookbook has been a labor of love...and hate. I voluntarily became a virtual prisoner in my home office. Luckily, I have great friends and attentive family members, so with their help, the book is finally in print.

In the beginning phase of a book—whether a novel or a cookbook—there are so many possibilities. The empty pages are challenging, and there you have a world of options. With each little detail you choose, with each chapter you complete, your options become smaller. When it's finally finished, you find that after all these long months, you are sad to let your "baby" go! Or it could be a touch of dementia from all the tedious work.

As to the unlikely title of this cookbook—*So Good..Make You Slap Your Mama!,* let me assure you it is simply an old South Louisiana phrase and in no way suggests any disrespect for mothers. Mamas are never, ever slapped in our genteel South! On the contrary, this title is simply a pat on the back for Mama for creating a dish or meal that is out-of-this world delicious!

Writing about food is simply my way to communicate what I feel about life. I believe an inviting table elevates the pleasure of eating into the art of dining. I grew up in a home where the kitchen was the heart of the home. That is where I acquired the gift of making people feel welcome and special—from both my mother and my father. I, in turn, passed this gift on to my children.

The beauty and wonder of life are not the big moments like weddings, reunions and parties. Those are just the punctuation marks. The beauty of life is in the simple things like sharing an evening meal—gathered around the dinner table with family, relating the events of the day and enjoying good food. The wonder is in the fun of friends and family cooking together, visiting and chatting in a warm, steamy kitchen. The words "cozy" and "comfort" describe those memorable experiences very nicely.

The simple acts of chopping vegetables, frying onions in hot oil and listening to the sizzle...all of this is enormously calming to me. I adore grocery shopping and can spend hours browsing the shelves. I sometimes fall into wonderful conversations with fellow shoppers—learning what they like to eat, some of the fantastic dishes they prepare and we often end up exchanging recipes.

Good cooking, and dining with kindred friends and family are all about being deliciously alive! Nothing is so fulfilling as entertaining in your own home, preparing marvelous dishes. Begin today using the fine china and crystal that's been stored since your wedding day—why wait for tomorrow?

As for the recipes, I never saw a cookbook until I got married, for my mom had all her specialties in her head...and in her heart. Through the years, I've come to the conclusion that there is no such thing as an "original" recipe. Everything for the past 100 years is simply a variation. Each recipe in this book has its own story, and when you use it, it becomes your story...your memories.

Justin Daniel Herpin

Appetizers

My *Food Lover's Companion* defines Hors D'oeuvres as "small savory appetizers...usually one-or-two-bite size...can be cold or hot...may be in the form of a fancy canapé or as simple as crudités."

Having been in the catering business for five years (a time which I refer to as my "five years hard labor"), I feel qualified to give you some advice on hosting a party.

When entertaining in your home, there are four basic rules to follow:

> 1. Keep the menu finger foods—no forks, no juggling plates.
> 2. Serve easy to eat foods. Have you ever had a slab of meat slapped on a roll that just got bigger and bigger the longer you chewed on it? It's not a pretty sight.
> 3. Make ahead—enjoy your party, leave only finishing touches for the last minute.
> 4. Choose a menu you are comfortable with. It is not the time to try a new recipe—stick with tried and true.

The appetizers in this chapter are designed to entice both the novice cook and the seasoned gourmet chef. Folks are busy these days and they are generally looking for something that is simple to prepare, yet delicious and beautifully presented.

Hosting a cocktail party is fun, for that is where you can "strut your stuff" with a variety of foods that appeal to all tastes. Molds and patés are perfect "stretchers" as they will feed the multitudes. A six-cup shrimp mold will feed about fifty people. Canapés that can be made ahead and frozen will only require a quick run through the oven to be hot and enticing. Cheese trays are lovely, heaped with fresh fruit. For a party sweet tray, make your motto: Keep it neat and not too sweet. Kahlua Brownies, Lemon Squares, and Pecan Tassies (see Index) are perfect sweets for party trays.

When I finished this chapter, my daughter Deb told me, "Mama, you've got too many appetizers—you should write a party book!" I washed her mouth out with soap!

PARTY BREADS

This chapter is all about gastronomic pleasures shared with friends in a social atmosphere. It's only fitting that I kick off with probably the most important ingredient to make every party special, whether it be a casual patio party or a formal reception for dignitaries—party breads!

Party breads come in many disguises: toast points, bruschetta, crostini, pita, English muffins, tortillas, baguettes... If I had to choose one item that is vital to a party, it would be toast points. Years ago, I was able to purchase large bags of these crispy buttered bread treats from my local grocer. One day when I called to order several bags, my friendly grocer broke the sad news: "The machine that made these gems has broken down...no more toast points." Alas! After combing area stores, I learned you can purchase gourmet toast points—garlic, onion, sundried tomato, basil—but the unflavored variety is not to be found. That was the day I began making my own. Now, let me warn you—there's a trick to baking perfect toast points, for they must be crispy, without being hard as brickbats. Beware of too much butter, for then they are soggy...you get the picture. Mine are not always perfect, but I think you'll like them. Make up a big batch and put them in airtight containers—they will keep fresh for two or three weeks. For a longer period, throw them in the freezer.

TOAST POINTS

2 freshly baked baguettes 2 sticks butter, melted
  or small French bread loaves Parsley flakes, to taste

Cut baguettes or loaves into about 1/4-inch rounds. Place on cookie sheets, sides touching. Add parsley flakes to melted butter and brush on bread rounds—not too heavily, but enough to taste. Place in a 275-degree oven and bake about 20-30 minutes, until golden and crisp. Check on them often while they are baking, making sure they don't turn brown. When done, remove from oven and cool completely on cookie sheet. Place in double plastic bags or airtight container. Serve with luncheon salads, party dips, cold seafood or cheese molds...
Yield: 150 rounds (approximate)
Note: Baguettes can be hard—I prefer to use French loaves.

BASIC PASTRY DOUGH RECIPE

Now you know how to make toast points.. the next best recipe to have in your files is Basic Dough. You may immediately think of this crust as for desserts only, such as Pecan Tassies (See Index), mini lemon or lime pies, fruit tarts, or a myriad of other wonderful delicacies. Let me assure you, this divine, crispy crust will turn out canapés that will make your mouth water, such as my Crawfish Croustades (See Index). They are great to have on hand in the freezer, either filled or ready to be filled.

1 (8-oz) cream cheese   2 cups all-purpose flour
2 sticks butter,

Place cream cheese and butter in a medium bowl; let soften at room temperature. Work flour into this mixture (with hands) until completely blended. Chill dough for at least one hour. Shape into small one-inch balls of dough; press each ball into an ungreased miniature muffin tin, shaping with fingers to fit up sides of tin. If preparing for freezer, bake in a 350-degree oven for about 20 minutes; after 5 minutes, remove by inverting pan and letting crusts gently drop out on paper towels. When cool, place in an airtight container or double plastic bags and freeze until ready to use. If serving now, fill and bake by recipe instructions.
Yield: 48 crusts

TOASTED NUTS

When a recipe calls for toasted or roasted nuts, many cooks are not sure how to prepare them. Let me say right up front: they burn very quickly! I've lost count of how many charred pecans have gone down my garbage disposal. Here's what I finally came up with:

1-2 lbs. pecans, almonds, walnuts   Butter-flavored spray
  or nuts of choice   Scant salt

Coat a long baking pan with butter spray. Place nuts, single layer, in pan; spray nuts lightly with butter and sprinkle with a little salt. Bake in a 300-degree oven for 5-6 minutes. Remove from oven and let cool.

MARLYN'S TRASH

There's no set recipe for making this wonderful snack—no magic involved. If there's a secret, it's in the seasoned butter, and you can make that as bland or as zesty as your taste buds dictate. It is important to roast trash slowly and toss or stir often, tasting as you go. This is my downfall—over tasting! I often resemble an inflated balloon when my trash is done. You may cut down this recipe for it will feed the multitudes. I bag it in cellophane, tie it with a pretty ribbon and give it to my favorite people just to say "you're special."

Sauce:

4-5 sticks butter	Red pepper, to taste
Tabasco, to taste	Creole or Cajun seasoning
Crushed garlic, to taste	Pinch sugar
1 Tbsp. Worcestershire	

Mix:

1 ½ lbs. pecan halves	2 lg. bags Chex Mix (Regular)
1 lb. whole walnuts	2 boxes Goldfish crackers (plain)
1 lb. whole almonds	1 box Wheat Thins (regular)
1 large can whole cashews	1 box Cheez-Its
1 large bag Gardetto's Snack Mix	

Melt butter in heavy saucepan; add remaining ingredients, tasting for flavor. It may require a little more Worcestershire or Tabasco. Using two turkey roaster pans, pour scant amount of the sauce in the bottom of each pan. Dividing ingredients between the two roasters, add all nuts and toss. Add remaining ingredients, tossing lightly and mixing well. As you toss, drizzle more sauce over mixture, looking for dry spots. Sprinkle a little garlic powder and seasoned salt as you toss, if you desire.

Place in a 275-300 degree oven; bake for a total of about 1-1/2 hours, stirring or tossing every 15 minutes. As you toss, garlic and other dry seasonings may be added, but go lightly on the salt.

Note: Let cool completely before putting trash in containers.

SWEET PARTY MIX

This sweet version of trash is very popular among the young crowd. The orange flavor blended with brown sugar adds a sweet tang to the mix. Feel free to add other mix ingredients if you choose.

Sauce:
1/4 cup butter, melted   1/4 cup frozen orange juice
1/4 cup brown sugar   concentrate, thawed

Mix:
1 box Corn Chex   1 cup almonds
1 box Wheat Chex   1/2 cup dried cranberries
1 box Rice Chex

Mix butter, brown sugar and orange juice concentrate; heat in microwave. Toss together cereal and almonds. In roaster pan, pour sauce mixture over cereal and toss well. Bake in a 300-degree oven for 30 minutes, stirring after first 15 minutes. Stir in cranberries and cool.

ROSEMARY CASHEWS

For gifts of snack food, these well-seasoned cashews fit the bill perfectly. This recipe comes from my cousin, Jeanne Marie Peet, who first sampled them at a wedding reception. She claims to have eaten a whole pound by herself. The first time I made them, it only took a taste to see why Jeanne ate so many, for they are delightfully addictive.

1 lb. whole cashews   1/2 tsp. cayenne pepper
2 Tbsps. fresh rosemary sprigs,   2 Tbsps. brown sugar
  chopped   1 Tbsp. butter, melted

Preheat oven to 350 degrees. Spread cashews out on a sheet pan with sides. Toast until warm—about five minutes. In a large bowl, combine rosemary, cayenne, brown sugar, and melted butter. Toss cashews with spiced butter; cool and store. Delicious served warm!

BRIE WITH RUM PECAN SAUCE

This is great to keep on hand for unexpected guests. The sweet, praline flavored sauce will keep in the refrigerator for several weeks—just heat in microwave and pour over brie. It's delicious on vanilla ice cream!

1 (16 oz.) Brie

Sauce:
1/4 cup butter   1/4 cup dark rum
2 cups brown sugar   1 tsp. vanilla
1 (12 oz.) can evaporated milk   1 cup coarsely chopped pecans

Scrape rind off top of Brie, leaving ¼" rim at edges. Melt butter in heavy saucepan; add brown sugar, and evaporated milk, mixing well. Cook over medium heat, stirring constantly until thickened, about 10 minutes. Add rum, vanilla and pecans; cook an additional 10 minutes until thick. Drizzle hot sauce over Brie; serve with crackers.
Yield: 25-30 servings

JAN'S CAMEMBERT

This delectable cheese dish is guaranteed to draw raves at your next party. I first tasted it at an L.S.U. tailgate party. Not only is it delicious, but the colorful cranberries and apricot preserves lend eye appeal. Thanks go to Jan LeBleu of Baton Rouge for this treat.

1/4 to 1/2 lb. Camembert or   1/4 cup dried cranberries
   Brie cheese wheel   1/4 cup chopped pistachios
1/4 cup apricot preserves

Place cheese wheel on a serving plate; top with preserves. Add a layer of dried cranberries and top with pistachios. Serve with toast points, crackers or apple slices.

For a moist cheese mold, always use freshly grated cheese.
Packaged grated or shredded cheese tends to dry out.

STRAWBERRY BRIE
A favorite for ladies' teas—delicate and creamy.

1 (1 lb.) Brie or Camembert   1 Tbsp. frozen strawberries
1 (3 oz.) cream cheese

Mix cream cheese and strawberries until fluffy, not runny. Scrape white coating off top and sides of Brie. Spread cream cheese mixture on top and sides; garnish top with fresh strawberries and mint. Serve with ginger snaps or buttery crackers.
Yield: 20 servings

CHUTNEY CHEESE MOLD
Cheese is greatly enhanced when fruit is added. This mold freezes well.

1 cup coarsely chopped pecans   1 small onion, finely chopped
1 lb. sharp Cheddar,   1 (8 oz.) pkg. cream cheese
 finely shredded   1/2 cup Major Grey's chutney

In a 300-degree oven, roast pecans for 5 minutes. Mix pecans, Cheddar, onion, and cream cheese, blending well. Place in a greased mold. Cut chutney in small pieces and pour over mold. Serve with crackers.

VEGETABLE CHEESE BALL
This old standby is still delicious—anyway you slice it!

3 (8-oz.) pkgs. cream cheese   1 small can chopped mushrooms
1 bunch green onions, chopped   1 small can chopped ripe olives
1 small jar diced pimientos   1 small jar chopped dried beef

Drain pimiento, mushrooms and chopped olives; shred dried beef. Mix all ingredients together; blend well. Form into a ball; refrigerate. Serve with assorted crackers.

CHEESE STRAWS

Cheese straws are a bit time consuming to make, but are well worth the effort. They fit in well with any party menu and are ideal for gift giving at holidays.

2 ½ sticks butter, softened
1 lb. sharp Cheddar cheese, grated
2 ½ cups flour
1/4 cup yellow cornmeal

2 tsps. baking powder
1 ½ tsps. garlic salt
1 ½ tsps. cayenne pepper

Blend butter with grated cheese, using your hands to distribute evenly. Measure and sift dry ingredients together; mix well. Incorporate dry mixture with cheese mixture. When well mixed, put into a cookie press and pipe out in slender strips on a cookie sheet that has been coated with non-stick spray. Bake in a 350-degree oven for 12-15 minutes. Do not overbake. Let cool and cut into lengths desired.
Note: If you do not have a cookie press, shape the dough into rolls, wrap and refrigerate for one hour. To bake, thinly slice and bake on sprayed cookie sheet.
Yield: 100 small straws (approximately)

BLUE CHEESE PUFFS

2 (8 oz.) pkgs. cream cheese
1 cup Hellmann's mayonnaise
1/4 cup green onion tops,
   finely chopped
1 cup crumbled blue cheese

1/2 tsp. cayenne pepper
1 loaf thinly sliced whole wheat
   bread
Paprika

Mix softened cream cheese and mayonnaise. Stir in green onions, blue cheese and cayenne pepper; set aside. Using a 2-inch round biscuit cutter, cut bread slices into rounds. Spread 1 tablespoon of cheese mixture on each round. Place puffs on a cookie sheet and bake in a 350-degree oven for 15 minutes. Sprinkle with paprika and serve immediately. These puffs may be frozen.
Yield: 30 rounds

ISLAND DELIGHT

My first reaction to this unusual combination was "toss it." Instead I decided to take it to a Hawaiian luau. It drew raves, both for flavor and presentation.

1 fresh pineapple
2 (8 oz.) pkgs. cream cheese
2 cans fruit cocktail,
  well drained

1 bunch green onion tops,
  chopped fine
Hellmann's mayonnaise for
  consistency

Scoop insides from pineapple, reserving ¼ cup pulp for filling. Mix all other ingredients; add reserved pineapple and put in pineapple shell to serve. Delicious with wheat crackers.
Yield: 40 servings

ONION AND CHEESE DIP

This is a great recipe to have in your files—you just throw it together and pop in the oven!

1 cup finely chopped sweet onion
1/2 cup Hellmann's mayonnaise
1/2 cup Swiss cheese grated

1/2 to 1/4 tsp. hot pepper sauce
1/4 cup grated Parmesan cheese
Paprika for top

Mix onions, mayonnaise, Swiss cheese and hot pepper sauce. Spread into a small baking dish or pie plate. Sprinkle with Parmesan cheese; bake in a 350-degree oven for 30 minutes until hot and bubbly. This dip is delicious with buttery crackers.

*Party dips were introduced in the '50's when an
innovative cook tried mixing onion soup mix with sour cream.
Look how far we've come today! The grocery shelves are filled with a
wide variety of hot and cold dips to suit even the most
discriminating palate. We've come a long way, baby!*

HOT BROCCOLI DIP

It wasn't until the late 60's that hot dips served in a chafer became popular. Until that time, cold dips, canapés and nuts were the usual party fare. It is believed that the hot broccoli dip was the first of its kind. After disappearing from the social scene for many years, it seems to be making a comeback. I'm glad because it is a very delicious appetizer.

1/2 stick butter	2 cans cream of mushroom soup
6 stalks celery, chopped	2 rolls garlic cheese
1 large onion, chopped	1 can sliced water chestnuts
1/2 lb. mushrooms, sliced	1 small pkg. sliced almonds,
2 pkgs. frozen chopped broccoli	toasted

Melt butter in a large Dutch oven; sauté celery, onion and mushrooms until soft. Cook broccoli as directed on package and drain well. Combine with the veggies and mushrooms; add mushroom soup. When piping hot and well mixed, add garlic cheese that has been cut into cubes. When cheese is melted, fold in drained water chestnuts and toasted almonds. Let simmer on low heat until flavors combine, being careful not to let burn on bottom. Serve in chafing dish with Melba rounds or toast points.
Yield: 30 servings

SPINACH/ARTICHOKE DIP

My daughter Donna has created a winner for your next gathering. With its profusion of flavors and light and airy texture, this dip is sublime.

1 (9-oz.) pkg. frozen creamed spinach, thawed	1/4 tsp. white pepper
	1 tsp. fresh lemon juice
3/4 cup freshly grated Parmesan (reserve ¼ cup for topping)	1 cup shredded mozzarella cheese
1 (14 oz.) can artichoke hearts, drained and chopped	

Combine all ingredients; place in a sprayed baking dish. Top with reserved Parmesan cheese. Bake in a 350-degree oven until hot and bubbly. Serve with toast points, Melba rounds, or wheat crackers.

MUSHROOM PATÉ

This paté is perfect for wedding receptions and cocktail parties. It can be doubled, tripled..multiplied to your party needs. For the folks who are not fond of liver, it is a welcome change. Since the brown specks of the mushroom tend to give the paté an unattractive color, it is fun to make an "icing" for it and dress it up with flowers, herbs, etc. This transforms a "plain paté" into a "feast for the eyes."

1/2 lb. fresh, chopped mushrooms   1 (8 oz.) pkgs. cream cheese,
2 Tbsps. butter   Frosting (see below)

Sauté mushrooms in butter until liquid has evaporated. Process all ingredients until smooth. Place in a pretty glass bowl, shaping into a dome; refrigerate, covered, for at least 4 hours before serving. Serve with toast points or Melba.
Yield: 15-20 servings

Party Version: Double the above ingredients, mix as shown, and place in a plastic wrap lined 8-inch cake pan. Let pate set at least 4 hours. When firmly set, remove paté from pan carefully and place on a pretty party plate. Spread top and sides with frosting:

Frosting:
16 ozs. cream cheese
1 squirt Tabasco
1/8 tsp. garlic powder

Mix together all ingredients and spread on pate. Garnish with parsley, flowers, sliced mushrooms, etc.
Yield: 40 servings (approximate)

*There was a time when all patés were en croute,
which means baked in a pastry.
A paté baked with pastry was called a paté en pot.*

HOT SAUSAGE DIP

1 lb. hot bulk sausage	1 jalapeno pepper, chopped
1 lb. ground chuck	1 large jar Picante sauce
1 lb. Velveeta cheese	1 can cream of mushroom soup

Fry sausage and ground chuck, stirring until broken up well. Add cheese that has been cut in chunks and stir until melted. Fold in chopped jalapeno, Picante sauce and cream of mushroom soup. Serve piping hot in a chafer with corn chips or tortilla chips.

BACON WRAPPED WATER CHESTNUTS

These are absolutely divine! When I make them, I eat the whole batch.

1 (8 oz.) can water chestnuts, drained and cut in half	1/2 cup brown sugar
1/2 cup soy sauce	5 slices bacon, each cut into four pieces

Marinate water chestnuts in soy sauce for 30 minutes. Roll in brown sugar and wrap in bacon pieces; secure with a toothpick. Bake in a 400-degree oven for 20 minutes on a rack in a broiler pan so chestnuts will not sit in bacon drippings. These can be made ahead and reheated for 5 minutes in a 350-degree oven right before serving.

JALAPENO APPETIZERS

10 large jalapeno peppers	10 bacon strips, halved
4 ozs. cream cheese, softened	

Cut jalapeno peppers in half lengthwise; remove seeds. Stuff each half with 2 teaspoons cream cheese. Wrap with bacon and secure with a toothpick. Place on a broiler rack that has been coated with nonstick cooking spray. Bake in a 350-degree oven for 20-25 minutes or until bacon is crisp. Serve piping hot.
Yield: 20 appetizers

SPINACH POM POMS

If you're a fan of Popeye, you will enjoy these party bites. The hot mustard sauce, much like a Chinese mustard is the secret to their success. One bit of advice: If you take a deep breath while you're cooking this tangy sauce, you are guaranteed to choke. Serve these Pom Poms in a chafer with the hot mustard sauce for dipping.

2 pkgs. frozen chopped spinach
2 cups packaged herb-seasoned
   stuffing mix, crushed
1 cup grated Parmesan cheese

1/2 tsp. nutmeg
6 eggs, beaten
3/4 cup butter, softened
Spicy Mustard Sauce

Thaw spinach and drain well, squeezing out all moisture; add remaining ingredients except spicy mustard sauce. Shape into 1-inch balls; refrigerate or freeze at this point. Place on lightly greased baking sheets and bake in a 350-degree oven for 10-15 minutes, until hot. Drain well on paper towels. Serve with toothpicks and Spicy Mustard Sauce.
Yield: 60

Hot Mustard Sauce:
1/3 cup dry mustard
1/2 cup white vinegar

1/2 cup sugar
1 egg yolk

Mix dry mustard and white vinegar in a small bowl. Cover and leave out at room temperature overnight. In a heavy saucepan, combine mustard/vinegar mixture, sugar and egg yolk. Simmer over low heat, stirring until slightly thickened. Cover, cool and store in refrigerator. Serve at room temperature with hot Spinach Pom Poms.
Yield: 1 ½ cups
Note: This sauce will keep in refrigerator for up to one month.

Vegetable canapés are easy on the budget,
and make for a good balance on the party table.

HOT ASPARAGUS ROLLUPS

My friend Beverly Pierce introduced me to these superb canapés several years ago. The blending together of blue cheese, cream cheese, and asparagus provides an unforgettable taste sensation. They are a little time consuming to prepare, but well worth the effort—and the praise!

20 slices thin white bread
3 ozs. blue cheese, softened
8 ozs. cream cheese, softened
1 egg, beaten
1/4 tsp. garlic salt

1/8 tsp. cayenne pepper
1/2 cup finely chopped green onion
20 canned asparagus spears
3/4 cup melted butter
1/2 cup finely chopped parsley

Trim crust from bread slices; flatten with a rolling pin. Mix cheeses, egg, garlic salt, and cayenne. Fold in onions. Spread bread slices generously and evenly with cheese mixture. Roll an asparagus spear in each slice of bread, sealing well by using a little cheese mixture to bind edge to roll. At this point, these can be frozen and thawed as needed. Roll each canapé in butter and place on an ungreased baking sheet. Bake in a 400-degree oven for 15 to 20 minutes until lightly browned. Garnish with chopped parsley.
Yield: 20 sandwiches

PROSCIUTTO SNACK

For an easy filler at a cocktail party, try these delicious bread sticks. Also a treat served with the salad course for an Italian dinner. Very attractive presentation.

12 Italian breadsticks
12 slices Prosciutto or
   thinly sliced honey ham

1/4 cup extra virgin olive oil
4 Tbsps. grated Parmesan or
   Romano cheese

Wrap each breadstick with one slice prosciutto. Brush with olive oil and sprinkle with Parmesan. Bake on a cookie sheet in a 300-degree oven for 15 minutes. Serve warm or cold.

CUCUMBER PINWHEELS

These Cucumber Pinwheels make an attractive presentation at a buffet table, especially for teas. As an added plus, they freeze well. The rolling process can be tedious; therefore, if you're short on time, feel free to simply make them into little sandwiches.

2 cucumbers, grated	1 stick margarine, softened
2 large loaves thin sliced white bread	1 (8 oz.) cream cheese
	1 drop green food coloring
1 jar whole sweet pickles	Dash garlic powder and salt

After grating cucumbers, place in colander and drain, squeezing out all moisture. Place on paper towels and continue draining. While cucumbers are draining, remove crusts from bread. Cut sweet pickles into long, thin strips; set aside. Blend together softened margarine and cream cheese; add food coloring, garlic powder and salt. Taking two slices of bread, overlap bread lengthwise and flatten with a rolling pin, until it is one long piece. Moisten edges of bread in order for them to adhere to one another when rolling. Spread filling on joined bread slices and place pickle strip at edge of long side of bread; roll into a pinwheel and wrap in waxed paper. Repeat procedure with each piece of bread. Place rolls in an airtight container, seal and freeze. To serve: cut partially frozen rolls with a serrated knife into 1-inch circles.
Yield: 90 pinwheels
Variation: For simple, easy-to-make sandwiches, cut crusts from bread and spread with cucumber mixture; cut into quarters and chill.

TORTILLA/HAM ROLLUPS

1 (3-oz.) cream cheese	8 ozs. thinly sliced ham
1 pkg. medium flour tortillas	1/2 cup chopped, drained green
Cayenne pepper, to taste	olives with pimentos

Spread cream cheese on tortillas; sprinkle lightly with cayenne pepper. Place one slice of ham on top and sprinkle with chopped olives; roll tightly. Chill and slice into 3/4-inch rounds. Serve with toothpicks.
Yield: 50 rollups

PARMESAN BREAD ROUNDS

2 (8-oz.) pkgs. cream cheese
3 tsps. minced onion
1 cup Hellmann's mayonnaise
1/2 tsp. cayenne pepper

4 Tbsps. chopped green onion tops
½ cup Parmesan cheese
2 loaves thin white bread

Combine all ingredients, except bread, mixing well. Cut bread into rounds and spread filling on each slice. Place on cookie sheet and bake in a 350-degree oven for 15-20 minutes. Freezes well.
·Yield: 40 appetizers (approx.)

JO ANN'S TOMATO CANAPÉS

These simple canapés are divine in flavor. There's only one catch—they must be served during the fresh tomato season to be truly authentic. My friend Jo Ann Faludi served these one evening before a dinner party. I ate so many, I almost ruined my appetite! Fat chance of that!

1 (8-oz.) pkg. cream cheese
1/2 cup Hellmann's mayonnaise
1/2 lemon, squeezed
1 cup minced pecans

1 loaf white or wheat bread
Small fresh tomato slices
Salt & pepper, to taste

Mix together cream cheese, mayonnaise, lemon juice, and pecans; set aside. Cut 2-inch circles from bread with a biscuit cutter. Spread cream cheese mixture on bread circles, place tomato slice on top and sprinkle lightly with salt & pepper.

*Food guru, James Beard wrote in his first cookbook,
"hors d'oeuvres and canapés are a rite, rather than a course...
their duty is to enchant the eye, please the palate and excite the
flow of gastric juices."*

CURRIED CHICKEN SPREAD

After sampling this wonderful blending of superb flavors at the home of friends Robert and Jeannie Barrett, we were hooked. It soon became a favorite to serve for both cocktail parties and as a luncheon entrée.

2 cups chopped cooked chicken
1 ½ cups almonds, toasted
2 Tbsps. chopped green onion
1/4 cup apricot preserves
8 ozs. cream cheese, softened

1/4 cup Hellmann's mayonnaise
2 tsps. curry powder
Salt, to taste
1 cup shredded coconut (optional)

Process in separate batches the chicken, almonds, and green onions in food processor until very finely chopped. Mix the chicken, almonds, green onions, and preserves in a medium bowl. Blend the cream cheese, mayonnaise, curry powder, and salt in a large bowl; stir in the chicken mixture. Chill thoroughly before serving. The mixture can be shaped into bite-sized balls and rolled in coconut, if desired, or shape into a mound and drizzle additional apricot preserves over it for a very attractive presentation.

APACHE BREAD

This dip is a true crowd pleaser. My friend Amy Prather brought it to a church gathering to welcome newcomers several years ago—it was the hit of the party, with everyone wanting the recipe.

8 oz. cream cheese, softened
3 cups shredded sharp Cheddar
1 small can diced chilies
1/2 lb. chopped ham
1 Tbsp. Worcestershire sauce

Onion powder, to taste
Garlic powder, to taste
Cayenne pepper, to taste
Black pepper, to taste
1 Hawaiian round bread loaf

Blend softened cream cheese with remaining ingredients, blending well. Place in hollowed out Hawaiian bread loaf and bake in a 325-degree oven for approximately 30 minutes. Serve with crackers.
Yield: 20-25 servings (approx.)

SUMMER SAUSAGE BREAD

Planning on giving a party? I've got a crowd pleaser for you! This old recipe is a winner for many reasons—it is delicious, it makes a nice presentation served in a large round bread, and it feeds the multitudes. At Occasions Catering, we made it a practice to bring a Lagnaippe dish to introduce to guests—something that was not on our menu. When this dip was kicked off, it went over like 4th of July fireworks—they loved it! Once when I was catering a cocktail party, I went out to get the bread round so it could be refilled while the second loaf baked. It was gone— the guests had actually eaten the "bowl"!

1 round loaf of crusty bread
8 oz. sharp Cheddar
8 oz. cream cheese, softened
1 ½ cups sour cream
1 ½ cups chopped summer sausage

1/2 cup chopped green onion tops
1/4 cup chopped, seeded jalapeno
   peppers
1 Tbsp. Worcestershire sauce

Remove insides of bread, being careful not to pierce through crust. Tear insides of bread into bite-sized pieces. Bake bread shell about 10 minutes to dry insides; reserve. Mix all remaining ingredients and place in bread cavity. Bake filled bread on cookie sheet in a 325-degree oven for 45 minutes. After first 20 minutes, place bread that has been torn into pieces around shell to let it crisp to use for dipping.
Yield: 20-30 servings

For 60 – 75 servings, triple recipe. This will fill about 3 large loaves. Filling can be baked separately and added when filling gets low in bread shell, but always have an extra scooped out bread on hand, just in case guests begin nibbling on the bread.

For 100 – 150 servings, 5 to 6 times the recipe – same as above.

*The word "Lagniappe" (LAN-yap) is French.
It is used primarily in southern Louisiana.
It means "a little something extra."*

SIMPLE PARTY MEATBALLS

1/4 cup plain bread crumbs
1 lb. ground beef
1 egg, lightly beaten
1/2 tsp. salt

1 tsp. garlic powder
1 (12 oz.) bottle chili sauce
1 (16 oz.) can whole cranberry
   sauce or 6 ozs. grape jelly

Place bread crumbs, beef, egg, salt, and garlic in a large bowl; mix well. Form into 1-inch balls. Place chili sauce and cranberry sauce in a large pot; heat until melted. Add meatballs and bring to a boil. Lower heat to simmer, and partially cover pot. Cook about 1 hour until meatballs are tender.
Yield: 30 meatballs
Note: Grape jelly makes a sweeter version of this sauce.

SAUSAGE BISCUIT BALLS

For an all-time favorite that kids absolutely adore, whip up several batches of this treat and freeze for snack times

1 (10-oz.) sharp cheese, grated
1 lb. bulk pork sausage

3 cups biscuit baking mix

Mix all ingredients well and shape into 1-inch balls. Bake in a 375-degree oven for 15 to 20 minutes. If frozen, set oven at 400 degrees and bake for 20 minutes.

COCKTAIL MEATBALL SAUCE

12 oz. ketchup
1 cup grape jelly
1/8 cup lemon juice

3 tsps. horseradish
Tabasco, to taste
Worcestershire, to taste

Combine all ingredients; serve with meatballs or cocktail sausages in a chafer. For 150 meatballs (5 lbs.) double the recipe.

SHRIMP MOLD

This classic shrimp mold was created by some ingenious chef in the late sixties, and soon became the rage in south Louisiana. My cousin, Deryl Hamilton of Baton Rouge sent it to me, with a note that said, "prepare to be the hit of the party." She was right—I brought it to a gathering of about 50 people and watched it disappear right before my eyes! The next time I made it for a crowd, I decided to show off and add lump crabmeat. Alas! When I unmolded it onto the party plate, I watched it glub, glub, glub right off the plate. The crabmeat had made the mold too juicy to set. That's what I get for showing off.

1 can tomato soup	3/4 cup chopped green onion tops
3 (3-oz.) pkgs. cream cheese	3/4 cup chopped celery
2 pkgs. plain gelatin	3 lbs. boiled, chopped spicy shrimp
1/4 cup cold water	Salt, pepper, Tabasco, to taste
1 cup Hellmann's mayonnaise	Scant mayonnaise

Heat 1 can tomato soup to boiling; add cream cheese. Blend well with electric mixer. Add gelatin that has been dissolved in cold water. Put mixture into refrigerator and let cool for at least 30 minutes. When cool, add mayonnaise, green onion tops, celery, and boiled shrimp. Add salt, pepper and Tabasco to your taste. Pour mixture into a 6-cup mold that has been well-greased with mayonnaise. To serve, unmold on a party plate and serve with crackers.
Yield: 40 servings

SHRIMP CUPS

1 cup grated Cheddar cheese	3 Tbsps. horseradish
1 cup Hellmann's mayonnaise	1 cup cooked shrimp
1/2 cup green onions, chopped	12 slices white bread
2 stalks celery, chopped	1 Tbsp. butter

Mix first 6 ingredients together, blending well. To prepare bread crusts: trim crusts from bread; thinly spread one side with softened butter. Press bread into 12 ungreased muffin cups, buttered side up. Fill cups with shrimp mixture and bake 12 minutes in a 375-degree oven.

SHRIMP PARTY SANDWICHES

These party sandwiches are delicious and simple to make, but don't let the "simple" fool you, for they are in the big league when it comes to truly gourmet flavor.

12 ozs. softened cream cheese
1 small quartered onion
1 can small shrimp, drained
1 Tbsp. Hellmann's mayonnaise

Cayenne pepper, to taste
Salt, to taste
1 large loaf thin sandwich bread

In a food processor, process cream cheese, onion, and shrimp. Blend in mayonnaise and seasonings. Spread on white or wheat bread which has had the crusts removed. Cut into quarters or strips. Refrigerate until serving.
Yield: 44 quarters

SHRIMP CANAPÉS

1 cup chopped cooked shrimp
1 cup grated sharp Cheddar cheese
2 large Kosher dill pickles, grated
1/2 cup Hellmann's mayonnaise
1/2 tsp. Tabasco

1/2 tsp. onion juice
1/2 tsp. black pepper
1/4 tsp. salt
1 clove garlic, minced
2 loaves white or wheat bread

Combine first 9 ingredients, blending well; set aside. With a cookie cutter, cut a 2-inch round from each slice of bread. Place rounds under broiler and toast one side. Spread mixture on toasted side of bread; bake in a 350-degree oven for 15 minutes until hot and bubbly.
Yield: 44 rounds

A good rule of thumb for sandwiches:
1 large loaf makes 11 whole sandwiches
and 44 quartered party sandwiches.

DODIE'S HOT OYSTER DIP

A friend of mine, Dodie Edwards Smith hosts a holiday tree-trimming party each year. How appropriate when she married five years ago that her wedding reception was a tree-trimming party. Guests had a ball placing ornaments on the gigantic fir tree. I know all this, because I was there..catering the happy occasion. Dodie is the ultimate hostess with her very own style—and a vast recipe library. This hot oyster delicacy is my favorite of all Dodie's gourmet dishes.

1/2 stick butter	3 dozen oysters
1 small onion, finely chopped	2 cans cream of mushroom soup
2 bunches shallots, chopped	White wine, to taste
1/2 bell pepper, finely chopped	Salt, cayenne pepper, and black
1 rib celery, finely chopped	pepper, to taste
Garlic, to taste	1 small jar diced pimiento

Melt butter in a large skillet and simmer onions, shallots, bell pepper, celery and garlic until soft. Check oysters for shells; cut into small pieces. Heat oysters with juice in a separate pan until edges curl. Drain and reserve oyster juice. Add oysters to onion mixture; blend in soup, wine and seasonings. Bring to a boil, stirring constantly. Remove from heat and add pimiento. If too thick, thin with reserved oyster juice. Serve dip in a chafing dish with party crackers or in tiny pastry shells.
Yield: 24 servings

DODIE'S CAVIAR MOLD

1 Tbsp. unflavored gelatin	1 tsp. Worcestershire sauce
2 Tbsps. cold water	2 Tbsps. Hellmann's mayonnaise
1/2 cup boiling water	2 cups sour cream
1 Tbsp. lemon juice	4 ½ ozs. black cavier

Soak gelatin in cold water, then dissolve in boiling water. Let cool, add lemon juice and Worcestershire. Fold in mayonnaise and sour cream; blend well. Add caviar; mix and pour into a well-greased mold. Refrigerate until set. Serve with toast points or your favorite cracker.
Yield: 25 servings

CRAWFISH CROUSTADES

These melt-in-your-mouth canapés combine crawfish, cream and Gouda cheese served piping hot in Basic Pastry Dough (See Index). They can be baked and frozen to give you an appetizer that will be work free on the day of your festivities. This filling provides a tantalizing entrée served in individual puff pastry shells.

1/2 stick butter
1 lb. crawfish tails
1/2 cup chopped green onion tops
1/2 cup chopped, fresh parsley
2 Tbsps. minced garlic
1/2 cup dry vermouth

1-2 Tbsps. Creole seasoning
1/2 cup half-and-half
3-4 Tbsps. Parmesan cheese
1/2 lb. Gouda, cut in small pieces
Pastry shells

Melt butter in large skillet; add next four ingredients and sauté about 5 minutes. Stir in vermouth and Creole seasoning. Simmer about 2 minutes and add cream and Parmesan cheese. Simmer until almost all liquid is consumed; fold in cut-up Gouda cheese and let cool. Place cooled mixture in Basic Pastry Dough (See Index) in mini muffin tins. Bake in a 350-degree oven for about 20-25 minutes. If freezing croustades for later use, bake only 15 minutes; remove from oven and cool slightly before removing from pans. Place in airtight container and freeze until ready to bake.
Yield: 36-40 canapés

Variations:
For a party of 60 guests, double batch of Basic Pastry Dough and filling. If you choose, you can pulse crawfish in food processor to make them smaller and easier to fit into small shells.

The word "canapé" is French for "couch".
These vessels simply complement the wonderful sauced fillings.

CRAWFISH DIP WITH PIZZAZZ

This creamy dip is a caterer's dream! It can be prepared a day ahead and heated in time for a party. The flavors of the soup, evaporated milk and seasonings blend together for a true, southern treat.

8 ribs celery, finely chopped
2 medium onions, finely chopped
2 bell peppers, finely chopped
2 sticks butter
2 small jars diced pimiento
2 cans cream of mushroom soup

2 (10 oz.) cans evaporated milk
Worcestershire, Tabasco, salt and
    black pepper, to taste
1 lbs. coarsely chopped crawfish
    tails
1 lb. sharp Cheddar, grated

Sauté celery, onion, bell pepper in butter until soft; blend in pimiento, soup, milk, and seasonings. When hot, fold in crawfish and simmer on low heat for 10 minutes, being careful not to burn. Stir in cheese and melt. Serve hot in a chafer with toast points or dipping corn chips.
Yield: 40-50 servings

HOT CRAWFISH DIP

My friend Jo Ann Rose brought this delightful dip to a party one evening—one blink of the eye and it was gone!

1 stick butter
1 onion, chopped
1 lb. crawfish or shrimp

1 can Ro-Tel tomatoes, drained
1 (8-oz.) cream cheese, softened
Creole seasoning, to taste

Melt butter in skillet; sauté onion until tender. Add crawfish or shrimp and simmer about 5 minutes. Add drained tomatoes and simmer 5 minutes longer. Fold in cream cheese and heat until cheese is melted. Sprinkle with Creole seasoning, to taste. Serve hot in a chafer with gourmet crackers.

MARINATED CRAWFISH

My daughter Donna sampled this outstanding dish Thanksgiving, 2004, at a holiday open house at Broadmoor Drugs. The recipe originated with Michael Sinitiere, son of Linda and Moise Sinitiere, owners of the now closed Broadmoor Drugs, an old Shreveport landmark. Donna served it on Christmas and even the pickiest eater of the bunch begged for the recipe. It is simple and delicious. Thanks to Linda and Michael for sharing.

1 bunch green onions, chopped
1 tsp. Cayenne pepper
2 tsps. celery seed
2 tsps. black pepper
2 garlic cloves, minced
2 tsps. onion powder

1 ½ tsps. curry powder
2 tsps. oregano
1 tsp. thyme
8-12 ozs. Italian dressing
12-16 ozs. crawfish tails
2 (8-oz.) blocks cream cheese

Mix together all ingredients except cream cheese. Refrigerate overnight. To serve: pour over cream cheese and serve with wheat crackers.
Yield: 20 servings (approximate)

MARINATED CRAB CLAWS

These crab claws do not appear on your serving table overnight—slow preparation is what marinating is all about, but believe me, it's worth the wait. This recipe has been in my files for so many years, it is yellowed with age.

1 cup chopped green onion
1 cup chopped celery stalks
    and leaves
6 cloves garlic, minced
1 cup parsley, chopped

2 cups extra virgin olive oil
2 cups tarragon vinegar
Salt and pepper, to taste
Juice of 4 lemons
1 lb. can crab claws

Mix together all ingredients except crab claws; let sit at room temperature for 48 hours. Add crab claws and let sit an additional 8 hours. Serve as an appetizer with hunks of French bread for dunking! Shrimp may be substituted.

CRABMEAT ELEGANTE

This hot chafer item is my favorite appetizer in the world! The original recipe hails from the kitchen of my old friend, Chloe Thornton. I have taken liberties with it—to name one, Chloe made it in the microwave and I prefer cooking on top the stove. This classic dish is simple to make, it freezes well, it makes great leftovers, such as breakfast egg omelets and a topping for broiled fish.. and most important, it is to-die-for delicious!

2 sticks butter
2 medium onions, finely chopped
2 (8 oz.) pkgs. cream cheese,
   cut into cubes

1 lb. lump or white crabmeat
White pepper, to taste
Tabasco, optional

Melt butter in large skillet; add onion and sauté slowly until it is soft. Do not brown. Add cubed cream cheese and beat in with electric mixer or whisk until well blended. Gently fold in crabmeat; sprinkle with white pepper. Keep warm until ready to serve in a chafer. Serve with toast points.
Yield: 25-30 servings

DONNA'S LUMP CRABMEAT DIP

When you want to show off for a special occasion, pull out all the stops with this luscious dip. My daughter Donna's "crowning glory" was the creation of this absolutely divine hors d'oeuvre. I would strongly advise making a double batch for it disappears very quickly!

1 stick butter
1 large onion, chopped
1/2 lb. fresh sliced mushrooms
1 (8 oz.) cream cheese, cut in cubes

1 can cream of mushroom soup
1 lb. lump crabmeat
Creole seasoning, cayenne
   pepper, and Worcestershire

Melt butter in Dutch oven and sauté onion on low heat until tender—do not brown. Add fresh mushrooms and sauté lightly. Blend in cream cheese cubes and mushroom soup, stirring and simmering slowly until cream cheese is melted. Carefully fold in crabmeat and seasonings. Serve piping hot in a chafer with toast points or Melba.
Yield: 20 servings

HOT CRABMEAT DIP

This simple little dip combines the zest of horseradish, the creaminess of cream cheese, and the crunch of almonds—it has it all! Can be prepared a day ahead and baked when ready to serve. It's also great on bread rounds for delicious canapés.

2 (8 oz.) pkgs. cream cheese   1/2 lb. lump or white crabmeat
1/2 cup horseradish   1/2 cup sliced toasted almonds
1/2 cup green onion tops,   Paprika, to taste
   finely chopped

Blend cream cheese, horseradish and green onions; fold in crabmeat. Spread mixture in a baking dish. Top with almonds and sprinkle with paprika. Bake uncovered in a 375-degree oven for 20 minutes. Serve with assorted crackers.
Yield: 20 servings
Variation: Place in a hollowed out French bread round to bake—classy!

CRABMEAT CANAPÉS

I tasted these at a Hawaiian Luau several years ago—before I could return for seconds, they were gone! Absolutely divine!

1 (6-oz) can lump crabmeat   1/2 tsp. Worcestershire sauce
1 cup grated Swiss cheese   1/4 tsp. salt
1/2 cup sour cream   1 can water chestnuts, drained and
2 Tbsps. minced green onion   chopped
1 Tbsp. lemon juice   1 large loaf sourdough bread

Drain and flake crabmeat. Combine crab, Swiss cheese, sour cream, green onion, lemon juice, Worcestershire and salt; blend well. Fold in water chestnuts. Slice sourdough bread into 1/4-inch rounds and spread mixture liberally on one side of each slice. Bake in a 400-degree oven for 15 minutes.
Yield: 20 canapés (approximate)

Adam Shane Herpin

Soups

There is an old Spanish proverb that goes something like this: "Of soup and love, the first is best." It's true that soup seldom disappoints. It acts as a culinary security blanket, giving one a sense of comfort.

In the old days, when I visited my grandmother, there was always a big pot filled with bones, meat, vegetables, herbs, and goodness knows what else, slowly simmering on a back burner. It's no wonder she was always so calm and composed! We live in a world of "hurry up", therefore very few stock pots are simmering on back burners—these are the times of bouillon cubes.

A stockpot of chicken soup or clam chowder is my remedy for relaxing and putting priorities back where they belong. I forget the deadlines, the bills to be paid, the stack of mail to be answered as I get back to basics with some serious soup making. It's a plus that I work from home so I can enjoy the aroma of soup slowly simmering all day.

We have a variety of soup-making choices. There are basic savory liquid soups or consommés such as good ole chicken soup for what ails you. Gourmet first-course cream soups, chowders or bisques are perfect for that sit-down dinner you're planning. And let's not forget the hearty main course soups and stews. All have their own special place in menu planning. Most soups freeze beautifully, so it's wise to whip up a triple batch if you're going to the trouble to make it.

The French have their bouillabaisse, the Italians their minestrone, the Texans their hot and spicy tortilla soup. Here in Louisiana, we have the ultimate—our beloved gumbo, brimming over with shrimp, crab, oysters, okra, crushed red peppers, and filé. Other bayou state favorites are our delicate bisques—crawfish, oysters, shrimp, and corn.

BLACK-EYED PEA SOUP

Everyone loves black-eyed peas—right? This dish is a perfect family entrée on a cool winter evening, served with salad and cornbread. For dessert, serve hot gingerbread like Grandma used to make, and I guarantee your family will be begging for more. Charlotte Peters shared this delicious soup with us. She and I worked in public relations together for several years, and had a ball planning social events for our company. With all the planning and tasting, I figure collectively, we put on about 80 pounds!

4 strips bacon
1 medium bell pepper, chopped
1 small onion, chopped
2 garlic cloves, minced
2 cans (15 ½ oz.) black-eyed
   peas, <u>undrained</u>
2 cans (14 ½ oz.) petite diced
   tomatoes, <u>undrained</u>

1 cup water
1 ½ tsps. salt
1 ¼ tsps. ground cumin
1 ½ tsps. ground mustard
1 tsp. chili powder
1/2 tsp. curry powder
1/4 tsp. sugar

In a heavy pot, cook bacon over medium heat until crisp—remove to paper towels. In the drippings, sauté bell pepper, onion and garlic until tender. Add peas, tomatoes, water and remaining ingredients; bring to a boil. Reduce heat, cover and simmer 15-20 minutes. Crumble bacon over soup when serving.
Yield: 6 servings

Black-eyed peas or cowpeas are a popular legume in the South. Originating in Asia, the black-eyed pea is thought to have been introduced through the African slave trade.

BLACK BEAN SOUP

My cousin Deryl Hamilton and long-time friend, Sybil Bateman concocted this luscious soup on one of their fun cooking days together. I serve it with regular or Mexican Cornbread (See Index).

1 medium onion, chopped
1 clove garlic, minced
1 Tbsp. ground cumin
2 Tbsps. vegetable oil
3 (16-oz.) cans black beans

2 (14-oz.) cans chicken broth
3 cups medium chunky Picante
  Sauce
Juice and grated peel of 1 lime
1/2 cup sour cream

Cook onion, garlic and cumin in oil in a 4-quart saucepot over medium heat until onion is tender, about 5 minutes; remove from heat. Puree 2 cans beans and their liquid in batches with chicken broth in electric blender; add to pot. Stir in remaining 1 can of beans, Picante, lime juice, and peel. Heat mixture to a boil, reduce heat to low and simmer for 30 minutes. Ladle soup into individual bowls; top with sour cream.
Yield: 6-8 servings

SAUSAGE BLACK BEAN SOUP

5 (15 oz.) cans chicken broth
1 bay leaf
5 (15 oz.) cans black beans
1 lb. smoked sausage, sliced
3 large onions, chopped
2 bell peppers, chopped

2 Tbsps. crushed garlic
2 Tbsps. olive oil
1 chopped jalapeno pepper
Salt, to taste
2 squirts Tabasco
Cooked rice

In a large soup pot that has been sprayed with nonstick spray, bring chicken broth, bay leaf and canned beans to a gentle boil. While mixture is simmering, place sausage, onion, bell pepper, garlic, olive oil, and jalapeno pepper into a heavy skillet; sauté gently until sausage is lightly browned and vegetables are soft. Add this mixture to the simmering soup, stirring well. Simmer on low heat for 20 minutes; serve over cooked rice. Garnish: dollops of sour cream, grated Monterey Jack cheese, jalapeno slices, and chopped black olives.
Yield: 8-10 servings

PARADISE IN A BOWL

This hearty soup makes a delicious family entrée. It is a favorite of my daughter Deb Fralix who lives in Houston, Texas.

1½ lbs. lean ground beef	1 (16 oz.) can crushed tomatoes
2 cups diced onion	2 Tbsps. Worcestershire sauce
1 cup diced carrot	1 tsp. red pepper sauce
1 cup diced celery	1/2 tsp. pepper, freshly ground
1 Tbsp. garlic, minced	1/4 cup butter
3 cans chicken broth	1/4 cup flour

Brown 1½ pounds lean ground beef in Dutch oven over medium-high heat. Add onions, carrots, celery and garlic; cook 10 to 12 minutes until vegetables are softened. Add next five ingredients; bring to a boil. Reduce heat, cover and simmer 15 minutes. Meanwhile, melt butter in small saucepan; stir in flour. Cook over medium high heat, stirring, until deep brown. Whisk into soup; cover and simmer 15 more minutes. Yield: 11 cups.

TEXAS TORTILLA SOUP

Another great soup from my Deb! Ole!

4 Tbsps. butter	1 lb. boneless, raw chicken, diced
1/2 cup oil	1 tsp. each: ground cumin, chili
1 large onion, chopped	powder, salt and lemon pepper
1 jalapeno, seeded and chopped	3 tsps. Tabasco
4 garlic cloves, minced	1 (14-oz.) can whole tomatoes
2 large carrots, diced	4 (10 ½ oz.) cans chicken broth
6 ribs celery, diced	Corn tortillas

Heat butter and oil in large kettle; add next 6 ingredients and simmer 5 minutes. Combine with cumin, chili powder, salt, lemon pepper, and Tabasco. Add tomatoes and chicken stock and simmer 1 hour. Cut corn tortillas into thin strips and drop into hot oil, frying until crisp. Garnish bowls with tortillas and add sour cream, avocado, and cheese. Yield: 6-8 servings

SOUPE A L'OIGNON (ONION SOUP)

One of my most prized cookbooks, A Treasury of Great Recipes, by Vincent Price (1965) is on the "most wanted" list of collectors' cookbooks. This handsome book features recipes and menus of famous restaurants from around the world. Mr. Price's Onion Soup is a delicious, rich rendition of an old favorite. I have adapted it to suit our family's taste.

3 tbsps. bacon drippings	Parsley, one sprig, chopped
4 large onions, chopped fine	Fresh thyme, one pinch
2 tbsps. flour	1 qt. chicken stock
1/2 tsp. salt	1 cup dry white wine
1/8 tsp. pepper	1 Tbsp. cognac (optional)
1 clove garlic, mashed	

In a deep heavy saucepan, heat bacon drippings; sauté onions in drippings. Cook over medium heat until onions are just soft. Add flour, salt, pepper, and garlic. Cook until mixture is golden brown but not burned. Add parsley, thyme, chicken stock and white wine; simmer for 45 minutes. Add 1 tablespoon cognac before serving.

Presentation: As a first course, serve in individual ovenproof bowls with 1 slice of toasted French bread in each. Or, as a first course or main dish, serve *gratinee* by placing in each bowl 3 layers of toasted French bread and sprinkling each layer with grated Parmesan cheese. Pour soup into bowls, top with more grated Parmesan cheese and a pat of melted butter. Place under broiler until the cheese melts and forms a brown crust.

Yield: 6 servings

A gratinee is a dish that is topped with cheese or breadcrumbs mixed with butter, then heated under the broiler until browned and crispy. Special gratin dishes are ovenproof and shallow— especially designed for individual servings.

CORN CHOWDER

This simple soup is creamy and comforting—the perfect dinner for a cool fall evening. Complete the meal with green salad and cornbread.

1/2 lb. bacon, cut up
1 large onion, chopped
2 ribs celery, sliced
3 cups diced red potatoes
1 tsp. salt

1/2 tsp. black pepper
1/4 tsp. pepper flakes
2 ½ cups water
1 (16-oz.) can cream-style corn
1 ½ cups half-and-half

Sauté bacon, onion and celery in Dutch oven until onion is transparent. Spoon off part of bacon drippings. Add potatoes, salt, black pepper, pepper flakes, and water; simmer for 20 minutes. Stir in corn and cream; heat until hot and bubbly. Sprinkle with parsley.
Yield: 6 servings
Note: Shrimp can be added to this chowder for additional flavor.

CHICKEN CORN CHOWDER

12 boneless chicken breasts,
   cut into bite-sized pieces
1 medium onion, chopped
2 garlic cloves, minced
4 Tbsps. butter
3 chicken bouillon cubes
1 cup hot water
1 tsp. ground cumin

2 cups half-and-half
8 ozs. Monterey Jack cheese
1 (16-oz.) can cream-style corn
1 can (4-oz.) chopped green
   chilies, undrained
1 tsp. hot pepper sauce
1 medium tomato, chopped
Fresh cilantro, for garnish

In a large Dutch oven, brown chicken pieces, onion and garlic in butter until chicken is no longer pink. Dissolve bouillon in hot water. Add to pan along with the cumin; bring to a boil. Reduce heat; cover and simmer 5 minutes. Blend in half and half, cheese (that has been cut in cubes), corn, chilies, and hot pepper sauce. Cook and stir over low heat until cheese is melted—do not boil; stir in chopped tomato. Serve immediately. Garnish with cilantro.
Yield: 6-8 servings

BROCCOLI-CHEESE SOUP

This recipe, which was featured in my original "..Slap Your Mama"
cookbook, is returning for a second bow. I looked in vain for a new
broccoli-cheese soup, but, in my opinion, there is no substitute. This
one, which I have updated a little, is the very best. Enjoy..again!

2 pkgs. frozen chopped broccoli   3 (12-oz.) cans evaporated milk
1 medium onion, chopped   8 ozs. pasteurized process cheese
1 stick butter   1 jalapeno pepper, chopped
2 cans cream of chicken soup   Dash of nutmeg
1 can cream of mushroom soup

Cook chopped broccoli according to package directions; drain and set
aside.   Sauté onion in butter; add soups and milk, blending well.
Simmer over low heat about 20 minutes. Cut cheese into cubes. Add
cheese, broccoli, chopped jalapeno and nutmeg to soup; simmer on low
heat, stirring often, for 15 minutes until cheese is melted and flavors are
well blended. This soup freezes well.
Yield: 6-8 servings

MUSHROOM BISQUE

This is another repeat—and one of my biggest requests.

1/2 cup butter   4 cups chicken broth
1/2 lb. fresh mushrooms, sliced   2 tsps. salt
1/2 small onion, chopped   1/2 tsp. coarsely ground pepper
1 Tbsp. minced garlic   Fresh parsley, chopped
1 Tbsp. fresh lemon juice   2 cups half-and-half
3 Tbsps. flour   2 Tbsps. dry sherry

Heat butter; sauté mushrooms, onion and garlic for 10 minutes. Add
lemon juice and blend in flour. Gradually add broth, salt, and pepper.
Bring to a simmer, stirring constantly until thickened. Stir in cream and
heat thoroughly. Add sherry and serve. Garnish with thin lemon slices.
Yield: 6 servings

CAULIFLOWER BRIE SOUP

This creamy potage is my rendition of the classic one on the menu at the famed New Orleans restaurant, Commander's Palace .

1 large head cauliflower
8 Tbsps. butter, divided
1 medium onion, diced
5 pods minced garlic
5 stalks celery, chopped
1 tsp. Kosher salt

White pepper, to taste
1 ½ pts. chicken broth
2 Tbsps. flour
16 oz. Brie cheese (rind removed)
  cut in cubes
1 cup heavy cream

Remove cauliflower leaves, core and cut into florets; set aside. Melt 6 tablespoons butter in a large soup pot. Add onion, garlic and celery; sauté, stirring often about 10 minutes. Add salt and pepper; stir in cauliflower and simmer for 10 minutes. Add chicken broth to mixture and simmer for 20 minutes until cauliflower is tender. Place mixture in a blender and puree until creamy white and smooth; return to pot and bring to a boil. In a small skillet, make a light roux by melting the remaining 2 Tbsps. butter over medium heat and slowly blending in flour. Stir until smooth—do not brown. Whisk roux into soup and bring to a simmer. Add cubed Brie, a few pieces at a time and blend until cheese is melted. Add cream and adjust seasonings to taste.
Yield: 6 entrée servings

OYSTER BISQUE

1 qt. oysters
2 slices bacon, chopped
1/2 cup chopped onion
1 (14-oz.) can potato soup

4 cups oyster liquor and
  half-and-half, mixed
Salt, to taste
Dash white pepper, parsley

Drain oysters, strain liquor; reserve. Fry bacon until crisp; remove and sauté onion in bacon drippings until tender; add soup. Combine oyster liquor and half and half to make 4 cups; add to soup, along with seasonings. Heat, stirring occasionally. Add bacon and oysters; heat for 5 minutes or until edges of oysters curl. Sprinkle with parsley and serve.
Yield: 6 servings

CLAM CHOWDER

This recipe, courtesy of Bill and Colette Males, has been a favorite of our family since 1983. "Madame" Males' home was in the Provence region of France. She was a much loved Latin teacher at Caddo Magnet High School. She and husband Bill, now deceased, enjoyed cooking together—especially French dishes. This chowder is the "real thing"—a heavenly taste that will transport you to the heart of Provence. It takes a little more time to make, but is well worth the effort.

1 doz. Cherrystone clams	1/4 tsp. Accent (MSG)
4 cups water	1 good shake nutmeg
3 medium potatoes	1 good shake curry powder
3 strips bacon	1/8 tsp. celery salt
1 medium onion, diced	1 cup half-and-half, scalded
2 Tbsps. flour	Salt and pepper, to taste
12 peppercorns	1 pat butter per serving

Wash clams well; place in a Dutch oven. Add water and boil until clams pop open. Remove clams (retain liquid in pot) and cut meat from each clam into at least 6 pieces. Drain the clam broth from the pot so as to leave the residual sand in the pot. Rinse pot and replace broth; add cut-up clams to pot. Dice potatoes into 1/2-inch cubes; add to clams and broth. Return liquid to boiling. Cut bacon into ¼-inch pieces and brown slightly in a skillet. Add diced onion to the bacon and cook until tender; stir in flour to thicken. Add mixture to soup pot. Add next 5 ingredients; cover pot and simmer on low heat for about ½ hour, or until potatoes are very tender. Remove from heat and add scalded half-and-half and salt and pepper, to taste. Serve in individual bowls with a pat of butter on top.

Chowder is any thick rich soup containing chunks of food.
The name comes from the French "chaudiere", a caldron
in which fishermen made their stews fresh from the sea.

CRAWFISH/ARTICHOKE SOUP

This creamy blend will, at first slurp, become a favorite in your home. With its distinct southern flavor, and robust color, this tasteful brew lends class either as a first course, or served as a main entrée with Caesar salad and crusty French bread. My sister-in-law, Ladye White, of The Bluffs shared this recipe. It is wonderful served with crispy toast points and Caesar Salad.

1 stick butter	1/2 cup all-purpose flour
1 medium onion, chopped	2 cups chicken broth
1 large stalk celery, chopped	3 cups half-and-half
1/2 bell pepper, chopped	2 lbs. crawfish tails (See note)
1 Tbsp. minced garlic	1 tsp. Louisiana Hot Sauce
1 tsp. dried thyme	1/2 cup chopped green onion tops
2 bay leaves	1/2 cup chopped fresh parsley or
2 (14 oz.) cans artichoke hearts	1/4 cup dried

Melt butter in a heavy Dutch oven. Add next six ingredients; cook for about 10 minutes. Drain and quarter artichoke hearts and add to pot; cook for an additional 5 minutes. Stir in flour; blend well. Add chicken broth slowly and let simmer about 5 minutes until broth starts to thicken. Slowly stir in half-and-half, crawfish and hot sauce; simmer on low heat for about 6-8 minutes, until shrimp are done and soup is smooth and blended. Stir in green onion tops and parsley.
Yield: 6-8 servings

Note: Shrimp may be substituted for the crawfish. If using frozen crawfish tails, place in a colander and rinse before adding to soup.

*Many Louisianans refer to their state as the
"crawfish capital of the world". The little crustaceans
are also popular in France where they are called écrevisses.
In Australia, they are referred to as "yabbies."
In South Louisiana, they're "mudbugs".*

BLENDER GAZPACHO

Gazpacho is a cold uncooked tomato-based soup made from a pureed mixture of fresh vegetables. In warm weather, paired with a green salad, crackers and iced tea, it provides a healthy cool addition to your lunch menu. I never really enjoyed it until I tasted my friend Kay Chance's kicked-up version.

2 cloves garlic	1/4 cup red wine vinegar
4-5 tomatoes, peeled and halved	Salt and black pepper, to taste
2 medium onions, chopped	Dash A-1 Sauce
2 green bell peppers, seeded	3/4 cup tomato juice
2 cucumbers, peeled and chopped	Lemon slices, fresh parsley, or
4 ribs celery, chopped fine	croutons

In an electric blender on "chop" combine first five ingredients. Blend well and add next five ingredients; blend about 1 minute longer; chill. Serve in bowls or mugs and garnish with thin lemon slices and chopped fresh parsley or croutons browned in butter.

MOLLY'S STRAWBERRY SOUP

Molly's strawberry soup is the creation of my friend and neighbor, Molly Weldon. This is the perfect dish for a ladies' luncheon or brunch. I love it so, I've been known to eat it for dessert! It's also great made with raspberries.

2 cups strawberries, sliced	1 cup half-and-half
1/4 cup sugar	2 Tbsps. brandy
1 cup sour cream	1/2 tsp. vanilla extract

Place all ingredients in blender; blend until smooth. Serve chilled.
Yield: 4 small servings

For a summer brunch, put cold soup in an attractive
glass pitcher – place pitcher on a festive tray
surrounded by glass punch cups.

Jillian (Jill) Leigh Duplichan

Salads

Salads come in many disguises. They no longer consist of limp lettuce, chunks of tomato and bell pepper, tossed with a bland bottled dressing. Today's salads are innovative, colorful, and flavorful, literally bursting with character. There are seafood salads, chicken salads, aspics, and cold rice or cabbage salads. These are some of the salads we identify with summer and warm weather. They are suitable main dishes which require only a chunk of crusty French bread or toast points (See Index) and a glass of iced tea.

Gourmet side salads are never boring—taste tempting Greek, Italian, and Caesar provide a spectacular palate of color as a first course for a dinner party. The addition of blue cheese, feta, goat or Romano cheeses will set the taste buds to tingling! Add a basket filled with fresh breads—bruschetta, pumpernickel, garlic, wheat, and some olive oil for drizzling. Your guests will applaud you.

With life in the fast lane, it's a good idea to have salads in the refrigerator that are ready to serve in a matter of minutes. I'm a big advocate for make-ahead meals—dishes that can be whisked out when the dinner bell rings. Pasta salads meet this chill-ahead requirement, and will take center stage for lovely presentation, paired up with thick slices of tomato, goat cheese, and basil. To round out the meal, add crisp, buttery French baguettes and a bottle of chilled Chablis Blanc.

During the holiday season, our thoughts go to congealed salads that are bursting with flavor and color. Nothing is more beautiful at Christmas than a red or green congealed salad on a holiday platter, surrounded by fresh pears, apples and branches of fresh herbs.

In this chapter, you will find a salad to fit your every need from the Classic Sensation Salad to Chet's Bridesmaid Chicken Salad—all the way to a grand finale—Holiday Cranberry Salad. Enjoy!

ITALIAN SALAD MIX

It is only fitting that I begin this chapter with the "crème de la crème" of salad mixes. As an enhancement to Italian salads and a variety of sandwiches, as a holiday food gift, or simply enjoying it straight from the jar, it cannot be beat. Simple to make, it yields seven pints, and will keep well for two or three months in the refrigerator. This savory salad mix is a staple in our home.

Italian Salad Mix

1 large bunch celery,
  coarsely chopped
3 large jars green olives with
  pimientos, chopped coarse
  (reserve liquid)
3 small cans sliced black olives,
  drained well
1/2 bunch chopped parsley

2 bunches green onions, chopped
4 heaping Tbsps. minced garlic
8 ozs. small capers
2 Tbsps. dried oregano leaves
10 ozs. extra virgin olive oil
1 small jar chopped pimiento,
  drained

Place all ingredients in large container; mix well, <u>including</u> the liquid from the <u>green salad olives and capers.</u> (Do not include liquid from black olives.) When well mixed, place in sterilized containers and refrigerate.

Yield: 7 pints or 14 half-pints

Note: For chopping the celery and green olives, a food processor works well, but be careful not to pulverize—coarsely chopped is perfect.

For Salad: Toss with mixed salad greens, sprinkle with fresh grated Parmesan cheese, croutons, salt and pepper and serve.

For Muffaletto Sandwich: On French or round Muffy bread, brush insides with olive oil and layer as follows: Virginia ham, slice of mozzarella cheese, <u>drained</u> Italian Salad Mix, slice of salami, and a slice of Provolone cheese. Place top on bread and brush crusty top with olive oil and sprinkle lightly with ground oregano. Wrap in foil and bake until sandwich is hot and all cheese is melted – 15 to 20 minutes. Delicious!

SENSATION SALAD

For a "sensational" favorite, Sensation Salad Dressing is legendary, with several Baton Rouge restaurants taking credit for creating the original. This is a recipe close to my heart, for I received the original version from the creator himself, Jake Staples. Jake and his brother, Bob, introduced this simple, yet superb dressing at their popular restaurant, Bob and Jakes, in the '50's. Through the years, it has been changed, adjusted, and sometimes mutilated, but Jake's is still the best.

1/3 cup olive oil	2 cloves garlic, pressed
2/3 cup vegetable oil	Juice of 1 lemon, more if desired
1/4 teaspoon coarse grind black pepper	1/2 tsp. salt
	7 Tbsps. Romano cheese, grated

Combine first six ingredients in a quart jar; add Romano cheese and shake well until blended. Refrigerate. To serve, shake well and toss with crispy lettuce of your choice. Sprinkle additional Romano Cheese and black pepper on top.

MOZZARELLA AND TOMATO SALAD

For a simple, clean taste, you can't beat this make-ahead salad.

1/2 lb. fresh mozzarella cheese	4 Tbsps. extra virgin olive oil
2 large home-grown tomatoes	Coarse grind pepper, to taste
1/2 tsp. salt	1/2 cup shredded fresh basil

Cut mozzarella cheese into 12 slices. Slice tomatoes and sprinkle with salt. On a platter, alternate tomato and cheese slices; drizzle with olive oil. Cover and chill 4 hours. To serve, sprinkle with coarsely ground pepper and strips of fresh basil; place on a lettuce leaf.
Yield: 6 servings

Fresh mozzarella is usually packaged in whey or water.
It is generally made from whole milk and has a soft
texture and a sweet, delicate flavor.
It is perfect for salads.

CHLOE'S SALAD DRESSING

This is another classic dressing. It has been my family's favorite since my friend Chloe Thornton shared the recipe many years ago. During my catering years, this became our signature salad, and often I made a gallon at a time when preparing for big dinner parties. There was definitely a "whole lotta shaking going on."

2 cups Crisco oil
10 Tbsps. white wine vinegar
6 Tbsps. sour cream
  (light or regular)
3 tsps. salt
1 tsp. dry mustard

4 Tbsps. sugar
1 ½ tsps. coarsely ground black
  pepper
4 tsps. chopped parsley
4 tsps. pureed garlic

Whisk together or shake in a quart jar all ingredients until sour cream is well blended and there are no lumps. Mix at least six hours before serving and refrigerate. When ready to serve: toss with spinach leaves, Romaine lettuce, sliced hard-boiled eggs, ½ cup Parmesan (or more), garlic powder, and croutons.
Yield: 1 quart dressing
Note: Dressing will keep in refrigerator about 3 weeks—if it gets very cold, it may "set up"—simply take out 30 minutes before serving.

BLUE CHEESE DRESSING

"This creamy salad dressing is fabulous on greens for a salad, on celery or crackers to serve as an appetizer, on asparagus, and on a spoon, right out of the jar." These are the words of originators of this recipe, *Brenda Dalton and husband Tom. It is a winner!*

1 qt. Hellmann's mayonnaise
  (do not use low fat)
1 ½ cups buttermilk
8 oz. blue cheese, crumbled

1/2 tsp. Beau Monde seasoning
3/4 tsps. garlic salt
1 Tbsp. lemon juice

Whisk together all ingredients, being careful not to break down the blue cheese too much. Refrigerate.
Yield: 2 ½ quarts

JILL'S GREEK SALAD

Our granddaughter, Jill, is blessed with a natural ability in the kitchen—whether cooking or setting a beautiful table. When she visits, she spoils us with meals that would grace the table of a gourmet restaurant. I think Jill's original salads are the most notable—this one is our favorite. Who would have thought of corn chips in a Greek salad? Trust me..it is outstanding. All the herbs are not required—simply use your favorites.

Romaine lettuce pieces   Yellow corn chips, crumbled
Spinach and red lettuce   4 oz. Feta cheese

Dressing:
1 can pitted whole black olives   Pinch of each:
2/3 cup extra virgin olive oil   Oregano leaves
Pinch of each: Thyme leaves
  Celery seed   Rubbed Sage
  Ground mustard   Cavender's Greek Seasoning
  Dill weed   Basil leaves

Mix olive oil with all ingredients; drain black olives and marinate in oil mixture. Refrigerate overnight. When ready to serve, toss lettuce, spinach, corn chips and Feta cheese; drizzle with dressing and black olives. Garnish with additional corn chips.

ARTICHOKE HEART SALAD

This salad is excellent served on a bed of spring lettuce with tomato slices and a sprig of parsley for garnish.

1 jar marinated artichoke hearts   1 Tbsp. olive oil
1 can water chestnuts, sliced   1 Tbsp. wine vinegar
8 large fresh mushrooms, sliced   1 tsp. salt
6 green onions, chopped   1/8 tsp. Tabasco sauce

Drain artichokes, reserving liquid; add water chestnuts, mushrooms and onions. To the reserved artichoke marinade, blend in remaining ingredients. Toss with artichoke mixture; refrigerate overnight. Serve on salad or keep on hand for snacking.

LAYERED SALAD

This layered salad is a lively combination of breezy vegetables, topped with an "icing" of mayonnaise and cheese. Ease plays a big role, for you can prepare this salad the day before and toss just before serving.

2 cups small shell macaroni
1/2 head lettuce, shredded
1 large can albacore tuna,
  broken up or 1 ½ cups thin
  strips of Virginia ham
1 10 oz. pkg. frozen green peas,
  thawed and drained
1 cup sliced purple onion

1 small can sliced black olives
3 hard-boiled eggs, sliced
1/2 lb. fresh mushrooms, sliced
1 can sliced water chestnuts,
  drained
2 cups Hellmann's mayonnaise
1 pkg. Ranch Style dressing mix
1/2 lb. mozzarella cheese, shredded

Boil shell macaroni in salted water until al dente; drain. In a large glass bowl, layer first 9 ingredients in the order listed. Mix mayonnaise with Ranch dressing mix and spread on top, all the way to edges. Sprinkle with cheese; cover tightly and refrigerate overnight. To serve, toss well.

PEAS AND ASPARAGUS MOLDED SALAD

This attractive molded dinner salad makes a beautiful presentation and will add class to any menu. My friend Sue Calhoun served it one evening with New York strip steaks and a light fluffy rice dish. It complemented the menu perfectly.

2 cans whole asparagus,
  reserve juice
1 can petit pois peas, drained
1 cup chopped celery

1 small bell pepper, chopped
2 envelopes Knox gelatin
3 (3-oz.) pkgs. cream cheese
1 (10-oz.) Durkee's dressing

Spray a 13x9x2-inch baking dish with cooking spray and layer vegetables in order given; set aside. In a saucepan, heat juice from asparagus and dissolve gelatin; set aside. With electric hand mixer, blend together cream cheese and Durkee's dressing; fold in gelatin mixture by hand. Pour mixture over vegetables and smooth out. Chill until cold and set. Cut in squares and serve on lettuce leaf.
Yield: 10-12 servings

CANDI'S SLAW

Candi's Slaw, a creation of Candi Ferachi of Baton Rouge, combines crispy Ramen noodles and slaw for a layered "ready to serve" salad that will enhance any menu—especially fried chicken or baked ham. When you want a unique dish for a reunion or pot-luck dinner, carry along a bowl of Candi's slaw for a guaranteed hit.

2 pkgs. beef ramen noodles	1 bunch green onions, chopped
2 (8 oz.) slaw mixes	1/3 cup sugar or sugar substitute
1 cup sliced almonds	3/4 cup vegetable oil
1 cup sunflower seeds (no shell)	1/3 cup apple cider vinegar

Crunch noodles; place in bottom of glass bowl. Layer as follows: slaw, almonds, sunflower seeds and green onions. Mix flavor packet from beef ramen noodles with sugar, oil and vinegar; pour over all. Do not toss. Cover and refrigerate for at least 10-12 hours; toss when ready to serve. Keeps well in refrigerator for one week.
Yield: 6-8 servings
Note: This slaw is fabulous using 2 pkgs. lime-shrimp ramen noodles in place of beef ramen, and adding boiled shrimp to salad

LUSCIOUS POTATO SALAD

My cousin Deryl Hamilton and Sybil Bateman, my old friend from schooldays, enjoy making this delicious potato salad—it's a takeoff from a Hellmann's mayonnaise recipe, which they adjusted.

1 cup mayonnaise	5 medium cubed cooked potatoes
2 Tbsps. vinegar	1 cup thinly sliced celery
1 ½ tsp. salt	1/2 cup chopped onion
1 tsp. sugar	1 small jar chopped pimiento,
1/4 tsp. pepper	2 chopped hard-boiled eggs

In a large bowl, combine first 5 ingredients. Stir in remaining ingredients; cover and chill.

PASTA SALAD

This delicious salad is from the files of my dear friend, Shelley Braswell.

1 lb. box vermicelli
1 red bell pepper, chopped
1 yellow bell pepper, chopped
1 can sliced water chestnuts
1 jar pimientos
1 can black olives, chopped

1 cup Hellmann's mayonnaise
2 Tbsps. lemon juice
1 Tbsp. Greek seasoning
1 Tbsp. Accent (MSG)
1 Tbsp. seasoned salt
1 Tbsp. lemon pepper

Cook vermicelli al dente; drain. Blend together all ingredients. Chill.
Yield: 6-8 servings

CHICKEN PASTA SALAD

This is a delicious salad that will feed the multitudes if the recipe is doubled or tripled. It's also marvelous with shrimp or crabmeat.

2 frying chickens
3 stalks celery, chopped
1 large onion, chopped
4-5 qts. water

Salt, red pepper, garlic powder,
  Creole seasoning, to taste
2 (16-oz.) bags medium pasta
  shells

Bring all ingredients except pasta shells to a boil in a large soup pot; boil until chicken is tender—about 1 hour. Remove chicken, cool, debone and cut into pieces. In the stock chicken was boiled in, cook shells until al dente—about 7 minutes; drain and set aside.

To cooled, drained pasta shells, add:
1 bunch chopped green onions
3 stalks celery, chopped
1 small bell pepper, chopped
2 small jars diced pimientos
2 small cans sliced black olives
1/2 cup green olives, chopped

Chopped parsley, to taste
1 jalapeno, chopped (optional)
1/2 lb. shredded mozzarella cheese
1 jar marinated artichoke hearts,
2-3 cups Hellmann's mayonnaise
2/3 cup Wishbone Italian dressing

Fold in chicken and toss well; adjust seasonings to your taste. Chill.
Yield: 10-12 servings

SHRIMP PASTA SALAD

6 ozs. angel hair pasta
  boiled and drained
3/4 cup chopped plum tomato
1/2 cup chopped red bell pepper
1/3 cup chopped green onion
2 Tbsps. fresh lemon juice
2 Tbsps. chopped pitted Kalamata
  olives
2 Tbsps. extra virgin olive oil

1 ½ tsps. chopped fresh thyme
1/2 tsp. white pepper
1/4 tsp. dried oregano
1 lb. spicy boiled shrimp,
  peeled and deveined
1 garlic clove, minced
1/2 cup crumbled Feta cheese
1 Tbsp. chopped fresh parsley
1 Tbsp. small capers

Combine all ingredients except Feta, parsley and capers. When well mixed, sprinkle with Feta, parsley and capers; chill.
Yield: 6 servings

WILD RICE SHRIMP SALAD

Since I hail from South Louisiana, I believe shrimp and rice go together like bread and butter..cookies and milk..cheese and crackers. This cold rice salad will hit the spot on a hot summer day. It is delicious served for a ladies' luncheon, garnished beautifully and accompanied by a icy cold glass of white Chablis.

1 box Uncle Ben's Wild Rice Mix
  (Original)
2 stalks celery, chopped fine
1/2 medium bell pepper
1/2 cup chopped green onion tops

1 lb. medium shrimp, boiled
1 tsp. Greek seasoning
Salt and pepper, to taste
1/2 cup Hellmann's mayonnaise
1/2 cup sour cream

Prepare wild rice by package directions; fold in next 6 ingredients. Mix mayonnaise and sour cream, sprinkling a little more Greek seasoning on it. Blend into rice mixture. Serve chilled on large lettuce leaves, garnished with small sprigs of grapes or melon slices.
Yield: 8 servings

CRABMEAT SALAD

What's more delectable than crabmeat? The marriage of crabmeat, creamy mayonnaise and French dressing in this recipe will excite all the senses, whether it is served as a first course salad, or an appetizer on bruschetta or crostini rounds.

1 lb. lump crabmeat   2 tsps. small capers
2/3 cups Hellmann's mayonnaise   1 tsp. chopped fresh parsley
3 Tbsps. French dressing   Fresh lemon juice, to taste
3 green onions, chopped fine

Mix mayonnaise, French dressing, green onions, capers, and parsley. Fold in crabmeat carefully. Serve over a bed of torn lettuce pieces, with two slices of tomato on the side. Squeeze lemon juice over salad just before serving.

CRAB LOUIS

There are many stories about this famous dish. Credit for its origin depends on where you are—some attribute it to the chef at Seattle's Olympic Club, while others claim it was created in San Francisco at the St. Francis Hotel. Whoever gets credit, there are many versions of this old favorite—all are delectable. It is great served for lunch or as a cold appetizer on toast points.

3/4 cup Hellmann's mayonnaise   1/2 tsp. Worcestershire sauce
1/4 cup chili sauce   1/4 tsp. prepared horseradish
2 Tbsps. minced parsley   1 tsp. fresh lemon juice
2 tsps. cider vinegar   1 lb. lump crabmeat

Combine first 7 ingredients. Pick over crabmeat for shell; fold into sauce. Chill until ready to serve. Serve on lettuce leaves, with wedges of tomato, hard boiled egg, and toast points.

*When heating olive oil, use pure olive oil.
The flavor of extra virgin olive oil tends to break down
at high temperatures, making the added expense a waste.*

CHET'S BRIDESMAID CHICKEN SALAD

The late Chet Beckwith of Baton Rouge was my friend and mentor for many years. His career was in the garment business—General Manager of Goldrings, then owner of Chebek a popular boutique in Baton Rouge. Upon his retirement he turned to his 1ˢᵗ love—cooking and entertaining. He wrote a column for InRegister, a Baton Rouge society publication and was the author of a cookbook entitled "Too Good To Be True." Most of all he was my wonderful buddy and I miss him. He had a delightful way of describing his dishes—he would declare something so good you would "swoon" or gravy so luscious you could "comb it through your hair." In his cookbook, Chet stated, "I have demonstrated this salad in cooking classes, on television, and married off more than a few brides with it. On a one-to-ten scale, it is a fifteen." That it is! I have made minor adjustments to suit our family's taste, but basically, it remains as Chet wrote it.

Salad Dressing:

1 ½ cups Hellmann's mayonnaise	2 tsps. grated lime peel
3/4 cup Major Gray's Chutney with	1/4 cup fresh lime juice
fruit chunks sliced thinly	1/2 tsp. salt
1 tsp. curry powder	

In a large mixing bowl, combine all dressing ingredients, blending well.

4 cups cooked chicken,	2 cups diagonally sliced celery
cut into small chunks	1 cup thinly sliced green onions
1 can (20 oz.) chunk pineapple,	1/2 cup toasted sliced almonds
drained well	

Gently fold chicken, pineapple, celery, onions and almonds into the sauce. Chill for 4 to 6 hours. Serve on crisp, chilled salad greens. Can be prepared the night before. Toss again before serving, making sure to go all the way to the bottom of container to blend in all the juices.
Yield: 8 to 10 generous servings

CEIL'S TOMATO ASPIC

My past experience with aspic left much to be desired. I found most versions sadly lacking in flavor. One evening I sampled Ceil Foster's aspic at a covered dish dinner and I was hooked! There was nothing bland about this one, and since my husband Ed is a fan of aspic, I gave him a taste, which earned a thumbs up. Another plus for this zippy dish—it was featured that evening on the Heart Healthy food table.

2 cups V-8 Juice (divided)   1/4 tsp. Tabasco
1 (3 oz.) pkg. lemon gelatin   1/2 tsp. Cajun Seasoning
1 Tbsp. Worcestershire   1/2 tsp. (heaping) Italian Seasoning
1 ½ tsps. lemon juice   1 tsp. instant minced onion flakes

Bring 1 cup V-8 juice to a boil; remove from heat. Add lemon gelatin and stir until it dissolves. Add onion flakes and all seasonings. Stir in remaining cup V-8 juice. Grease 6 custard cups with Wesson Oil and pour equal amounts of mixture into each cup. Chill until jelled.
Yield: 6 servings

GRAPE SALAD

For a light, sweet fruit selection, this super salad will have both the kids and the adults begging for more. My first taste of this attractive and delicious salad was when Connie Calhoun served it on Thanksgiving—to rave reviews!

8 oz. cream cheese   1 cup chopped pecans
7 oz. marshmallow cream   4 cups red seedless grapes
1 cup shredded Cheddar cheese

Beat cream cheese and marshmallow cream; stir in cheddar cheese and pecans. Fold in grapes and chill.
Yield: 8-10

AVOCADO, GRAPEFRUIT, ORANGE SALAD

I sampled this recipe at an outdoor birthday party—it was a hot day on the water and this dish hit the spot. It was shared by Shelley Braswell and created by Katy Merriman. This celery seed dressing is divine!

1 avocado   1 grapefruit
1 Tbsp. lemon juice   Lettuce leaves
1 large orange   Celery Seed Dressing (follows)

Slice avocado and sprinkle with lemon juice. Using a sharp paring knife, peel the skin and outer pulp from orange and grapefruit. Slice toward the center, along the side of each membrane and remove fruit sections. Arrange the avocado and fruit sections on lettuce leaves. Serve with Celery Seed Dressing (recipe follows).

Celery Seed Dressing:
3/4 - 1 cup sugar   1/2 tsp. celery salt
1 tsp. salt   1/3 cup white vinegar
1 tsp. dry mustard   1 cup salad oil
3 Tbsps. grated onion   2 Tbsps. celery seed

Combine first 6 ingredients in blender on low speed. Add oil a little at a time—this is important. Blend in celery seed. Taste and add a touch more sugar or dry mustard as needed.

SUMMER PEACHES

2 (3 oz.) pkgs. cream cheese   3 (15-oz.) cans peach halves or
2 Tbsps. apricot preserves   6 fresh peaches, halved, seeded
1 cup pineapple tidbits, drained   Leaf lettuce

In a small mixing bowl, beat the cream cheese and preserves until blended. Stir in pineapple tidbits. Place peaches, cut side up, on a lettuce-lined serving platter; fill with cream cheese mixture. Garnish with fresh mint leaves.
Yield: 15 servings

NONNON'S AMBROSIA

According to Greek mythology, ambrosia (meaning "immortality") was the food of the gods on Mt. Olympus. To my husband Ed, ambrosia brings memories of his grandmother Mary "Nonnon" Yeagley and her bountiful holiday table. He fondly recalls watching her prepare fresh coconut for this cherished dish, extracting the milk, cracking it open and grating it by hand. Ambrosia can be served as a salad or as a dessert.

1 fresh pineapple
3 large navel oranges
1 grapefruit
6-8 maraschino cherries, drained well

1/4 cup orange juice
3 Tbsps. sifted powdered sugar
1/4 -1/3 cup flaked coconut

Peel and trim eyes from pineapple; remove core. Cut pineapple into ½ to 1-inch chunks; place in a bowl. Peel oranges and grapefruit and separate into sections, removing seeds; add to pineapple. Add cherries. Sprinkle with orange juice, powdered sugar, and coconut. Toss lightly. Yield: 8 servings

PEAR AND BLUE CHEESE SALAD

2 heads Romaine lettuce
1 (6-oz.) bag baby spinach
1 (14-oz.) can artichoke hearts
1/2 cup toasted pecans

2 ripe red Bartlett pears, cored,
    quartered and sliced
4 ozs. Blue cheese, crumbled

Clean Romaine; cut leaves into 1-inch strips, including ribs. Remove stems from spinach and combine in large bowl with Romaine. Rinse artichoke hearts, pat dry and cut into quarters; add to bowl. Add pecans, pears, and blue cheese. Toss with Citrus Dressing and serve.

Citrus Dressing:
1/2 cup Italian dressing
1/4 cup orange juice concentrate
1/2 tsp. grated orange rind

1 Tbsp. fresh lemon juice
1/2 tsp. Tabasco

Combine dressing ingredients; shake well to blend.

BLUEBERRY DELUXE SALAD

There are few congealed fruit salads in my repertoire. I would like to give a reason for this, but there is none. The few I have are wonderful and we just keep on making the same ones—year after year! This one is from my dear cousin, Deryl Hamilton of Baton Rouge.

2 (3-oz.) boxes black cherry gelatin 　1/2 pt. sour cream
2 cups boiling water 　1/4 cup sugar
1 (8-oz.) can crushed pineapple 　1/2 tsp. vanilla
1 Tbsp. lemon juice 　1 can prepared blueberry pie filling
1 (8-oz.) pkg. cream cheese

Put dry gelatin in a bowl. Pour boiling water over gelatin and stir until completely dissolved. Add crushed pineapple, lemon juice and pie filling. Put this mixture in a lightly greased dish; refrigerate until set. Soften cream cheese and blend into the sour cream. Stir in sugar and vanilla; blend until smooth. After the salad has congealed, spread the cream cheese mixture over the top. Serve on lettuce leaf.
Yield: 12 servings

HOLIDAY CRANBERRY DELIGHT

This luscious congealed salad will draw smiles at your dinner table. It is perfect for a holiday buffet dinner.

1 (20-oz.) can crushed pineapple, 　3 Tbsps. lemon juice
　juice drained and reserved 　1/2 tsp. grated lemon peel
1 cup water 　1/2 tsp. ground nutmeg
1 (6-oz.) pkg. strawberry gelatin 　2 cups sour cream
1 (16-oz.) can whole-berry 　1/2 cup chopped pecans
　cranberry sauce 　Fresh strawberries, optional

Combine pineapple juice and water in a 2-qt. saucepan; heat to boiling. Remove from heat and add gelatin; stir until it dissolves. Stir in cranberry sauce, lemon juice, peel and nutmeg. Chill until mixture thickens slightly. Add sour cream; stir until thoroughly combined. Fold in pineapple and pecans. Pour into an 8-cup lightly greased mold; chill until firm. Unmold onto a serving plate and garnish with strawberries.

Courtney Claire Czarnecki

Meats

This chapter has a very short and simple name, considering it covers a multitude of choices from chicken to veal.

Chicken is probably the most versatile of all the meats available. There is nothing more basic than perfectly roasted chicken, yet it will grace even the most elaborate table. On the other end of the spectrum, there are few things more sinful than fried chicken with its golden-brown crispy skin. We eat chicken a lot in our home for the sake of economy, but most of all we love it because it can be prepared in literally hundreds of ways—all wonderful!

When it comes to veal, in Italy, they do wondrous things with scallops of veal—or veal medallions as they are often called. Veal is a delicacy people of every country enjoy, prepared in their own special way. Veal is costly; therefore, it's good to remember that chicken can be substituted in many veal recipes. Veal Piccata and Veal Marsala (See Index) are my two favorite ways to prepare this delicate meat.

And beef...heartiest of meats! What is more American than a fat juicy hamburger? Or, there's the gourmet filet of beef that is my favorite cut. I seldom order steak in a restaurant because my husband Ed is a master at cooking a filet, a beef tender or a standing rib roast. He has perfected the art, for both on the grill or oven cooking. Ed's Beef Tender with Bearnaise Sauce (See Index) is what legends are made of...

I have saved the wonderful, succulent, "other white meat" for last. In the past, pork had the reputation of being full of fat and, therefore, bad for us. In the old days, when my mama prepared our fresh pork ham at holidays, she probably could have cooked it for three days and, with all the fat marbling, it would have still been juicy. Not so today... Today, pork loins and tenderloins are virtually fat free and that's one reason they should not be overcooked. I miss Mama's fresh pork roasts, stuffed with garlic and drizzled with gravy that would make you swoon!! Her cornbread dressing enhanced with pork gravy always took center stage at Thanksgiving.

SOUTHERN FRIED CHICKEN

As a Southerner, I feel no cookbook is complete without a good Southern fried chicken recipe. My husband Ed can rival "the Colonel" himself with his succulent rendition. Our kids' and grandkids' favorite dinner is Papaw's fried chicken, fluffy mashed potatoes with country gravy, baby lima beans, cornbread and blackberry cobbler for dessert. I love those Sunday dinners when he's in charge.

1 fresh fryer, cut up
2-3 cups buttermilk
2 cups Crisco oil (approx.)
1-2 cups all-purpose flour

Salt, black pepper, and Cayenne
   pepper, to taste
Country gravy (recipe follows)

Wash chicken pieces well; pat dry and sprinkle with salt. Place in a large bowl with buttermilk and refrigerate for at least 6 hours. When ready to fry, drain chicken in a colander. In a large, heavy skillet or Dutch oven, heat oil to medium-high. (A black iron pot browns the chicken too fast—do not use) Mix flour, black and red pepper. Dredge chicken pieces, one at a time, in flour mixture and place in oil. Reserve the leftover flour for making gravy. Turn heat to medium and fry uncovered for about 15 minutes, or until golden. Turn chicken and cover lightly, leaving room for steam to escape; fry another 15 minutes. Drain well.
Yield: 4-6 servings

Country gravy:
1/2 cup chicken drippings
1/3 cup reserved flour

1 cup milk (approx.)
Salt, to taste

Pour off all but about ½ cup chicken drippings; stir in reserved flour, blending well. Do not brown this mixture. Gradually add 1 cup milk, stirring constantly. If too thick, add more milk; if too thin, blend in a little more flour. Taste and add a little salt if necessary. Serve with mashed potatoes.

Fresh, free-range chickens are the birds that have been raised outside cramped cages and generally have a more old-fashioned flavor. For Southern fried chicken, there is no substitute—fresh is the best!

CHICKEN POT PIE

Another Southern staple is chicken pot pie. My grandmother made the best pot pie in the world, but alas! she never wrote down any of her wonderful recipes. This is my take-off and it's not bad, if I say so myself.

3 qts. water
1 frying chicken, washed
Salt and pepper, to taste
2 pods garlic, minced
1/2 medium onion, finely chopped
3 Tbsps. flour

1 hard-boiled egg, chopped
1 can LeSeuer Petit-Pois peas, drained well
1 can sliced carrots, drained and diced
1 refrigerated prepared pie dough

Place water in stock pot and add chicken, salt, pepper, garlic and onion. Boil until tender; reserve broth and chill. When chicken cools, debone and cut into medium sized chunks. Combine flour with 2 cups chilled chicken broth to make a thick paste. Mix chicken, chopped hard-boiled egg, peas, carrots and broth mixture; place in a greased pot pie baking dish. Roll out pie dough and place on top of pie dish—seal and crimp edges. Place pot pie in a 350-degree oven; bake until hot and bubbly and the crust is golden.
Yield: 6 servings

ED'S GRILLED CHICKEN

2 (3 lb.) frying chicken, cut up
1 cup olive oil
1 Tbsp. lemon pepper

1 Tbsp. garlic powder
1 Tbsp. dried parsley
1 Tbsp. Worcestershire sauce

Light coals in grill; let heat up for 20-30 minutes. While coals are heating, prepare basting sauce by mixing olive oil with remaining ingredients. When coals are hot, place chicken pieces on grill; cook on low-to-medium fire for 15 minutes, with grill cover closed. After 15 minutes, turn pieces over and begin to baste with sauce. Continue turning and basting every 15 minutes until chicken is done—about 45 minutes (keep grill cover closed). Barbecue sauce can be added at last basting, or when chicken is done.

CHICKEN CASSEROLE
It doesn't get any easier than this—layer, cover, and bake. Delicious!

6 large boneless chicken breasts
1 can cream of chicken soup
1 can cream of mushroom soup
1/4 cup dry white wine

1 large can artichoke hearts,
    drained
1 small can chopped mushrooms
1 ½ cups garlic croutons

Salt and pepper chicken breasts and place in a 13x9x2-inch baking dish. Layer with the remaining ingredients in order given. Cover and bake for 1 hour in a 350-degree oven. Serve with mashed potatoes or fluffy rice.
Yield: 6 servings
Note: This casserole can be made with boneless pork chops in place of chicken.

CHINESE CHICKEN
This recipe is courtesy of my dear friend and sous chef, Sylvia Norton. Sylvia and I present cooking classes several times a year at the Woman's Department Club. Working with this special person is a true joy.

4 cups cooked, cubed chicken
2 cups cooked rice
1 ½ cups mayonnaise
2 tsps. chopped onion
2 tsps. lemon juice
2 cans cream of chicken Soup
2 cups fresh mushrooms, sliced

2 (4-oz.) cans water chestnuts,
    drained and sliced
2 tsps. salt
1/2 cup margarine
1 cup slivered almonds
2 cups corn flakes

Mix all ingredients except almonds, corn flakes and margarine; put in greased baking dish. Melt butter, add almonds and cornflakes; place on top of chicken-rice mixture. Bake 35 minutes in a 350-degree oven.
Yield: 12-14 servings
Note: This is delicious with steamed asparagus or broccoli spears.

CHABLIS CHICKEN

This was one of the first company dishes I learned to cook as a young bride. I am sure my friends were happy when my repertoire began to include a little more variety. It is delicious served with Lemon Rice (See Index) green bean casserole, and a Caesar salad.

4 chicken breasts	1 medium onion, sliced
Salt, pepper and garlic powder,	2 stalks celery, coarsely chopped
to taste	6-8 fresh mushrooms, sliced
4 Tbsps Crisco oil	3/4 cup white Chablis

Season chicken breasts with salt, pepper, and garlic powder; brown in oil in a medium skillet. Add onion, celery and mushrooms and sauté lightly. Pour wine over all, cover and simmer for 45 minutes.
Yield: 4 servings

BREAST OF CHICKEN GOURMET

6 Tbsps. butter, divided	1/3 medium onion, finely chopped
4 boneless chicken breasts	1/2 pt. sour cream
3/4 cup white Chablis, divided	Salt and white pepper, to taste

Melt 4 tablespoons butter in a skillet; add chicken breasts and simmer uncovered until just brown, turning occasionally. Sprinkle breasts with ½ cup Chablis; cover and steam until tender—about 20 minutes. Melt the remaining 2 tablespoons butter in another pan and sauté onion—do not brown. Stir in the remaining Chablis and sour cream; remove from heat. When chicken is tender, drizzle some of the sour cream sauce over it. Add salt and white pepper to taste: heat only long enough to warm the cream sauce again. Place remaining sauce in a gravy boat and serve with fluffy rice.
Yield: 4 servings

*Do not use a wood cutting board to cut up raw chicken.
After cutting it up, be sure to sterilize the work area.*

SHERRIED ARTICHOKE CHICKEN

This elegant dish was a most requested item in my catering business—second only to Chicken Tetrazzini. There are many pluses to this masterpiece, one being that it can be made a day ahead and baked when ready to serve. Another plus is that it can be multiplied easily if you're feeding lots of people. The biggest plus is the delectable gourmet flavor. For a perfect menu, pair it with fluffy rice, glazed baby carrots, Caesar Salad and hard crusty rolls.

6 large boneless chicken breasts
Salt, pepper and paprika, to taste
1 stick butter, divided
1 (14-oz.) can artichoke hearts,
  drained and halved

1/2 lb. fresh mushrooms, sliced
1/2 cup chopped green onions
3 Tbsps. flour
3/4 cup chicken broth
1/4 cup cream sherry

Sprinkle chicken breasts with salt, pepper, and paprika. Melt ½ stick butter in a large skillet and brown chicken pieces. Place chicken in a sprayed 13x9x2-inch baking dish and place artichoke hearts around chicken pieces. Add remaining butter to the drippings in the skillet; sauté mushrooms and green onions until tender. Sprinkle flour over the mushrooms and blend well; stir in broth and sherry. Stir over low heat, blending well and pour over chicken and artichoke hearts. Cover baking dish tightly with foil and bake in a 375-degree oven for 1 hour.
Yield: 6 servings

Oloroso sherries are sweet, full-flavored wines. They are usually aged longer than their dry counterparts, and are more expensive. They are often labeled "cream" or "golden". When cooking with sherry, it is your own personal taste that determines which sherry to use. When drinking sherry, it is the dry that is most popular.

PAULA'S CRUNCHY CHICKEN

I first sampled this delicious chicken dish at the home of Paula and Tom Chavanne. This husband-and-wife team turned out a captivating meal that evening. Accompanying Paula's chicken were Tom's potatoes au gratin, green beans, and a very special salad made with goat cheese. Served with a delicate white wine, it was quite a feast.

2 cups buttery cracker crumbs   2 tsps. salt
3/4 cup grated Parmesan cheese   1/8 tsp. pepper
1/4 cup chopped fresh parsley   4 boneless chicken breasts
1 tsp. minced garlic   1 cup margarine, melted

Combine cracker crumbs, cheese, parsley, garlic, salt and pepper. Dip chicken pieces in margarine; roll in crumb mixture. Arrange chicken in a sprayed shallow roasting pan. Pour remaining margarine over chicken and bake uncovered, at 350 degrees for 1 hour. Do not turn chicken.
Yield: 4 servings

SWISS CHICKEN

Another layered delight—this recipe is from the kitchen of my friend and gourmet cook, Jean Boyette. Young brides need to take note of this one, for it is easy, but tastes as if you've been in the kitchen all day.

6 boneless chicken breast halves   1 can cream of chicken soup
1/8 tsp. garlic powder   1/4 cup milk
1/8 tsp. black pepper   2 cups herb stuffing mix
6 (4-in.square) slices Swiss cheese 1/4 cup butter or margarine

Place chicken in a greased 13x9x2-inch baking dish; sprinkle with garlic powder and pepper. Top each breast with cheese. Combine soup and milk, stirring until smooth; pour over chicken. Sprinkle with stuffing mix and drizzle with butter. Bake 50 minutes in a 350-degree oven.
Yield: 6 servings

GLAZED CORNISH HENS

There are few meals more romantic than a special dinner for two of delicate Cornish hens. If you're looking for time with that special someone, you can either prepare them in a slow cooker, or bake in the oven. Either way, your meal will be happily cooking while you sip on cocktails and munch on light appetizers.

2 Cornish hens	1 cup Catalina salad dressing
Salt and pepper, to taste	1 cup apricot preserves

The night before serving, sprinkle the hens lightly with salt and pepper; mix together Catalina dressing and apricot preserves. Marinate hens overnight, until ready to cook. Put hens, along with the marinade, in the slow cooker that is set on low and cook for eight hours.
Yield: 2 servings
Note: Oven method: marinate hens same as above. When ready to cook, place in a small roasting pan and bake in a 350-degree oven, uncovered, for 30 minutes; remove from oven, baste with sauce, then cover roaster and bake an additional 40 minutes or until tender.

SHERRIED CHICKEN

If my memory serves me right, the original recipe for Sherried Chicken came out of the ever popular River Road Recipes Cookbook from the Baton Rouge Junior League, the first cookbook I ever owned. I have adjusted it through the years. This great dish is simplicity at its best.

2 frying chickens, cut up	4 Tbsps. dry onion soup mix
Salt and pepper, to taste	2 stalks celery, chopped fine
1/2 stick butter	1 ½ cups dry sherry

Season chicken with salt and pepper; brown in butter in a heavy skillet. Arrange pieces in a large roasting pan, skin side up. Sprinkle chicken with onion soup mix, then celery. Drizzle with sherry; cover roaster. Bake in a 350-degree oven for one hour.
Yield: 4-6 servings

TO-DIE-FOR HOLIDAY ROAST TURKEY

Fried or smoked turkeys have become very popular during the last fifteen years, but I still prefer the traditional baked bird like grandma used to make. There are hundreds of ways to bake a turkey and I have tried them all—baking it breast side down (boiled taste), baking it open (dry), baking it in a bag (fell apart!).   Finally, I came up with the perfect method for our clan--one that gave me pride in the serving. This baking method produces a golden, crispy-skinned turkey that is incredibly moist inside--one that could grace the cover of a gourmet magazine. Its natural gravy is a rich, golden brown. I think you'll love it.

1 stick butter	Salt and pepper, to taste
Juice of 1/2 lemon	1/2 large onion, cut in half
2 Tbsps. flour	3 large pieces celery
1/8 teaspoon garlic powder	1/2 cup cornstarch
1 medium-large fresh turkey	1 cup water (room temperature)

Soften butter (do not melt) and add lemon juice, flour and garlic powder, blending well. Remove giblets from turkey carcass and wash turkey well; pat dry. Salt and pepper turkey, both inside and out. Place onion and celery in carcass. Rub butter mixture over breasts and legs, coating well. Place in turkey roaster and bake uncovered about 45 minutes in a 350-degree oven. Remove from oven, cover, and bake about 20 minutes per pound. Do not overcook. When done, remove turkey from roaster. Mix cornstarch and cool water until smooth. Thicken turkey drippings with this mixture. Drizzle gravy on sliced turkey breast and dressing. Note: You can also add cooked, chopped giblets to gravy, if desired.

*One of those Kodak memorable moments was the Christmas
I baked the turkey with all the giblets inside the cavity, still in their
little paper sack. That taught me to listen to my Mama when she
told me to "wash the turkey well, Marlyn—inside and out."
The pork roast was a hot item that holiday.*

TURKEY AND SHRIMP JAMBALAYA

I grew up in Baton Rouge amid LSU Tiger fever. I was a part of the cheering crowd when Billy Cannon made his legendary touchdown in 1958 and during the seasons when Paul Dietzel's Chinese Bandits wooed the fans. My fondest memories, however, are of the buzz and excitement of unforgettable parties and the lavish Southern feasts served there. With my many delicious memories, it was no wonder I was excited when I was asked to write a special feature story about the 1994 L.S.U. Championship game in the Sugar Bowl. With the help of friends, I had a ball whipping up some luscious dishes for the special day. This jambalaya recipe is from the files of Minnett Thornton, an avid Tiger fan who, with husband Blocker, never misses a game. This is one of Minnett's favorites to take to tailgate parties. For the Cajun touch, Andouille sausage makes this dish especially appealing.

1/2 lb. andouille sausage, sliced	2 cups raw long grain rice
1 lb. raw turkey breast, diced into ½ inch pieces	1 (1-lb.) can tomatoes, crushed with liquid
1/4 cup vegetable oil	2 cups hot chicken stock
2 cups onion, chopped	1 lb. raw peeled shrimp
4 cloves garlic, minced	4 green onions, sliced
1 bell pepper, chopped	1/4 cup chopped parsley
2 stalks celery, chopped	Salt and pepper, to taste
3 bay leaves	Tabasco sauce, to taste
1/2 tsp. dried thyme	

Sauté sausage and turkey in oil for several minutes; remove meat and set aside. In the same oil (adding a little extra if needed), cook the onions and garlic until soft. Add the bell pepper and celery; cook until tender. Add bay leaves and thyme. Add raw rice and stir until coated in oil. Add tomatoes, chicken stock, and reserved meat; bring mixture to a boil. Reduce heat, cover and simmer for about 30 minutes until rice is done. Add shrimp; cook until shrimp are pink. Just before serving, add green onion, parsley, salt, pepper, and hot sauce.
Yield: 10-12 servings

PIG ROAST (COCHON DE LAIT)

Are you familiar with the term "living high on the hog"? I hail from South Louisiana, where it often describes a gathering of friends to roast pigs, eat hearty and sip a few cold ones. In Cajun country, this type of revelry is known as a Cochon de Lait (French for suckling pig). Here in North Louisiana, it's a pig roast. When members of our boating group, the Shreveport Power Squadron, are not enjoying life from the deck of a boat, one of our favorite parties of the year is the annual pig roast at the home of Sam and Linda Duggan. Sam learned about pig roasting at an early age, for there were many pig roasts at the Duggan family camp located on the Cane River in Natchitoches, with one hosted each year during the Christmas Lights Festival. As Sam tells us, "when you have a family of seven children and lots of kin folks, there is no better way to feed a crowd." Two of Sam's sisters became engaged at pig roasts, causing Sam's dad to swear there would be a pig roast until he "married off" all his daughters! The first pig roast Sam and Linda hosted together was for their wedding reception in 1986. My husband Ed and I also had a Cochon de Lait when we married—our rehearsal dinner. Held on the banks of a sleepy old bayou in South Louisiana, our celebration was attended by 150 friends and lasted for two days. It may well have been the longest rehearsal dinner on record.

For those of you who are adventurous and would like to start your own pig roasting tradition, Sam has shared his secrets with us. Preparing and executing a pig roast is not for the weak, for it is much akin to boiling crawfish— both require lots of labor to be a success. I do, however, guarantee if you follow these instructions, the results will be the most delectable pork imaginable.

The Planning and Prepping:
A successful pig roast requires advance planning, for the pig, as well as the firewood must be ordered several weeks ahead. The pig is put on the fire the evening prior to the roast. This is referred to as the "Pig *Watch*" as friends begin arriving to help Sam split cords of firewood. These loyal helpers go home about midnight, while Sam keeps watch, banking the fire several times during the night. Keeping the fire hot is a vital part if the pig is to be ready by the following afternoon.

Preparing the Pig: Split pig open and insert garlic pods under the skin, sprinkling with salt and black pepper. Place heavy wire on the front and back of the pig, securing it in place. Sam Duggan's pig roaster consists of four poles set into the ground, with tin on three sides (for reflecting the heat), and a metal pole placed on top the roaster. A rotisserie is attached to the pole and the pig encased in the metal wire is attached to an electric rotisserie. The pig then turns slowly over an open fire for fifteen to sixteen hours. During the night, as the pig turns and begins cooking process, the fire must be banked two or three times in order for the pig to be cooked in time for next day's occasion. The entire cooking procedure takes about a half cord of wood, for the fire must be kept hot. How quickly the pig cooks is controlled by moving the pole closer to, or farther from, the fire. Pig is done when it stops dripping.

On the big day, workers arrive early to relieve Sam for awhile, and guests begin arriving mid-morning, laden with mouth-watering appetizers, desserts, and casseroles. Everyone congregates outdoors— sipping, snacking, and enjoying the sight of the golden-brown pig while it slowly rotates over the blazing fire. Around 2:00 p.m., the crispy-skinned entrée is taken off the fire, removed from the wire grill, and placed on a table where the skin and bones are removed, and the choice meat is put on platters for ravenous guests.

Some dishes that go well for an outdoor roast are broccoli rice, candied yams, black-eyed peas, fruit salads, cornbread, bread pudding, and German chocolate cake for dessert.

CROWN PORK ROAST

It will be a "grateful gathering" at your home on Christmas day when you pull out all the stops with this stunningly beautiful crown pork roast. My husband Ed discovered this treasured recipe in an old Southern Living cookbook years ago and, after some testing and adjusting, declared it to be his favorite. The stuffing, which can be made a day ahead, is superb, and the crown pork roast cannot be beat for flavor and tenderness. If you're planning on serving this cut of roast, call your butcher and order at least a week ahead. He can advise you on the size of roast you will need to accommodate your guests. This is the epitome of class, served with baked sweet potatoes, fresh green beans, ambrosia, and Southern pecan pie with whipped cream.

1 crown pork roast
Salt and pepper to taste
2 (8 oz.) pkgs. seasoned
   bread stuffing
2 Tbsps. grated lemon rind
1/2 cup finely chopped onion
2 Tbsps. dried parsley

2 sticks butter, melted
3 Tbsps. freshly squeezed
   lemon juice
1 ½ cups chicken broth
1/2 cup sauterne wine
Gravy (see recipe below)

Trim excess fat from roast and season with salt and pepper. Place in a greased open roasting pan. Combine remaining ingredients and mix well. Place stuffing in center of roast. To remaining stuffing, add about 3 tablespoons chicken broth and place in a greased baking dish; set aside. Bake roast in a 350-degree oven about 20 minutes per pound or until meat is tender. After one hour of cooking, place foil loosely over stuffing to prevent drying. Baste with dry white wine several times during cooking to prevent dryness. Forty-five minutes before serving, place reserved stuffing in oven and bake until hot and bubbly.

For gravy: Drain off fat and add 1 cup chicken broth to drippings; simmer 5 minutes. To thicken, stir in cornstarch that has been mixed with cool water. Drizzle over meat and/or dressing.

To serve: Garnish roast with spiced apples or peaches. Top the rib crowns with boots or cherry tomatoes. Picture perfect!

MARY'S PERFECT COMPANY PORK

My dear friend, Mary Rademacher is a master at cooking pork that will make you swoon. This splendid dish requires very little effort—simply whip up the marinade the evening before and pour it over the tenderloin. I've been known to forget and put it in to marinate only a few hours before baking—it's still a winner. Broccoli rice and a tossed green salad will round out your menu for a perfect meal.

1 bottle Catalina salad dressing
1 box (2 pkts.) dried onion soup
   mix

1 can (whole berry) cranberry
   sauce
1 ½ - 2 lbs. pork tenderloin

Mix first 3 ingredients, blending well. The night before serving, place tenderloin in baking dish and pour marinade on top. Do not add water. Cover and refrigerate. Remove from refrigerator about 2 hours before baking. Bake uncovered in a 325-degree oven for 20 minutes; cover and bake until meat reaches an internal temperature of 165 degrees—about 20 minutes.
Yield: 4 servings

MARLYN'S PORK LOIN

For a dinner party one evening I decided to experiment with sauces. This is what I came up with—the blending of sweet Catalina dressing and apricot preserves, the tang of horseradish and dry mustard, and the exotic flavor of cream sherry produced a gravy that was "slap your mama" good.

1 cup Catalina dressing
1 cup apricot preserves
1 Tbsp. dry mustard

1 Tbsp. horseradish
1/2 cup cream sherry
1 large pork loin

Combine first 5 ingredients, blending well. Place pork loin in a medium roaster that's been coated with nonstick spray. Pour sauce over pork. Bake covered in a 350-degree oven for about 20 minutes per pound. Serve thickly sliced pork with hot sauce drizzled on top.

TEQUILA LIME PORK TENDERLOIN

This recipe is courtesy of our friends Harlan and Lil Appel. It's a real winner accompanied by Lime Cilantro Mayonnaise and Roasted Red Pepper Mayonnaise. This fun couple love cooking together and can always be depended upon to come up with something new and innovative.

1 pork tenderloin
Lawry's Tequila Lime Marinate
2 to 3 tsps. red pepper flakes

1/4 cup lime juice (about 2 large limes)

Rinse and dry tenderloin; pull off any white skin and put tenderloin in a heavy plastic bag. Add tequila lime marinate to cover loin in bag. Add lime juice and the rind of the limes to bag, with the red pepper flakes. Massage bag to mix marinade and distribute evenly around the tenderloin. Marinate for 30 minutes at room temperature. Cook on an outdoor grill, or bake in a 325-degree oven until internal temperature of 160 degrees is reached. Serve with sliced rounds of French bread baguettes or small rolls and Lime Cilantro Mayonnaise and Roasted Red Pepper Mayonnaise. Recipe follows:

Lime Cilantro Mayonnaise
1/2 cup mayonnaise
1 ½ Tbsp. cilantro, chopped

1 ½ to 2 tsps. lime peel, grated
1 tsp. lime juice

Combine all ingredients and mix well; refrigerate.

Roasted Red Pepper Mayonnaise
1/2 cup mayonnaise
1/4 tsp. dried oregano
1/4 tsp. garlic and herb no salt
   seasoning

1/8 tsp. cayenne pepper
1/4 tsp. Tabasco
3 Tbsp. roasted red peppers,
   chopped

Combine all ingredients and mix well. Refrigerate.

PORK TENDERLOIN WITH MUSTARD SAUCE

I begged for this recipe one night at a dinner party—it is wonderful!

1/4 cup soy sauce
1/4 cup bourbon
1/2 tsp. dry mustard

2 Tbsps. brown sugar
2 (1 lb.) pork tenderloins
Mustard sauce (recipe follows)

Mix first 4 ingredients in a Zip-Loc bag or a plastic dish. Add tenderloins and marinate for at least 2 hours, turning occasionally. Remove pork, discarding marinade; place pork on a rack in a shallow roasting pan. Bake in a 325-degree oven for 45 minutes or until meat thermometer inserted into thickest part registers 165 degrees. Slice and serve with mustard sauce.

Mustard Sauce:
2/3 cup Hellmann's mayonnaise
2/3 cup sour cream

2 Tbsps. dry mustard
Chopped green onions for garnish

Combine all ingredients; cover and chill. Serve drizzled on pork.

PORK CHOPS AND WILD RICE

This dish will do honor to your table whether serving a sit-down dinner for guests, or for an evening family meal. My very talented friend Mary Rademacher is the creator of this marvelous rice dish. Paired up with Susan's Roasted Asparagus (See Index) and Baked Apricots (See Index), this dish will reign supreme!

1 cup raw wild rice
1 ½ cups water
1 can cream of mushroom soup
2 cans mushroom, undrained

3 Tbsps. granulated chicken
  bouillon
4 thick center-cut pork chops
Salt and pepper, to taste

Place rice in a 13x9x2-inch baking dish that has been coated with non-stick spray. Mix together water, soup, mushrooms and bouillon; spread over rice. Salt and pepper chops and brown in a little oil; place on top of rice and sauce. Bake covered in a 325-degree oven for two hours.
Yield: 4 servings

PORK MEDALLIONS

This is a sinful, but divine dish, and one of my son Danny's favorites. It ran about 20 years ago in a Louisiana Conservationist Magazine. This publication which, to our chagrin, is no longer in print, was a favorite in our home. We especially enjoyed the food column, Bayou Kitchen which featured popular Louisianans and their favorite dishes. We could always count on a great selection of South Louisiana favorites.

2 lbs. pork tenderloin, well
  trimmed, cut crosswise into
  1-inch thick medallions
1 tsp. salt
1/2 tsp. pepper
1/2 cup flour
2 eggs
1/4 cup water

1 cup dry bread crumbs
6 Tbsps. butter
2 Tbsps olive oil
1/2 cup dry white wine
1/2 lb. mushrooms, sliced
1 Tbsp. lemon juice
2 Tbsps. finely chopped fresh
  parsley

Dry pork medallions with paper towels. Combine salt, pepper and flour; dredge medallions. Shake off excess. Beat eggs with water; dip medallions in egg and coat with bread crumbs. Press meat with heel of palm to adhere bread crumbs; dry 10 minutes. In a Dutch oven, heat butter and oil; sauté medallions 8 minutes on each side. Remove browned meat, and drain on paper towels. After all medallions have cooked, transfer to a heated platter and keep warm. Remove pan from heat. Add wine and, over high heat, deglaze pan, scrapping brown bits on bottom and sides of pan, until liquid is reduced by half, about 3 minutes. Add mushrooms and cook, stirring 2 minutes. Add lemon juice and cook, stirring 1 minute. Pour sauce over meat, garnish with parsley, and serve immediately.
Yield: 6 serving

Leftover pork can be as flavorful as the original dish.
Chop meat and mix with barbecue sauce for a delicious sandwich on a
bun, or chop and stir fry pork, adding Chinese veggies, rice, green
onions, seasonings and soy sauce for a great oriental entrée

BAKED PORK CHOPS

My cousin, Deryl Hamilton and I have been exchanging recipes for as long as I can remember. She and I grew up together in Baton Rouge and the bonds we made are for life. We learned to appreciate good food from our grandmother and our mothers, who were perhaps the best cooks ever. We never tasted boudin, andouille sausage or tasso until we were grown, for these women were strictly French Creole cooks. My mother is awfully proud of her ancestors from Bordeaux, France. Deryl's baked pork chops are simple to prepare and very flavorful. I love to serve this with macaroni and cheese and petit pois peas or baby lima beans.

6 thick pork chops   1 tube Ritz crackers, crushed fine
1 egg, beaten with 1 Tbsp. water

Dip chops in egg; roll in cracker crumbs—repeat procedure to make thick coating. Spray a baking sheet with non-stick spray and place chops on it. Bake in a 325-degree oven for 30 minutes. Turn chops and bake another 30 minutes.
Yield: 6 servings

PORK CHOP CASSEROLE

This tasty dish will cook while you're helping the kids with homework, stretched out enjoying a novel, or soaking in a tub of bubbles. Just throw it together and pop in the oven. Since it has a luscious creamy sauce, I usually cook a pot of rice to accompany it.

3 Tbsps. cooking oil   2 cans cream of mushroom soup
6 thick boneless pork chops   1/2 cup dry white wine
1/2 small onion, sliced   1/2 cup sour cream
1 Tbsp. chopped bell pepper   Salt & pepper, to taste

In large oven-proof skillet, heat oil and cook pork chops about 5 minutes on each side. Combine remaining ingredients and pour over chops. Bake covered in a 350-degree oven for 1 hour.
Yield: 6 servings

ORANGE JUICE PORK CHOPS

This divine pork recipe is a favorite recipe of Shelley and Robert Braswell and their girls, Alexa and Carly. Shelley graciously agreed to share it and it has now climbed to the top of our favorite list also.

6 pork chops
Salt and pepper, to taste
4 Tbsps. olive oil (approximate)
1 large onion, thinly sliced
1 tsp. minced garlic
1 tsp. ground ginger
1/4 tsp. cayenne pepper
3 dashes Tabasco

1 Tbsp. Worcestershire sauce
2 cups orange juice
2 cups chicken broth
1 pkg. Lipton Onion Soup Mix
3 Tbsps. cornstarch
1 cup water
3 Tbsps. chopped green onions

Salt and pepper pork chops. Brown in olive oil with sliced onions and garlic, about 5 minutes per side. When brown, sprinkle chops with ginger, red pepper, Tabasco, and Worcestershire; place chops in a 13x9x2-inch baking dish; set aside. In a mixing bowl, combine orange juice, chicken broth and onion soup mix until smooth. Pour orange juice mixture to cover pork chops in pan. Cover and cook over low heat for 1 – 1½ hours, stirring occasionally, until pork chops are tender. Remove chops from baking dish. In small bowl, add cornstarch to 1 cup water and stir until smooth; add to baking dish to thicken sauce and make gravy. Return pork chops to baking dish and keep warm. Sprinkle with green onions and serve over fluffy rice.

PORK TENDERLOIN FOR BEGINNERS

1/2 cup yellow mustard
1/2 cup brown sugar (approximate)

1 ½ lbs. pork tenderloin
Salt, pepper, garlic powder, to taste

Mix mustard and brown sugar, blending well. Mixture should be tart/sweet to suit your taste. Sprinkle tenderloin with salt, pepper, and garlic powder. Liberally coat meat with mustard blend. Place in a sprayed baking dish; bake uncovered in a 350-degree oven for about 1 hour. Do not overcook!
Yield: 2-4 servings

BEEF TENDERLOIN WITH BEARNAISE SAUCE

This is the best beef tenderloin ever! My husband, Ed came up with this recipe about 15 years ago and it never failed to draw accolades from catering clients, as well as dinner guests. For a cocktail party, served with tea rolls and horseradish mayonnaise, this is the epitome of class. The sugar coating is the secret to the success of this dish.

1 (5 lb.) tenderloin, strap removed   Garlic powder, to taste
Cracked pepper, to taste   1/4 cup granulated sugar (approx.)
Lemon pepper, to taste

Season tenderloins with cracked pepper, lemon pepper, garlic powder and sugar, coating tops and sides of meat. Let stand at room temperature for two hours. Cook on an outdoor grill on low fire for 20 minutes each side, or until desired doneness is reached. Let meat stand for 15 minutes before cutting.
For oven baking, season tenderloin same as above. Preheat oven to 500 degrees. Place tenderloin on a rack in a greased roaster or pan. As soon as you place tenderloin in oven, reduce heat to 325 degrees. Cook uncovered for 20 minutes per pound. Meat will be medium-rare. Let tenderloin stand for at least 15 minutes before cutting. Serve with Bearnaise Sauce (recipe follows)
Yield: 12 servings

Bearnaise Sauce
2 egg yolks   1/4 tsp. soy sauce
1/2 Tbsps. lemon juice   1 stick butter, softened
1/2 Tbsps. tarragon vinegar   2 Tbsps. chopped green onion tops

In a blender put egg yolks, lemon juice, tarragon vinegar and soy sauce. Blend on high speed. Melt butter in microwave; very slowly pour into egg mixture as the blender is going. Blend until thickened. Add chopped green onion tops and blend for about 10 seconds. Pour some of the sauce over meat and save reminder for serving with meal.

Using meat thermometer: Rare— 120-125 degrees
                           Medium Rare— 130-135 degrees
                           Medium— 140-150 degrees

SAUCY BEEF BRISKET

If you're in the market for an economical cut of meat that will stretch well, try my daughter, Debbie's Saucy Brisket. This is a breeze to prepare, it is tender, and has an exceptional flavor. Deb's friend, Dinah Zapatka is the creator of this well-seasoned roast.

4-5 lb. beef brisket   1 (15-oz.) bottle soy sauce
Coarse grain black pepper

Sprinkle brisket liberally with pepper; place in a 2-gallon plastic bag. Pour one-half bottle soy sauce over it and place in the refrigerator for 24 hours, turning a few times. To bake, remove from bag, discarding soy sauce. Place brisket in a 13x9x2-inch baking dish and cover top and bottom with remaining soy sauce. Cover tightly with foil (otherwise, no gravy) and bake in a 275-degree oven for 5-6 hours.
Yield: 10-12 servings
Note: This slow method of cooking renders a flavorful, tender roast.

MARINATED BRISKET

This is a recipe I've had for at least 30 years. The marinade is so divine I used it often at Occasions Catering—guests cleaned their plates and came back for more!

4-5 lb. beef brisket, not trimmed

Marinade:
1 cup soy sauce   1/4 cup (Accent) MSG tenderizer
1/2 cup dry sherry   2 cloves garlic, minced
1/2 cup white wine   1/2 cup sugar
Dash of Worcestershire   1/2 cup lemon juice
3 cups pineapple juice   Salt, to taste

Blend together all marinade ingredients; marinate meat for 48 hours. Cover tightly and bake in a 275-degree oven for 5 hours.
Yield: 10-12 servings
Marinade Variations: Use Italian dressing; add dry sherry, garlic, sugar, lemon juice and Accent.

CAROL'S RUMP ROAST

This rump roast could easily be labeled "The Best of the Best". It is the product of Carol Schexnaildre, a New Orleans lady who can hold her own when it comes to Creole or any southern comfort cooking. Her son, Mark Schexnaildre, has been bragging about his Mom's rump roast for years. One night at a family crawfish boil at Mark's home, I had the pleasure of meeting Carol and sampling this succulent roast. Mark had not exaggerated—it is simply divine. That evening, it was served as an appetizer, with gravy and small rolls—I lost count after my third serving. A few years ago, Mark's sister put together a cookbook of all her mothers' favorite dishes and sent me a copy. I'm so proud of this treasure, I refer to it as my "Joy of Cooking". We love this roast for Sunday dinner, served with rice, smothered okra, candied yams, ambrosia and cornbread. Don't let the length of the recipe scare you— it is very simple to prepare.

1 (5-6 lb.) rump roast
5 cloves garlic, sliced
Cayenne pepper, to cover roast

1 box (2 pkgs.) dry onion soup mix
1 can Beefy Mushroom soup
Tony Chachere's Roux, to taste

Place heavy duty aluminum foil in the bottom of a roasting pan, with enough to wrap roast air tight. Make various slits in the roast and stuff it with garlic. Coat the roast in the cayenne pepper. Sprinkle soup packages over the entire roast, in addition to the can of beefy mushroom soup. Place roast in the foil/pan with the fat side up for extra flavor while cooking. Preheat oven to 400 degrees; cook roast for one hour. After one hour, turn oven down to 225 degrees and cook roast for 30 minutes per pound. (A 5-lb. roast will cook for 3.5 hours.) Once roast is finished cooking, remove from foil, put on a platter and scrape remaining fat off of it.
Yield: 10-12 servings

Options: Pour gravy out of the foil into a container. For a fat-free gravy, refrigerate it until fat solidifies; skim all fat off the top and discard. Refrigerate roast so it can be sliced easily. Heat gravy on stove and add Tony Chachere's Roux, or your favorite roux mix until desired consistency.

LINDA'S MARINATED ROAST BEEF

This deli-style roast beef, courtesy of my friend Linda Duggan, is perfect for picnics, boating trips, or luncheons. It is also delicious sliced paper thin and served as an appetizer with small rolls and a variety of cheeses, mustards and horseradish, or to top off a green salad. It is scrumptious.

4 lb. boneless round roast,   Salt and pepper, to taste
   cut about 3 inches thick
Marinade:
1 cup red wine vinegar   1 tsp. coarsely ground black pepper
1 ½ cups light olive oil   1/4 tsp. oregano
2 pods garlic, chopped, or   2 Tbsps. parsley, minced
   2 tsps., minced   1 bay leaf

Salt and pepper meat liberally. Bake uncovered in a 350-degree oven for two hours, or until meat is done; refrigerate. When cold, remove visible fat and slice very thin. Place sliced roast in a shallow container. Blend together marinade ingredients and pour over roast. Store roast in refrigerator for three days.

ED'S BEEFY NOODLE DISH

My husband Ed throws this dish together with little effort while I prepare cornbread and green beans. I added the sugar to the recipe to cut the acid from the tomatoes.

1 medium onion, chopped   1 Tbsp. minced or pureed garlic
2 Tbsps. cooking oil   2 (14-oz.) cans diced tomatoes
1 ½ lbs. lean ground beef   Pinch of sugar
Salt and pepper, to taste   1 cup elbow macaroni (uncooked)

Sauté onion in oil until transparent; add ground beef. While stirring and browning ground beef, add salt, pepper and garlic. When beef is no longer pink, add a pinch of sugar, tomatoes and juice. Blend well and bring to a simmer; stir in elbow macaroni. At this point, add about ¼ cup water. When it begins to simmer again, cover skillet tightly and turn heat to low. Let cook about 30 minutes or until noodles are tender.
Yield: 4-6 servings

NEW ENGLAND BOILED DINNER

This dish is not South Louisiana by any stretch of the imagination, but it surely does provide a comfort meal on a cold winter night.

3 lbs. boneless beef round
  or lean chuck roast
2 Tbsps cooking oil
2 cans Campbell's Onion soup
2 Tbsps. prepared horseradish
1 medium bay leaf
1 medium clove garlic, minced
4 turnips, sliced

6 medium carrots,
  cut in 2-inch pieces
8 small whole potatoes
1 medium head cabbage,
  cut into 6 wedges
1/2 cup water
1/4 cup cornstarch

In a large heavy Dutch oven, brown roast in oil; pour off fat. Add onion soup, horseradish, bay leaf, and garlic. Cover and cook over low heat for 2 hours; add turnips and carrots. Cook for 30 minutes, stirring occasionally. Add potatoes; place cabbage on top. Cook 30 minutes longer, or until done. Remove meat and vegetables to a serving platter; keep warm. Meanwhile, blend water into cornstarch until smooth; slowly stir into sauce. Simmer, stirring until thick; serve with roast.
Yield: 8 servings

BEEFY CORNBREAD CASSEROLE

2 eggs, slightly beaten
1 cup yellow cornmeal
2 tsps. baking soda
1 tsp. salt and pepper
1 (17-oz.) can cream corn
1 cup milk

1/4 cup cooking oil
1 ½ lbs. ground beef
2 cups shredded Cheddar
1 large onion, chopped
2 jalapeno peppers, chopped

Combine first 7 ingredients; set aside. Sauté ground beef until brown; drain and set aside. Pour half cornmeal mixture into a greased 13x9x2-inch baking dish or large iron skillet. Sprinkle mixture with beef; top with cheese, onion and peppers. Pour remaining batter on top. Bake in a 350-degree oven for 1 hour.
Yield: 6 servings

HAMBURGER CASSEROLE

If you're looking for a new family favorite, look no more. This hearty and delicious casserole is a classic holiday dish on Christmas Eve for my son Danny's family. My daughter-in-law's mother, the late Margie Sutton, started this tradition many years ago. Margie was a bright, talented lady—a master seamstress and designer, gourmet cook, admired teacher, and a cherished mother. We miss her vibrant energy!

1 lb. ground chuck
1 Tbsp. butter
1 clove garlic, crushed
1 tsp. salt
1/4 tsp. pepper
1 tsp. sugar
2 (8-oz.) cans tomato sauce

1 (3-oz.) pkg. cream cheese
1 carton (8-oz.) sour cream
6 green onions, finely chopped
1 (5-oz.) pkgs. egg noodles
1/2 cup grated medium Cheddar
   cheese

Brown meat in butter. Add remaining ingredients, except noodles and cheese; simmer. Meanwhile cook noodles according to package directions; drain and add to meat mixture. Place in a greased 13x9x2-inch baking dish; top with grated cheese. Bake in a 350-degree oven, uncovered, for 30 minutes, or until heated through.
Yield: 6 servings

SHERRIED BEEF

This warm, homey dish is perfect for a cold winter evening when you're looking for some stick-to-the-ribs food for your family. It literally cooks itself. Cook a can of green beans and a pot of cornbread and you've got a winner.

3 lbs. stewing beef
2 cans cream of mushroom soup

1 pkg. dry onion soup
3/4 cups cooking sherry

Combine all ingredients in a large greased casserole. Cover and bake in a 325-degree oven for 3 hours. Serve with noodles or rice.
Yield: 6 servings

CLASSIC MEATLOAF

This is comfort food at its best. I made it for a covered dish dinner and it was an instant success, with everyone begging for the recipe. If "tasting is believing", then I made believers out of a lot of those church members that evening.

3 Tbsps. butter
2 cups finely chopped onion
3/4 cup finely chopped bell pepper
1 large celery rib, finely chopped
1 tsp. dried thyme, crumbled
2 lbs. ground beef
2/3 cup rolled oats
   (Quick may be used)

2 Tbsps. minced garlic
2/3 cup buttery or saltine crackers
1 cup ketchup, divided
2 eggs, beaten
2 tsps. salt
1 ½ tsps. black pepper
4 slices bacon, halved

In a medium skillet, melt butter. Add next four ingredients; cover and cook, stirring once or twice, for 10 minutes. Remove from heat and let cool. In a large bowl, combine ground beef, cooled onion mixture, oats, garlic, crackers, 1/3 cup of the ketchup, eggs, salt and pepper; mix well. Place meat mixture in a 13x9x2-inch baking dish; shape into a flat loaf. Spread the remaining 2/3-cup ketchup over the loaf; arrange the bacon strips on top. Bake in a 350-degree oven for about 1 ¼ hours. Lower temperature to 325 degrees and bake an additional 20 minutes. Let meat rest about 10 minutes before slicing.
Yield: 8 servings

Note: For next-day meat loaf sandwiches, all you need is two thick slices of wheat bread with thinly sliced onions and lots of mayonnaise. Or serve it warm on hot Italian bread, topped with slices of mozzarella cheese and drizzled with seasoned tomato sauce.

Meatloaf has been described as "poor man's food."
Where else can you feed a family of eight for
the price of two pounds of ground meat?

CABBAGE ROLLS

1 lb. ground beef
1 lb. ground pork
1 ½ cups raw rice
2/3 stick butter, melted
1 ½ cups onion, chopped
1 ½ stalks celery, chopped
1/2 cup bell pepper, chopped

2 small cans tomato sauce
4 tsps. salt
1/2 tsp. cayenne pepper
1/2 tsp. black pepper
2 large heads cabbage
7-8 strips bacon

In a large bowl, mix meat, rice, butter, vegetables, 1 can tomato sauce, salt and peppers, blending well. Core cabbage and place in boiling water. As leaves wilt, peel off and drain well. Wrap about 1 tablespoon of meat mixture in each cabbage leaf, starting at the stem edge and rolling; fold ends over. Put rolls in a large roaster. Place bacon strips on rolls, add water almost to cover, and drizzle remaining can of tomato sauce over all. Bake in a 350-degree oven for 1 ½ hours.

BEEFY STUFFED GREEN PEPPERS

This recipe is the creation of an old friend, Carol Guilmino. This gal is such a wonderful cook, she could make even a mud pie taste good!

6 large bell peppers
1 lb. ground beef
3/4 cup chopped onion
1/4 cup chopped bell pepper
1 clove garlic, crushed
1/3 cup chopped celery

1 (17-oz.) can cream-style corn
1/4 tsp. pepper
Red pepper, to taste
1/2 cup Italian breadcrumbs
1/2 cup shredded Cheddar cheese

Cook peppers for 5 minutes in boiling salted water; drain. Cook ground beef with next 4 ingredients until beef is brown and vegetables are tender, stirring often; drain off drippings. Add corn, salt and peppers, and cook, stirring often, until thoroughly heated. Fill peppers with meat mixture; place in a 9-inch square baking dish. Combine breadcrumbs and cheese; sprinkle over peppers. Bake in a 350-degree oven for 15 minutes.
Yield: 6 servings

VEAL

Veal is a delicacy—young, tender, and appealing to all the senses! Though there are no exact age standards for veal, the term is generally used in describing young calves from one to three months old. When you see the term "milk-fed" veal, it means the calves are under twelve weeks old and still on their mother's milk. This meat is white, with a pale pink tinge. Formula-fed veal can come from calves up to four months old. The meat from formula-fed veal is coarser than milk-fed veal. Calves between six and twelve months old are described as baby beef, and this meat is coarser and pink to light red in color. Baby beef requires a little more cooking. Veal, with its lack of natural fat, is easy to overcook, so careful attention must be paid to its preparation. Although I enjoy veal cutlets and chops, veal scallops, or medallions, are my favorite cut for ease in preparation—there is no pounding, it cooks fast, and it is guaranteed to be delicate and tender.

*For authentic **Italian** veal recipes—Veal Piccata, Veal Marsala, and Veal Francesca—see Beyond Our Borders Chapter.*

VEAL IN CREAM SAUCE

2 Tbsps. butter	8 thin slices veal scallops
4 white mushrooms, sliced	1/2 cup dry white wine
2 Tbsps. flour	1/2 cup heavy whipping cream
Salt and fresh ground pepper	Chopped fresh parsley

Melt butter in a large skillet; add the mushrooms. Cook over low heat for 5 minutes; do not brown. Season flour with salt and pepper; coat veal with flour. Turn up the heat and add veal. Cook each side of veal for 2 minutes. Remove veal from the skillet; set aside. With a whisk, gradually add the wine to the pan, mixing it into the flour residue; bring to a boil. Cook, stirring until liquid is reduced by half. Add the cream; simmer 2 minutes more. Serve veal immediately, with sauce on top and garnished with chopped parsley.
Yield: 4 servings

VEAL ROLL-UPS

2 ½ lbs. veal cutlets	1 egg, slightly beaten
8 thin slices ham	4 Tbsps. whipping cream
8 slices Swiss cheese, halved	1 cup seasoned bread crumbs
Sauce:	
1/4 cup white wine	1/2 cup homogenized milk
1 (10-oz.) can cream of	1/2 stick butter, melted
mushroom soup	1/2 cup bread crumbs

Cut veal into 8 serving pieces; pound with a mallet into 1/8-inch thick cutlets. Layer ½ slice of cheese, 1 slice ham, and another ½ slice cheese onto each cutlet. Roll each jellyroll fashion and secure with a toothpick. Mix egg and cream; dip each roll in this mixture, then in bread crumbs. Place, seam-side down, in a shallow 13x9x2-inch baking dish. Make sauce by combining wine, soup and milk and heating until bubbly, stirring. Pour over rolls, cover dish and bake 1 hour. Remove cover, sprinkle with mixture of melted butter and bread crumbs and bake another 10 minutes. Delicious served with rice or noodles.
Yield: 8 servings

LEG OF LAMB WITH ORANGE GLAZE
This lamb dish, with its sweet, succulent flavor, is a true winner. It's possible it's as good as my Greek Lamb (Slap Your Mama #1)

1 (4-5 lb.) leg of lamb	2 Tbsps. Grand Marnier liqueur
4 Tbsps. teriyaki sauce	1 clove garlic, crushed
2/3 cup orange juice	1/2 cup orange marmalade

Place leg of lamb in a greased roaster pan. Mix teriyaki sauce with next 3 ingredients; pour over lamb, coating well. Cover and bake in a 325-degree oven for about 20-30 minutes per pound, until tender, basting occasionally. For the last 30 minutes of cooking time, glaze roast with marmalade and return to oven, uncovered, for the remaining cooking time.
Yield: 6-8 servings

Alec Scott Daniel

Seafood

"Jambalaya, crawfish pie, filet gumbo...son of a gun, we'll have big fun on the bayou." The words of that song depict what South Louisiana is all about—carefree living and good eating. We are blessed with the freshest and finest seafood in the country—shrimp, crab, oysters, trout, red snapper—a never ending supply from the Gulf of Mexico.

Some of my favorite recipes, such as Oysters Bienville, Rockefeller, en Brochette, Scalloped...and crab dishes such as Crabmeat AuGratin and Stuffed Crabs were featured in my original *So Good..Make You Slap Your Mama!* cookbook. I do not have a "next best" recipe for those particular classics. However, in this Volume II, you will find classics that are equally inviting—crab cakes, crawfish pie and etouffee, oyster pie, perfect boiled shrimp, fried shrimp, shrimp Creole... One taste, and you will adopt these marvelous dishes as your own.

There are also some sublime salmon recipes (See Index) in this chapter. Since my experience with cooking fresh salmon has been minimal, the grilled salmon recipes in this chapter are courtesy of a talented friend who holds the title of "master" in cooking salmon.

When it comes to seafood, two of our children keep us well supplied. Our son Danny is generous with his bounty from the Gulf, such as speckled trout, amberjack, red snapper, and tuna. Then, every so often, he will surprise us with an ice chest filled with gigantic fresh shrimp. We have such fun packaging these beauties in water in quart containers and lovingly placing them in the freezer. I tend to want to "hoard" them, while my Ed wants to cook some every night! Donna, our daughter in Lake Charles provides us with fresh lump crabmeat from the Gulf. This delicious, moist crabmeat has been so well picked over, it has virtually no shell. This is royal dining at its best.

How privileged we are to live in a state where we can reap the benefits of such treasures! And, how blessed we are to have kids who love to share!

NO-FAIL BOILED SHRIMP

There is an art to boiling shrimp. Many of us tend to overcook them and the result is a tough, dry shrimp. This no-fail method for boiling perfect shrimp was shared by a fellow caterer, and to this day, it has never failed me. I do confess I added my own touch—sugar and garlic—but the basic preparation is the same, and it works everytime! On Friday evenings my husband Ed and I enjoy boiled shrimp with cocktail sauce or remoulade sauce, potato salad or coleslaw, crusty French bread, and icy cold white wine. The leftovers can be peeled for a luscious shrimp salad the next day or to use in Ed's famous Shrimp in Shells (original Slap Your Mama! cookbook) as a first course to dinner that night.

5 lbs. large raw shrimp	2 Tbsps. salt
8 to 10 quarts water	3 Tbsps. McCormick Season-All
2-3 Tbsps. cayenne pepper	1 lemon, quartered
3 Tbsps. sugar	2 boxes Zatarain's Crab Boil

Fill 12-15 quart pot with water; add all ingredients, except shrimp. Bring to a rolling boil; add shrimp. When the water returns to a full boil, remove from heat, cover tightly and let sit for five minutes. After five minutes, place shrimp in large colander and immediately cover with ice to stop the cooking.
Yield: 10-15 appetizer servings

Tip: Do not boil more than 5 lbs. shrimp at one time. If cooking more, retain boiling, seasoned water and return to stove to use for a second batch. One caution on using the original water: Shrimp will be hotter and spicier than the first batch.

Tip: If cooking shrimp for 40 people, boil about 12 pounds.

*When using frozen raw shrimp for a recipe, remember
they have absorbed lots of liquid. It's a good idea
to thaw them on paper towels before using.*

FRIED SHRIMP

When I lived in South Louisiana, I got spoiled with the bounty of fresh shrimp and crab. Each spring my family would go shrimping in Big Lake, a beautiful lake which opens into the ship channel and into the Gulf of Mexico. At daybreak, we would drop the net into the water and drag all day, heading the shrimp after each catch was pulled up. My kids and I became champs when it came to heading shrimp. I loved the magic of sitting in a quiet boat watching the sun rise over the lake. And, it never ceased to be a thrill when the net was pulled up filled with assorted fish, shrimp, crabs...My young son Danny would have his little pail of water and we would give him the tiny squid to play with. When he got bored with that, I would open a can of Vienna sausage and crackers—his favorite snack on the boat. Icy cold shrimp and crab salad was the fare for the rest of the family—the ultimate refreshment on a hot day in the sun! When we got home, the neighbors would often gather and we would fire up the outdoor cooker and boil the crabs we had caught, along with new potatoes and onions. How very fortunate we were to have those memorable moments. We ate a lot of fried shrimp, for it was the kids' favorite. It's time-consuming to fry shrimp, but if you'd like to give it a try, this is a foolproof method. The batter is light and the seasonings lend a marvelous flavor.

2 eggs, beaten	1 tsp. baking powder
1 cup milk	1/2 tsp. garlic puree
1 cup flour, divided	Cajun or Creole seasoning, to taste
Salt and red pepper, to taste	2 lbs. large peeled shrimp

Beat milk and eggs; slowly stir in just enough of the flour to make a *light* paste. Add remaining ingredients, except shrimp. Dip shrimp into the batter, which should drip *slowly* off the shrimp—neither too thick nor too thin. Dip immediately in the remainder of the flour which has been well seasoned with salt and red pepper, garlic and Cajun seasoning. Fry in oil in a heavy Dutch oven or electric skillet (not black iron pot) until golden brown, about five minutes—do not overcook or shrimp will become tough.

Yield: 4-6 servings

Note: For perfect golden fried shrimp, peanut oil is the oil of choice.

SHRIMP IN LEMON BUTTER

Got twenty minutes and two pounds of shrimp? That's all it takes to put a gourmet company meal on the table—twenty minutes! In that time, you can cook a pot of Lemon Rice (See Index), toss a Caesar Salad and chill a bottle of white wine. By the way, don't forget to pick up a dozen chocolate éclairs at the bakery on your way home.

1 cup butter	1/2 tsp. coarsely ground black
Juice of two lemons	pepper
1 clove garlic, minced	1/2 tsp. salt
1 tsp. chopped parsley	1/4 tsp. garlic powder
1 tsp. Worcestershire sauce	2 lbs. large or jumbo shrimp,
1 tsp. soy sauce	peeled and deveined

Melt butter in a large skillet; add next 8 ingredients and bring to a boil. Add shrimp and cook over medium heat for 5 minutes, stirring occasionally. Garnish with additional parsley and lemon wedges.
Yield: 6 servings

BAKED SHRIMP

How easy can you get? This is one of the many old family recipes in the files of Shelley Braswell—this one from her Aunt Bonnie Chavanne who lives in New Roads. Be sure to have some hot fresh bread for dipping!

1/2 lb. margarine	2 tsps. salt
1/2 lb. butter	3 tsps. pepper
3 cloves garlic, minced	1/2 tsp. Tabasco
2-3 freshly squeezed lemons	4-5 lbs. shrimp

Mix all ingredients except shrimp; heat in a saucepan. Pour over shrimp that's been placed in a baking pan; bake in a 400-degree oven for 20 minutes. Serve hot! Peel while you eat! Serve with piping hot crusty French bread.
Yield: 6 servings (approx.)

ORANGE SHRIMP

This recipe is from the kitchen of my hair stylist and good buddy, Sandy Toney. This well-seasoned cook enjoys only one thing more than creating innovative meals, and that is dining in sensational restaurants. I recently tried this recipe with red snapper—divine!

2 dozen jumbo shrimp	4 Tbsps. soy sauce
1/2 stick butter	Sesame seeds for garnish
2/3 cup orange juice	(Optional)

Peel shrimp, leaving tail intact; devein and set aside. Melt butter and whisk in orange juice and soy sauce. Pour mixture over shrimp and toss. Refrigerate for 1 hour. When ready to serve, place shrimp and marinade in a large skillet; cook on high heat for 4 minutes on each side. Spoon shrimp and sauce over a bed of white or wild rice; serve immediately. Yield: 2 servings

Note: Shrimp and marinade can be placed on a baking sheet with sides and broiled or grilled with marinade 4 minutes on each side. For a lovely presentation on rice, thread the shrimp on bamboo skewers.

SHERRIED SHRIMP

This is great when you have weekend guests coming—simply keep in refrigerator until ready to put on the table. It is great with potato salad.

10 lbs. large shrimp, boiled and peeled	2 tsps. salt
1 lb. fresh mushrooms	Cayenne pepper, to taste
1 qt. olive oil	2 lemons, sliced
1 ½ cups garlic vinegar	6 onions, thinly sliced
1 ½ cups dry sherry	1 Tbsp. Creole seasoning
	1 Tbsp. Tabasco

Layer shrimp and mushrooms in large container. Mix together next 6 ingredients; pour over shrimp mixture. Cover and refrigerate for three days, stirring frequently. After 24 hours, add onions, Creole seasoning and Tabasco; continue stirring frequently until ready to serve.

CHAVANNE SHRIMP CREOLE

This is from the files of Shelley Chavanne Braswell and is just one of the many old family classics handed down from her paternal great-grandmother. Shrimp Creole is a true southern dish, and this rendition is the best I have ever tasted. Since Shelley is a "little of this—little of that" type cook, she decided to prepare a trial batch of Shrimp Creole to be sure of her ingredient amounts. She shared dinner with us that evening and it was heavenly! So heavenly that for breakfast the next morning, we enjoyed leftover Shrimp Creole hot and steaming served on grits cakes, paired with curried fruit. We imagined ourselves sitting in a courtyard in the French Quarter enjoying a Sunday morning brunch!

3 lbs. medium raw shrimp	1/2 cup chopped parsley
1/2 cup oil	4 green onions, chopped fine
1 Tbsp. flour	Salt and pepper, to taste
2 medium white onions, chopped	2 bay leaves
2 large bell peppers, chopped fine	1 Tbsp. Kitchen Bouquet
3 cloves garlic, chopped fine	1 tsp. Tabasco sauce
2 cans tomato paste	1/3 cup red wine
2-3 cups water	2 Tbsps. sugar
1/4 tsp. red pepper	

Peel shrimp; sprinkle with salt and pepper. Add oil to cover bottom of heavy pan. Brown 1 tablespoon flour in the oil over medium heat about 5-10 minutes, stirring constantly. Add white onions, bell peppers, and garlic; sauté until soft, about 10 minutes. Add shrimp, stirring constantly, until pink, about 3-4 minutes. Add tomato paste and continue to stir until brown, about 5 minutes. Add 2-3 cups water, red pepper, parsley, green onions, and salt and pepper, to taste; stir well. Add bay leaves, Kitchen Bouquet, Tabasco, red wine, and sugar. When bubbling, cover and cook on low heat for 30 minutes, stirring often. Taste and adjust seasoning, if necessary. Serve over white rice.
Yield: 6 servings

Creole cookery reflects the full-flavored combination of the best of French, Spanish and African cuisine. Creoles favor tomatoes, cream and butter, while Cajuns rely on spices. Both cuisines place emphasis on the "holy trinity—bell pepper, onions and celery.

SEAFOOD FEAST

This glorious feast is a repeat from So Good..Make You Slap Your Mama Volume 1. In the first printing, the recipe was incorrect . To those of you who made this dish and ended up with a sticky mess, please give it another try. Teamed up with a Caesar Salad, crusty French bread and white wine, it is a great party dish. On the day before your dinner party, prepare the casserole and refrigerate it. Clean Romaine lettuce for the salad, spin almost dry, and place loosely in a plastic bag; refrigerate. Prepare the salad dressing, grate Parmesan cheese, and boil two or three eggs for slicing. Prepare the French bread with butter, and wrap in foil. Whip up a beautiful Peach and Raspberry Trifle (See Index) Voila! You can lie around and eat bon-bons the next day!

1 stick butter	1 Tbsp. pureed or minced garlic
1 (8 oz.) pkg. cream cheese	Tabasco, to taste
3 Tbsps. butter	1 tsp. white pepper
1 large onion, chopped	2 cups cooked rice
1 small bell pepper, chopped	4 Tbsps. white wine (optional)
3 ribs celery, chopped	1 lb. fresh white or lump crabmeat
1/2 lb. fresh mushrooms sliced	8 ozs. sharp Cheddar, grated
1 ½ lbs. raw shrimp, peeled	1/2 cup cracker crumbs
1 can cream of mushroom soup	

Melt butter in 2-quart saucepan; add cream cheese that's been cut into cubes and stir until it is melted. In a heavy Dutch oven, sauté onion, bell pepper and celery in 3 tablespoons butter. Add sliced mushrooms and shrimp; simmer 5 minutes, stirring constantly. Add the melted cream cheese and butter mixture. Blend in soup, seasonings, rice and wine. Fold in crabmeat and place in a greased 13x9x2-inch baking dish. Toss Cheddar and cracker crumbs together and sprinkle over top. Bake in a 350-degree oven for approximately 30 minutes, until bubbly and golden. Yield: 8-10 servings

*To devein or not to devein—that's a good question!
This is a matter of personal preference. Small and medium shrimp do not need deveining; however, the intestinal vein of large and jumbo shrimp contains grit and should always be removed.*

MARK'S BOILED CRAWFISH

As we southerners know, the crawfish has been an inherent part of our Louisiana culture since the first settlers. Crawfish boils are not just about eating crawfish, considering the labor it takes to peel those little devils. No..the secret is in the pageantry of gathering friends outdoors, enjoying lively conversations and laughter as we consume mounds of crawdads, corn, potatoes, mushrooms and sip a few brews.

From the time I was young, I knew how to prepare many sumptuous crawfish dishes, but I had never boiled crawfish until one memorable day many years ago. My teenage son Danny and I decided to take the plunge—to kick off the weekend with a crawfish boil. Before you could say "crawdaddy," Danny and I had purchased and lugged home a huge sack of live, squirming crawfish and all the accouterments needed for a backyard boil.

My Cajun cookbook told me, "crawfish must be purged in very salty water so they will expel mud from their systems." Nowhere in those sketchy instructions was I told what to do when the little varmints began to climb out of the pot and run amuck all over my backyard. By that time, my teenager had lost interest and escaped with a carload of friends, so I did what any sane person would do—I climbed on the patio table and screamed for help! Luckily my guests showed up and saved the day—pursuing the escapees and returning them to the pot. The guys took over the cooking and we were soon enjoying our first crawfish boil.

When we visit Baton Rouge in the spring, we often are invited to a crawfish boil at the home of Mark and Kelly Schexnaildre, friends of Danny and his wife, Carol. Mark is a master at boiling crawfish in his state-of-the-arts outdoor kitchen. Our last visit, he boiled 80 lbs., and while Kelly had planned to make crawfish pies with the leftovers, she had not anticipated the keen appreciation of their guests, for there was nary a mudbug left!

See next page for Mark's crawfish boil procedure.

Mark's Crawfish Boil (Continued):

1 (35-40 lb.) sack live crawfish
10-12 lemons
5 onions
5 stalks celery
4 pods garlic
1 (4.5 lb.) bag La. Crawfish boil
1 (8 oz.) bottle liquid crab boil

1/2 of a 13-oz. box of salt
15-20 whole mushrooms
3-6 links cooked sausage
1 bag small red potatoes
6-8 ears frozen corn on the cob
   (at least one for each person)

Fill a crawfish boiling pot (80-120 qt.) about halfway with water and begin heating on burner. Meanwhile, purge the crawfish by placing in an ice chest or large container and rinsing well with salted water. Cut lemons, onion, celery and garlic in halves. When water in pot comes to a rolling boil, add bagged and liquid crab boil and salt. Squeeze lemons into the mixture and discard the rinds in the boiling basket. (The squeezed lemon is the key to the eventual outcome.) Pour drained crawfish into the basket with the remaining ingredients, with the exception of the corn. Lower the basket into boiling pot and stir; cover. Enjoy the smell! Once mixture comes to a rolling boil once again, let it boil for 3 minutes and turn off the gas to burner. Add corn to the mixture, stir and leave soaking uncovered for approximately 20-30 minutes or longer, depending on taste. Lift the basket and let it drain for a couple of minutes. Pour the crawfish onto a large table that's been covered with newspaper. Dip for crawfish: mix ketchup, horseradish sauce, lemon, Worcestershire, salt and pepper. ENJOY!

The great majority of the United States crawfish harvest comes from the waters of the Mississippi basin. Many Louisianans refer to their state as the "Crawfish Capital of the World." The South Louisiana town of Breaux Bridge is famous for its Crawfish Festival which is held every year—the first weekend in May.

KELLY'S CRAWFISH PIES

Kelly Schexnaildre of Baton Rouge makes the best crawfish pies I have ever tasted. When there are leftover crawfish from one of her and husband Mark's crawfish boils, Kelly whips up several batches of these mouth-watering individual pies, and puts up an ample supply in the freezer. This is Mark's mother, Carol Schexnaildre's recipe. I, too, make a big batch each spring so we can enjoy them year round.

1 large onion, chopped
1/4 cup green onion, chopped
2 cloves garlic, minced
1/2 bell pepper, chopped
2 ribs celery, chopped
1 stick butter
1 can cream of celery soup
4 Tbsps. tomato sauce

1 cup milk
1/4 cup parsley, chopped
*1 lb. crawfish tails
1/2 cup seasoned breadcrumbs
1 tsp. salt
1/2 tsp. cayenne pepper
Black pepper, to taste

Sauté first 5 ingredients in butter until soft. Add soup, tomato sauce, milk, parsley and crawfish tails. Cook for 10 minutes. Add remaining ingredients and cook 5 minutes. Place mixture in a large pie shell or in individual tart shells. Cover with a top shell if desired. Bake at 350-degrees for 30-35 minutes.
Yield: 1 large pie or 18-20 small tart shells
*If using frozen crawfish tails, rinse and drain in a colander before adding.
Variation: To serve this filling as a crawfish sauce for pasta or rice, omit breadcrumbs—it's outstanding!

Considering they were once in the lowly position of providing bait for fishermen, the crawfish has come a long way in the past thirty years. Nowadays, they can be found in the neatest places—on the dinner table, baked in a golden piecrust.. in our backyard, happily boiling, along with corn and potatoes, in a kettle… or on an elaborate party table in a silver chafing dish as a party dip.

CRAWFISH ÉTOUFFÉE

This étouffée is the world's best! I first tasted it when we were attending a spring conference in San Destin, Florida with Harold and Helen Turner. One evening, I helped Helen whip up a batch for a group of friends. It was a smash hit! Helen does everything well—cooking, sewing, decorating—but her best role of all is wife and mother.

3 sticks butter, divided	Salt and pepper, to taste
1 cup flour	Tabasco, to taste
3 large onions, chopped	1 ½ cups water
1 large bunch celery, chopped	1/2 cup chopped fresh parsley
3 large bell peppers, chopped	2/3 cup chopped green onion
6 pods garlic, minced	3 Tbsps. cornstarch (optional)
5 lbs. peeled crawfish	6 Tbsps. water
Creole seasoning, to taste	

Make a dark roux with 2 sticks butter and 1 cup flour, cooking and stirring until dark penny brown. Add onion and sauté until transparent; add celery, bell pepper, and garlic; sauté until tender. Add remaining stick butter, crawfish, Creole seasoning, peppers, and Tabasco. Let simmer on low heat for 30 minutes. Taste and adjust seasonings, if desired. Add water, parsley and green onion. Mix cornstarch with water if gravy is too thin.
Yield: 18-20 servings
Note: When using fresh crawfish, include the fat. If using frozen, rinse crawfish in a colander before adding; the juice can be strong tasting.

EASY CRAWFISH CASSEROLE

This dish takes 1st prize in two categories: easy and delicious!

1 lb. crawfish tails,	1 can cream of mushroom soup
(rinse and drain if frozen)	2/3 cup uncooked long grain rice
1 can cream of onion soup	1/4 tsp. red pepper

Mix all ingredients well. Bake covered in a sprayed 2-quart casserole, in a 350-degree oven for 1 hour and 10 minutes.
Yield: 4 servings

CRAWFISH PASTA

I sampled this tantalizing casserole at a dinner party given by Beverly and Jack Pierce. Although Bev, the ultimate hostess, was raised on bona fide Norwegian food in North Dakota, she is a gifted southern cook. She paired this dish with Caesar Salad and buttery rolls, and for dessert, she chose a light touch with gourmet cheeses, fresh fruit and coffee.

1 stick butter or margarine
2 medium onions, chopped
1 bell pepper, chopped
2 stalks celery, chopped
3 cloves garlic, minced
1 jalapeno pepper, seeded and
   chopped
4 Tbsps. flour
1 pt. + 1/4 cup half-and-half
2 Tbsps. dried parsley flakes
   or 1/2 cup fresh, chopped

1 lb. pasteurized process cheese,
   cut in cubes
Salt and pepper, to taste
Cayenne pepper, Cajun seasoning,
   seafood seasoning, to taste
1 ½ tsps. Worcestershire sauce
2 lbs. crawfish tails
1 (12-oz.) pkg. linguine or other
   pasta of choice, cooked al dente
1 cup Parmesan cheese, grated

In a large skillet, melt butter and sauté chopped onions, bell pepper, celery, garlic, and jalapeno until soft—about 20 minutes. Add flour and simmer, stirring constantly, for 10 minutes. Slowly add half-and-half and stir until hot. Add parsley and cheese cubes; stir until cheese is melted and blended. Add seasonings; fold in crawfish and pasta. Divide between two buttered 9x13x2-inch baking dishes and cover with grated Parmesan cheese. Bake covered in a 350-degree oven for 30 minutes or until hot and bubbly. Do not over bake.

Yield: 12-14 servings

Note: For insured moistness, this dish can be tossed and served immediately, skipping the baking process entirely.

When we think of crawfish, we think immediately of rice, however, there is no dish more flavorful than one which combines crawfish and pasta—it is truly divine.

CRAWFISH AND CORN CASSEROLE

1/2 cup chopped onion
1/4 cup chopped bell pepper
2 green onion tops, chopped
4 Tbsps. butter

1 can Ro-tel tomatoes, drained
2 (11-oz.) cans whole kernel corn
1 (15-oz.) can cream style corn
1 lb. crawfish tails

Sauté first 3 ingredients in butter until tender. Add drained tomatoes; simmer for 5 minutes. Add corn and crawfish; pour into a 2-quart baking dish and bake in a 350-degree oven for 30 minutes.
Yield: 8 servings

POT LUCK CRAWFISH CASSEROLE

I created this dish for a covered dish dinner. There was not a smidgen left when the party ended!

6 Tbsps. butter
1 medium onion, chopped
1/2 small bell pepper, chopped
1 cup chopped celery
1 Tbsp. minced garlic
1 can Ro-tel tomatoes
1 (10-oz.) can French onion soup
1 (10-oz.) can cream of
  mushroom soup

1 cup uncooked rice
2 lbs. crawfish tails
1/3 cup dried parsley
2/3 cup grated Monterey Jack
  cheese
Black pepper, to taste
1 Tbsp. Creole seasoning
1 ½ cups grated sharp Cheddar
  cheese, for topping

Melt butter in a Dutch oven; sauté onion, bell pepper, celery and garlic until tender. Fold in all remaining ingredients except Cheddar cheese, blending well. Pour into a 13x9x2-inch baking dish. Cover tightly and bake in a 350-degree oven for 45 minutes. Remove from oven; uncover and sprinkle with grated cheese. Return to oven and bake another 15 minutes.
Yield: 8-10 servings
Note: If using frozen crawfish, drain and rinse in a colander before adding to casserole.

FRIED SOFT-SHELL CRABS

Back in the days when we went shrimping on our boat in the spring, whenever we caught any soft-shell crabs in the net, we were ecstatic. They would go into the ice chest to be frozen later. As soon as we had enough for a meal, we would batter and fry them—what a feast!

3 large eggs	1/2 tsp. salt
6 Tbsps. whipping cream	1/2 tsp. cayenne pepper
1/4 tsp. salt	1/2 tsp. black pepper
1/2 tsp. coarsely ground pepper	1/2 tsp. garlic powder
1 doz. soft shell crabs, cleaned	Creole or Cajun seasoning, to taste
2 cups flour	2/3 cup vegetable oil (approx.)
2 tsps. baking powder	or peanut oil

In a large shallow pan, whisk eggs with cream, salt and pepper. Dip crabs into mixture, turning to coat well; leave in pan. Combine flour and next 6 ingredients. Remove crabs from egg mixture and dredge in seasoned flour. Let stand 4-5 minutes and dredge once again in flour mixture. Pour oil into a large heavy skillet to about ½ inch in depth. Fry crabs in hot oil for 3-4 minutes on each side, or until golden brown. Drain well on paper towels; serve immediately with tartar sauce.
Yield: 1 dozen

CRABMEAT IMPERIAL

1 large bell pepper, diced	3 Tbsps. Hellmann's mayonnaise
1 (2-oz.) jar diced pimientos, drained	2 eggs, lightly beaten
	3 Tbsps. dry sherry
1/2 tsp. salt	1 tsp. Old Bay seasoning
1/2 tsp. white pepper	2 lbs. white or lump crabmeat
1 Tbsp. dry mustard	Paprika, to taste

Mix together bell pepper and pimiento. Add next 7 ingredients; mix well. Carefully fold in crabmeat so as not to break up lumps; place in a buttered casserole. Spread with additional mayonnaise and sprinkle with paprika. Bake uncovered in a 350-degree oven for 20 minutes.
Yield: 6 servings

CRABMEAT LE MARIN

While visiting some of our favorite restaurants in the Biloxi, Mississippi area, we discovered a restaurant by the name of Trilby's in nearby Ocean Springs. This elegant restaurant, which is now closed, served fresh seafood that was absolutely divine and beautifully presented. My favorite was Crabmeat Le Marin—this is my take-off of the recipe.

8 Tbsps. butter, divided	1 1/3 cups cheese sauce
1 lb. large fresh mushrooms,	(recipe follows)
stems removed	Water
1 lb. lump crabmeat	

Melt 4 tablespoons butter in skillet and sauté mushroom caps about 1 minute on each side. Place 1 teaspoon water in bottom of four round greased casserole dishes; top with mushrooms, stem side up. Top with ¼ pound crabmeat per person. Melt remaining 4 tablespoons of butter and drizzle over the crabmeat. Pour cheese sauce (recipe below) over each dish and bake in a 400-degree oven until the cheese bubbles and is slightly brown. Transfer to a warm dinner plate by sliding mushrooms on top of toast round and serve with a broiled tomato and Lemon Rice (See Index).

Cheese Sauce:

1 Tbsp. butter	Salt, to taste
1 ½ Tbsps. flour	Dash nutmeg
1 pt. boiling milk	4-6 ozs. mild Cheddar or Colby

In a heavy saucepan over medium heat, melt and heat the butter. Whisk in the flour and bring to a golden color. This is a white roux, so don't let the sauce get too dark. Immediately incorporate the hot milk, stirring constantly with a wooden spoon to keep it from scorching and from forming lumps. Add salt to taste and the nutmeg. Boil the sauce for 3 minutes in order to cook the flour well, stirring all the time, otherwise you will taste the flour. Add grated cheese and stir only until melted. Pour over the Crabmeat Le Marin and bake as directed. Note: The above sauce without the cheese is also known as white sauce or Bechamel Sauce.

CRABMEAT AND ASPARAGUS

1/4 cup chopped green onion
2 Tbsps. butter, melted
1 Tbsp. flour
1/2 tsp. salt
Dash cayenne
1 cup half-and-half
1/4 cup salad dressing
(not mayonnaise)

1 lb. lump crabmeat
picked over for shells
4 Tbsps. sherry or vermouth
1 (10-oz.) pkg. frozen asparagus
or 1 lb. fresh asparagus, steamed
lightly
1/4 cup Parmesan cheese

Sauté onion in butter until tender; blend in flour, salt and cayenne. Add cream; cook, stirring constantly, until thickened. Remove from heat; stir in salad dressing, crabmeat and sherry. Arrange asparagus in a 1 ½ qt. baking dish. Spoon crab mixture over asparagus; sprinkle with Parmesan. Bake in a 350-degree oven for 30 minutes

DAVID'S CRAB CAKES

These delectably light crab cakes are the creation of my friend, David Whitener. They come highly recommended by everyone who has had the privilege of feasting on a meal of crab cakes at David and wife Carol's home. They're delicious served with new potatoes and fresh asparagus.

1 lb. jumbo lump crab meat
picked over to remove cartilage
3 green onions, finely chopped
1 heaping Tbsp. good mayonnaise
1 ½ tsps. Dijon mustard
1/2 tsp. cayenne pepper
1 tsp. Old Bay Seasoning

1 tsp. salt
Dash of Worcestershire
2 eggs, beaten
Fresh breadcrumbs, made from
3 slices wheat bread
4 Tbsps. butter

Mix all ingredients in a large bowl, being careful not to break up crabmeat. Form 6 large crab cakes by hand and place in refrigerator for 30 minutes. Melt butter in a skillet and sauté crab cakes on medium heat until lightly browned on each side.
Note: David often uses pasteurized crabmeat for a moist, delicious crab cake.

LOUISIANA FRIED OYSTERS

Although purists prefer their oysters raw with a zippy cocktail sauce, fried oysters are probably the most requested. The secret to a crispy crust is hot oil and fast cooking.

1 qt. fresh medium-large oysters
Creole seasoning, to taste
Tabasco
2 eggs, beaten lightly
4 Tbsps. milk
1 tsp. mustard
2 cups cornmeal or cracker crumbs
Cooking oil

Check oysters for shell; lay out on paper towels. Sprinkle oysters lightly with Creole seasoning and shake some drops of Tabasco over all. To eggs, add milk and mustard. Dip oysters in egg mixture and roll in cracker crumbs or cornmeal. Drop into hot cooking oil and fry for about 2 minutes; drain on paper towels and serve immediately.
Yield: 4 servings

BAKED OYSTERS

In Louisiana, we're blessed with the some of the finest oysters in the country. This dish is delicious served with stuffed baked potato and steamed asparagus.

1 ¼ sticks butter
1/2 cup olive oil
1/2 cup chopped green onions
1/4 cup chopped fresh parsley
2 Tbsps. minced garlic
1 1/3 cup seasoned bread
   crumbs
1/2 cup grated Parmesan cheese
1 tsp. salt
1/2 tsp. black pepper
1/4 tsp. cayenne pepper
1 tsp. basil
1 tsp. oregano
2 qts. oysters, picked over for shell
   and drained on paper towels

In a large skillet, heat butter and oil; sauté onion, parsley and garlic. In a bowl, combine bread crumbs, cheese, salt, black pepper, cayenne, basil and oregano. Add to skillet and mix well. Remove from heat and add oysters. Stir gently and place in a sprayed 2-quart baking dish. Bake in a 425-degree oven for 15 minutes or until brown.
Yield: 6 servings

CREAMED OYSTERS

1/2 cup chopped onion	Salt and pepper, to taste
1/2 cup chopped celery	Dash cayenne
4 Tbsps. butter	1 cup light cream
1 pt. fresh oysters	2 Tbsps. dry sherry
2 Tbsps. flour	4 English muffins, split and
1 tsp. yellow mustard	toasted

Cook onion and celery in butter until tender. Check oysters for shell, strain and reserve oyster liquid. Add oysters and liquid to onion and celery and cook until edges curl. Stir in flour, mustard, salt, pepper and cayenne. Add cream and cook, stirring constantly, until bubbly. Add sherry and heat through. Serve on split English muffins or pastry shells.
Yield: 4 servings

OYSTER PIE

This luscious pie is delicious with baby limas or petit pois peas and a fruit salad. A perfect fall dish, Oyster Pie will comfort you with memories of home and grandma.

5 Tbsps. flour	Tabasco, to taste
1 stick + 2 Tbsps. butter	Cayenne pepper, to taste
1 small onion, chopped	Pinch of thyme
3 stalks celery, chopped	1/2 cup chopped green onion tops
2 qts. oysters, reserve liquid	1/2 cup half-and-half
2 slices lean bacon, cooked and	1 can regular biscuits
crumbled	

Make a penny-brown roux with flour and butter. Add onion and celery; sauté until tender. Add oysters, oyster liquid (strained), bacon, seasonings and green onions. Simmer 5 minutes and blend in half and half. Place in a greased 11-inch baking dish; slightly flatten out uncooked biscuits and place on top of mixture. Bake in a 375-degree oven for 20 minutes.
Yield: 6 servings
Note: If mixture is too thick, add a little more cream before baking.

BILL BERGER'S FAMOUS FISH

Bill Berger and his wife Jeanelle, are long-time boating friends. These folks embrace the simple life—living on their boat in Florida, dining at unique restaurants, traveling, visiting their daughters and grandsons, and creating new dishes. When they visit Shreveport, Billy and I talk "cooking" so much, everyone is bored to tears! This fish dish is a winner—especially when hosting a company dinner. It is to-die-for good when paired up with Lemon Rice (See Index) and Spinach Madeline (See Index) or Bacon Wrapped Green Beans (See Index).

8-10 fish fillets
1/2-2/3 cup lemon juice
Creole Seasoning, to taste
Salt & pepper, to taste
Flour to dredge fish
2/3 cup vegetable cooking oil

1 (14-oz.) can artichoke hearts
1 (14-oz.) can pineapple chunks
2 cans mandarin oranges
1 stick butter
4 Tbsps. dried dill weed

Wash fish fillets and cut out any dark sections. Drizzle each piece liberally with lemon juice. Place in refrigerator overnight. When ready to cook fish, drain well and sprinkle liberally with Creole Seasoning and salt and pepper; dredge in flour. Fry fish in hot oil in a large skillet, cooking about 5 minutes on each side. Remove from skillet and place on a sprayed large baking pan or cookie sheet. (This can be set aside at this point until ready to bake.) When ready to bake, drain artichoke hearts and cut into quarters; drain pineapple and mandarin oranges. Place on top of fish. Melt butter and add dill weed; drizzle over all. Bake in a 350-degree oven for 20-30 minutes.
Yield: 4 servings

When choosing fish for a recipe, bear in mind that the most healthy cuts are tilapia, salmon, mai-mai, and cod. These fish are rich in Omega 3 fatty acids and are reputed to be free of mercury.

DANNY'S FRIED SPECKLED TROUT

Our son Danny has perfected the art of frying crispy, moist fish. Danny and his family enjoy fishing at their camp in Cocodrie, a fisherman's paradise just south of Houma. At home, Danny's state-of-the-arts outdoor kitchen provides the perfect spot for frying fish, as well as the delicious side dishes that go well with it—hush puppies, icy cold slaw, crispy French fries, sweet onion rings, and a bowl of fresh tomato relish.

12-15 speckled trout filets
   or catfish filets

Marinade:
1 pt. milk (approx.)   1 egg, beaten well
6-8 ozs. beer   Creole seasoning, to taste

With a whisk, mix well the above ingredients; add fish filets and soak in the marinade for several hours in refrigerator.

Batter:
2/3 cup cornmeal   Onion powder, to taste
1/3 cup flour   Garlic powder, to taste
Salt and cayenne pepper

Cooking oil for frying

Mix batter ingredients and place in a plastic bag. To fry, place pieces of fish, a few at a time, in bag; shake to coat fish. Fry in hot cooking oil until golden brown. Do not overcook.
Yield: 4-6 servings

If you're watching fats, in place of battered and deep-fried fish, pan fry it in a mixture of olive oil and light butter. This will yield a filet that is golden and crispy on the outside and moist and tender on the inside.

BAKED CATFISH

My favorite way to eat catfish is fried, but as we all know, it's better for us baked or broiled. Catfish is a mild fish and lends itself to any method of preparation. We enjoy this baked dish for its zippy flavor.

2 lbs. catfish filets
Salt and pepper, to taste
3/4 cup thinly sliced onions
3 Tbsps. butter
1 cup mayonnaise

1/4 cup Dijon mustard
2 Tbsps. dry vermouth
1/2 tsp. Tabasco
1/4 cup chopped fresh parsley

Arrange fish in a shallow baking dish; salt and pepper liberally. Cover with sliced onion and dot with butter. Bake 20 minutes in a 350-degree oven, or until fish flakes easily. Combine mayonnaise, mustard, vermouth and Tabasco. Pour over fish and broil 2 to 3 minutes, until brown and bubbly. Sprinkle parsley over top; serve with lemon wedges.
Yield: 6 servings

ITALIAN FISH

6-8 catfish or Tilapia filets
Salt and pepper, to taste
1/4 cup lemon juice
1/2 cup Italian bread crumbs

1/4 cup Parmesan cheese
1 lemon, sliced
1 bell pepper, sliced
1/4 to 1/2 cup olive oil

Arrange filets on a lightly greased cookie sheet. Season filets with salt and pepper and drizzle with lemon juice. Combine Italian bread crumbs and Parmesan cheese and sprinkle liberally over fish. Add slices of lemon and bell pepper, drizzle top with olive oil and more lemon juice. Bake in a 375-degree oven for 25 minutes, uncovered.
Yield: 4 servings

SUSAN'S HALIBUT—SEATTLE STYLE

Our daughter, Susan lives in Seattle where fresh fish is at its best.
This delicious dish is a family favorite.

2 lb. halibut filet   1 cup mayonnaise
4 ozs. Parmesan cheese, shredded   1 Tbsp. lemon juice
1 small onion, finely chopped

Preheat oven to 450 degrees. Place fish in a buttered pan; cook for 10
minutes. Pour off liquid. Mix other ingredients and pour over fish.
Bake for 15-25 minutes, until light and puffy brown.

ORANGE FISH

This easy broiled fish is to-die-for delicious with fluffy rice or potatoes.!

6-8 tilapia or catfish filets   2/3 cup orange juice
1/2 stick butter   4 Tbsps. soy sauce

Place filets in a greased baking pan. Melt butter and whisk in orange
juice and soy sauce. Pour mixture over fish; let sit for about 30 minutes.
To cook: place fish under broiler and cook about 6 minutes on each
side. Serve immediately.
Yield: 4 servings

FISH ELEGANTE

This recipe is courtesy of my talented friend and neighbor, Molly
Weldon. It is simple and so very tasty!

1 lb. fish filets   1 can cream of shrimp soup
Black pepper, to taste   1/4 cup grated Parmesan cheese
2 Tbsps. butter   Paprika, to taste

Place filets in greased baking dish; sprinkle with pepper and dot with
butter. Mix remaining ingredients and pour over fish. Bake in a 400-
degree oven for 20-25 minutes.

SALMON FOR TWO

Salmon is truly a gourmet dish. Featured in the finest restaurants in the world, it is universally enjoyed by the most discriminating gourmands. I, personally, have never broiled, grilled, or baked a salmon that would earn me a blue ribbon; however, I do know someone whose salmon dishes cannot be beat—my friend, Dot Hensley. The three featured salmon recipes are hers—each delightfully different—each fabulous!

2 Tbsps. honey
2 Tbsps. dry vermouth
Salt & pepper, to taste
1 ½ tsps. grated fresh ginger

1 ½ tsps. Dijon mustard
1 (10-12 oz.) salmon filet
center cut, same thickness

Mix honey, vermouth, salt and pepper, ginger and Dijon mustard; set aside. Oven cooking: Preheat broiler. With foil, make a small "pan" to hold the salmon and liquid. The sauce tends to burn, due to the honey. Broil salmon 14-15 minutes, using sauce half way through and at the end. There is no need to turn the salmon.

Grill cooking: Leave skin on the salmon. Spray the skin side with Pam and place on the grill skin side down.

SALMON WITH DILL

With this dish Dot is tempting our taste buds with lemon and dill.

4-6 Tbsps. butter, melted
Juice of one lemon
Salt & pepper, to taste

1 Tbsps. dry dill
1 salmon filet with skin left on

Combine butter, lemon juice, salt and pepper, and dill. Spray the skin side of salmon with Pam. Brush the fish side with butter mixture. Place on a pre-heated grill, skin side down, and baste with sauce to keep it moist. If the filet is not the same thickness, cut the thin end off before placing it on the grill, as it will not take as long to cook. Do not turn the salmon. Cooking time is about 15 minutes, depending on the temperature of the grill. As a rule, cooking time for most fish is 8-10 minutes per inch of thickness.

HONEY PEPPER SALMON

For this zesty dish, Dot Hensley put together a blend of spicy peppers combined with the sweetness of honey.

2 large salmon filets, skin on
1 Tbsp. fresh cracked pepper
1/2 tsp. cayenne pepper
1/2 chili pepper
1/2 tsp. paprika

1 tsp. fresh rosemary, minced
1/2 tsp. garlic powder
1/2 tsp. sea salt
1/4 cup honey
1/4 cup rice vinegar

Combine all ingredients except salmon. Spray skin side of salmon filets with Pam. Place skin side down, on a platter and cover filets with one-half sauce. Let the fish rest for 5-10 minutes. Place salmon, skin side down, on pre-heated grill; cover with lid. Baste fish often with sauce to keep it moist. Grill about 8-10 minutes per inch of thickness.

MILDRED LYNCH'S SALMON FRITTERS

This fritter recipe is from the files of the late Mildred Lynch. Her daughter, Charlotte Peters, shared this gem with me many years ago. There's nothing that tastes like salmon fritters!

1 (9-oz.) can salmon
Milk
1 egg, slightly beaten
1 tsp. lemon juice
1 cup buttermilk baking mix

1/2 tsp. seasoned salt
1/4 cup finely chopped celery
2 Tbsps. chopped bell pepper
2 Tbsps. chopped onion

Drain salmon, reserving liquid. Add enough milk to salmon liquid to make ½ cup. Combine egg and lemon juice. Combine seasoned salt and baking mix; add liquid and blend in salmon and vegetables. Drop batter by spoonfuls into hot oil (375-degrees); fry about 3 minutes or until golden brown.

SALMON LOAF

This delicious loaf is perfect family fare—comfort food! The recipe is from the files of my friend, Beverly Pierce. The dill sauce would fit the bill for almost any seafood dish. I particularly enjoy it slathered liberally on fish, shrimp or oyster poboys. My family enjoys this salmon loaf served with macaroni and cheese and petit pois peas—to complete the comfort food menu.

1 (8 oz.) can salmon	1 Tbsp. dried onion flakes
1 (8-oz.) pkg. cream cheese	1 cup chopped walnuts or pecans
1 Tbsp. lemon juice	3 tsps. horseradish
1/4 tsp. liquid smoke	Salt & pepper, to taste

Clean salmon. Mix all ingredients, except half of the nuts. Mold salmon loaf into desired shape (loaf pan or other). Sprinkle top of loaf with remaining nuts. Bake in a 350-degree oven for 30-40 minutes. Serve with dill sauce.
Yield: 6 servings

Dill Sauce:
1/2 cup Hellmann's mayonnaise	1 Tbsp. chopped dill
2 Tbsps. lemon juice	Dash of cayenne pepper
1 Tbsp. whole baby capers	

SMOKED SALMON

We receive lots of smoked salmon from our daughter Susan who lives in Seattle—the home of smoked salmon and Dungeness crabs. For a lovely lunch or snack, I like to pig out on cold salmon and potato salad.

6 ozs. smoked salmon	1/2 small bottle capers, drained
1 bag baby bagels	1 (8-oz.) cream cheese, or soft
1/2 medium sweet onion, chopped	salmon flavored cream cheese

On a large platter, place salmon and split baby bagels. Place remaining ingredients in small bowls; arrange on platter with salmon and bagels. To serve, place salmon on bagel and top with remaining ingredients.
Yield: 2 servings

Carol Ann Daniel

Veggies / Sides

Southern cooks are famed for their talent in enhancing vegetables with delicious seasonings and sauces.

As a young child, I learned to eat what my friends termed "gross" things like eggplant, okra, squash and peas. My dad had the neatest, most productive garden in the neighborhood; so in the summer, Mom fed us a steady diet of dishes like eggplant casserole, smothered okra and tomatoes, purple hull peas cooked with the most amazing onion relish, and tomato pie! I can see her now in the garden, picking okra pods or peas and carrying them into the kitchen in the ample skirt of her blue and white tissue gingham apron. There I'd be, a little girl trailing along behind her Mom, munching on a big red radish.

When my crafty little Mom cooked vegetables, you never realized you were eating healthy, for she made them tasty and fun to eat!! My Dad's favorite thing was tomatoes. He believed there is absolutely nothing in the world as delicious as a homegrown tomato. Mom did all kind of fancy things with those tomatoes, but secretly, I knew Dad preferred to just sit in his lawn chair in the garden and bite into one freshly picked off the vine, and let the juice run down his chin. My precious father passed away forty-two years ago, but I still miss him each and every time I bite down on a fresh tomato.

What enhances a dinner table better than the cozy comfort of side dishes—cornbread dressing, macaroni and cheese, homemade mashed potatoes, sweet potatoes swimming in butter, and brown sugar, fluffy rice dishes, deviled eggs? It's all right here in this chapter.

This chapter features many great recipes—recipes that will offer new approaches and ideas for your favorite vegetables and side dishes, both the simple and the elegant. Enjoy!

GREEN BEAN AND CORN CASSEROLE

This recipe is from the kitchen of a very dear lady, Lou Nicholas. The welcome mat was always out at Lou's lovely home, whether we needed a hostess for a progressive dinner or a covered dish for a boating occasion. Lou is a beautiful person who will never grow old—and a darned good cook, too!

1 can whole green beans, drained
1 can shoe-peg corn, drained
1 can cream of chicken soup
1/2 cup sour cream
1/2 cup grated sharp cheese

1/2 cup grated onion
Salt and pepper, to taste
1 tube buttery crackers, crushed
1 stick butter, melted
1/2 cup sliced almonds

Mix first 7 ingredients together; blend well. Place in a greased baking dish. Blend crushed buttery crackers with melted butter; add almonds and sprinkle mixture on top. Bake in a 350-degree oven for 45 minutes.
Yield: 6 servings

SOUTHERN-STYLE GREEN BEANS

2 strips lean bacon
½ cup chopped onion
2 cans whole or cut green beans,
   drained
2 Tbsps. hot pepper vinegar

1 tsp. sugar
Salt, pepper, and garlic powder,
   to taste
Slivered toasted almonds, optional

Fry bacon in a skillet; remove and crumble. Fry onion in bacon drippings about 3 minutes. Add green beans, vinegar, sugar, crumbled bacon and seasonings. Cover pot and simmer on low for about 20-30 minutes. For an added treat, when green beans are done, drain them and toss in slivered almonds before serving. Delicious!
Yield: 6 servings

KENTUCKY WONDERS

I grew up on Kentucky Wonder green beans. In my Dad's garden, the green beans were propped up by poles that crossed near the top—the perfect hiding place for a little girl. Mom would often send me out to pick a big basket full of these "wonders", along with a few new potatoes. No one every cooked a pot of Kentucky Wonders like my Mom! Memories…

2 lbs. Kentucky Wonder beans   1 tsp. sugar
1/4 cup olive oil   1 garlic pod, minced
Salt and pepper, to taste   1/2 cup chopped onion
2 Tbsps. lemon juice   Parsley

Toss beans with olive oil and cook slowly in a Dutch oven for 30-40 minutes until beans are glazed, tossing frequently. Add remainder of ingredients, a little water, cover and simmer on low for about one hour.
Yield: 6 servings

BILL'S BACON WRAPPED GREEN BEANS

Our friend Bill Berger wowed us one evening with these beans. He certainly didn't get this recipe out of a cookbook—he also did not specify measurements, so I took the liberty of making them up!

2 lbs. fresh whole green beans   1 stick butter, melted
   or 3 cans whole green beans   1/2-1/3 cup brown sugar
1/2 lb. lean bacon, cut in half

Wrap 5-6 green beans in bacon and place in a greased baking dish. Repeat procedure until all green beans are used. Blend together melted butter and brown sugar; drizzle over bean/bacon bundles and bake in a 350-degree oven for about 25-30 minutes.
Yield: 6 servings

CAROL'S SIMPLE GREEN BEANS

My daughter-in-law, Carol, came up with this delicious method of cooking green beans. The zip of the Tony's seasoning and the sweetener makes for a winning combination. Carol is not shy when sprinkling the Tony's and that's what makes it so good.

1 can whole green beans
2 packets sugar or sweetener

Tony Chachere's Creole
Seasoning, to taste

Drain green beans and replace with water. Place in a 2-quart saucepan; sprinkle with sweetener and Tony's. Cover and cook about 30 minutes.
Yield: 2-3 servings

LADYE'S SMOTHERED SPINACH

My sister-in-law, Ladye White, tipped me off to this flavorful spinach dish. The combination of garlic and olive oil add life to bland spinach.

4 Tbsps. olive oil (approx.)
2 pods garlic, minced

1 lb. bag fresh spinach
Salt and pepper, to taste

Heat olive oil in a large skillet; add garlic and let simmer on low about 5 minutes—do not brown garlic. Add cleaned and well-drained fresh spinach; sprinkle with salt and pepper. Cover and steam spinach until tender.
Yield: 2 servings

Popeye, the sailor man's famous saying was, "I Yam So Strong Cause I Eats My Spinach" His comic strip appeared in1929, and by 1933, Popeye cartoons were in the movies. Now, seventy years later, he's going strong on the cartoon channel. That's quite a career based on a leafy green, iron-packed vegetable!!

SPINACH MADELINE

Perhaps the most celebrated spinach dish in Louisiana is Spinach Madeline, the creation of a lady by the name of Madeline Nevil. For me, the joy of spinach came when I had my first helping of her savory dish. A few years ago, I visited Mrs. Nevill at her beautiful plantation-style bed and breakfast, Green Springs, in the Tunica Hills Nature Area of St. Francisville, Louisiana. Mrs. Nevill graciously shared her story of the creation of Spinach Madeline. When she was a young bride, while preparing creamed spinach for a bridge luncheon, she blended in a new product—a six-ounce roll of jalapeno cheese. Spinach Madeline was born! This delightful dish was featured in the first Baton Rouge Junior League cookbook—River Road Recipes. Now, forty-five years later, the popularity of Spinach Madeline has never waned. Since the six-ounce Jalapeno cheese roll is no longer available, I now substitute with Velveeta and minced jalapeno. This is my rendition.

2 pkgs. frozen chopped spinach	3/4 tsp. garlic salt
4 Tbsps. butter	Salt, to taste
2 Tbsps. flour	8 ozs. Velveeta cheese,
2 Tbsps. chopped onion	cut in chunks
1/2 cup evaporated milk	1 jalapeno pepper, minced
1/2 cup vegetable liquor	1 tsp. Worcestershire sauce
1/2 tsp. black pepper	Red pepper, to taste
3/4 tsp. celery salt	

Cook spinach according to directions on package. Drain and reserve liquor. Melt butter in saucepan over low heat. Add flour, stirring until blended and smooth, but not brown. Add onion and cook until soft but not brown. Add liquid slowly, stirring constantly to avoid lumps. Cook until smooth and thick; continue stirring. Add seasonings and cheese which has been cut into small pieces; stir until melted. Combine with cooked spinach. This may be served immediately or put into a casserole and topped with buttered bread crumbs and refrigerated. When ready to serve, bake in a 350-degree oven for 40 minutes. This dish freezes well.
Yield: 6 servings
Note: Madeline has a new version of this dish: in place of Velveeta and jalapeno, use 4 tablespoons Green Tabasco and 1 tube garlic cheese.
Note: This is great served in a chafer with crispy toast points.

SPINACH CASSEROLE

1 (10-oz.) pkg. frozen chopped
  spinach
1 tsp. sugar
1 can cream of chicken soup
1 egg, beaten

1 cup shredded sharp Cheddar
2 slices bread, cut in cubes
3 Tbsps. melted butter
Dash red pepper
Dash garlic powder

Cook spinach by package directions; drain very well. Combine spinach with next 4 ingredients; place in a 2-quart baking dish. Toss bread cubes with butter, pepper and garlic powder—place on top of spinach. Bake in a 350-degree oven for 1 hour.
Yield: 4 servings

MOM'S SPINACH CASSEROLE

This creamy spinach dish is great for a dinner party served with baked pork loin and a light rice dish. For a holiday dinner, it is splendid served with turkey and dressing.

3 pkgs. frozen chopped spinach
4 Tbsps. butter
1 onion, chopped
1 (8-oz.) pkg. cream cheese

1/2 cup Parmesan cheese
1 can cream of mushroom soup
1/2 tsp. garlic powder
Salt and pepper, to taste

Cook spinach as directed on package; drain well and set aside. Melt butter in a large skillet and sauté onion. Cut cream cheese into cubes and blend into butter and onion; heat until cheese melts. Add Parmesan, soup, garlic powder, salt and pepper; fold in spinach and mix well. Place in a greased baking dish and bake in a 350-degree oven for 20-30 minutes, until hot and bubbly.
Yield: 6-8 servings

SUSAN'S ROASTED ASPARAGUS

Our daughter Susan is very aware of the benefits of preparing healthy meals for her family. With this roasted dish, she's enhanced the flavor of the asparagus with olive oil and garlic pepper. It's very simple to prepare—pop in the oven and serve as soon as it comes out. Give these savory spears a try—your family will love them.

1 bunch fresh asparagus
2 Tbsps. olive oil

1/4 tsp. garlic pepper seasoning

Preheat oven to 400 degrees. Place one bunch of asparagus, ends trimmed, in a Ziploc bag. Add olive oil and garlic pepper to bag; shake to coat. Place in a single layer on foil-lined baking sheet. Cook for 10-15 minutes, depending on the size of asparagus, until lightly browned and tender.
Yield: 4 servings

BAKED ASPARAGUS

This delicious casserole is a fine company dish. The crunch of the water chestnuts combined with the creaminess of the cheese enhances the clean, fresh taste of the asparagus. It's a favorite in our home.

2 cans whole asparagus, drained
1 can petit pois peas, drained
1 can cream of celery soup
1 can sliced water chestnuts,
   drained

2 cups mild Cheddar cheese,
   grated
3 slices bread, cubed
1 stick butter, melted

Drain asparagus well and place in the bottom of a greased 13x9x2-inch baking dish. Mix peas, soup and water chestnuts. Pour mixture over asparagus layer and sprinkle with grated cheese. Place bread cubes in melted butter in a large skillet—sauté until golden. Place cubes on top of cheese layer. Bake in a 325-degree oven for 30 minutes, or until hot and bubbly.
Yield: 4-6 servings

ASPARAGUS MORNAY

1 ½ lbs. fresh asparagus, trimmed
2 Tbsps. butter
2 Tbsps. flour
1 cup half-and-half
1/2 tsp. chicken bouillon granules

1/8 tsp. ground nutmeg
Salt and white pepper, to taste
1/2 cup shredded Swiss cheese
4 Tbsps. crushed buttery crackers

Cook asparagus in a large skillet in a small amount of water about 6 minutes; drain. Arrange spears in the bottom of a greased 13x9x2-inch baking dish; set aside. In a 2-qt. saucepan, melt butter over low heat. Add flour; cook and stir for 1 minute. Whisk in half-and-half, bouillon, nutmeg, salt and pepper; bring to a boil over medium heat. Cook, stirring constantly, for 2 minutes. Remove from heat; stir in cheese until melted. Pour over asparagus; sprinkle with cracker crumbs. Bake in a 375-degree oven for 15 minutes, or until top is lightly browned.
Yield: 6 servings

EASY, EASY ASPARAGUS

When our daughter, Debbie, lived in Bangkok, her cook prepared this regularly for my grandson Adam by popular demand. So delicious!

3 Tbsps. sesame or olive oil
1 clove garlic, minced
1 bunch fresh asparagus, trimmed

6 Tbsps. soy sauce
Sesame seeds

Heat oil in a large skillet; sauté garlic about 3 minutes—do not brown. Add asparagus spears; sprinkle with soy sauce. Cook 6-8 minutes, gently rolling spears until all sides are golden brown and tender. Sprinkle with sesame seeds and serve immediately.
Yield: 4 servings

When trimming fresh asparagus, as you wash each spear, bend at the hard end; the tough part will snap off. If asparagus stems are tough, remove the outer layer with a potato peeler.

ULTIMATE ASPARAGUS CASSEROLE

The combination of hard-boiled eggs and asparagus makes this a real pleasing company dish.

1 ½ lbs. fresh asparagus spears,   1/2 cup evaporated milk
   cooked (reserve the liquid)   2/3 cup corn flake crumbs
2 Tbsps. butter   2 hard-boiled eggs, chopped
1 Tbsp. flour   1 cup Cheddar cheese, grated

In a saucepan, melt butter; stir in the flour and add evaporated milk and 1 cup of reserved asparagus liquid.   Cook, stirring constantly, until smooth; add salt and pepper, to taste. In a greased 13x9x2-inch baking dish, place asparagus.   Top with the crumbs, eggs, and cream sauce. Sprinkle with the cheese and bake in a 350-degree oven for 30 minutes. Yield: 6 servings

SQUASH CASSEROLE

This is my favorite squash dish in the whole world! The buttery crackers lend a sweet taste that defies description! You do not have to use three kinds of squash—it is equally wonderful with just yellow and pattypan— or yellow squash by itself.

1 stick butter, divided   1/2 tsp. black pepper
5 yellow squash, sliced   1 cup Hellmann's mayonnaise
3-4 pattypan squash, cut in chunks   1 cup grated Cheddar cheese
3 zucchini squash, sliced   1 tube buttery crackers, coarsely
1 medium onion, chopped   crushed
1 tsp. salt

Melt ½-stick of the butter in a large heavy skillet or Dutch oven.   Add squash, onion, salt and pepper, and simmer until crisp-tender. Blend together mayonnaise and grated cheese and add to squash mixture.   Pour into a 13x9x2-inch baking dish.   Top with crushed crackers and dot with remaining butter that has been cut into slices.   Bake uncovered in a 350-degree oven for 30 minutes. Yield: 6-8 servings

SIMPLE SQUASH

4 Tbsps. butter
6 medium yellow squash,
  cut in 1-inch rounds
1 tsp. salt
1/4 tsp. sugar
4 or 5 green onions, chopped

1 (8-oz.) carton sour cream
  (can use low-fat)
4 oz. shredded Cheddar cheese
1/2 cup Parmesan cheese
1 cup plain bread crumbs

Melt butter in large skillet; add squash, salt, sugar and green onions, blending well.   Cover skillet and simmer over low heat, stirring occasionally, about 15 minutes, or until squash is tender; fold in sour cream and cheeses.   Pour into a greased baking dish. Top with bread crumbs.   Bake in a 350-degree oven for 30 minutes.
Yield: 6-8 servings

LADYE'S STUFFED ZUCCHINI

My sister-in-law, Ladye White, is a master at cooking vegetables. This is one of her oldest, and favorite, recipes. It pairs up well with pork loin and a green salad. This dish can be made a day ahead and baked when ready to serve.

6 zucchini squash
2 eggs, lightly beaten
1 ½ cups sharp Cheddar cheese
1/2 cup cottage cheese
2 Tbsps. chopped parsley

2 Tbsps. chopped onion
Salt and pepper, to taste
1/2 cup plain bread crumbs
2 Tbsps. melted butter

Cook whole zucchini until tender (12 minutes).   Drain and cut each in half, lengthwise.   Scoop out center to make a "boat"; invert and drain. Combine eggs, Cheddar, cottage cheese, parsley, onion, and salt and pepper.   Fill zucchini boats.   Sprinkle bread crumbs and butter on top. Bake in a 350-degree oven for 25 minutes.

SQUASH DRESSING

3 cups cooked yellow squash
1 stick butter, melted
1 onion, chopped
1 pkg. cornbread mix, baked

1 can cream of chicken soup
1 can chicken broth
1 egg, beaten
Scant salt & pepper

Lightly mash drained squash. Melt butter in a skillet and sauté onion. Crumble baked cornbread. Mix together all ingredients and place in a greased 2-quart baking dish. Bake in a 350-degree oven for 30-40 minutes, until hot and bubbly.
Yield: 6 servings

OVEN FRIED ZUCCHINI WITH DIPPING SAUCE

These are great battered and fried, but as we all know, that's forbidden.

1/2 cup seasoned bread crumbs
2 Tbsps. grated Parmesan cheese
3-4 zucchini squashes
2 large eggs, beaten

1/4 cup olive oil
Spicy Dipping sauce
  (recipe follows)

Preheat oven to 400 degrees. Spray a baking sheet with baking spray. Combine bread crumbs and Parmesan in a large bowl; set aside. Cut zucchini into ½-inch wedges. Dip zucchini wedges in beaten eggs; then coat with bread crumb mixture. Place on greased baking sheet and drizzle lightly with olive oil. Bake until golden—about 30 minutes. Serve with Spicy Dipping Sauce.
Yield: 4 servings

Spicy Dipping Sauce
1/4 cup ketchup
1/2 cup mayonnaise
2-3 Tbsps. prepared horseradish
1/2 tsp. cayenne pepper
Mix well. Serve with Oven Fried Zucchini.

TOMATO-SQUASH BAKE

This juicy dish can be prepared with almost any combination of fresh veggies. I often add a layer of eggplant that's been sautéed in olive oil. Veggies can be chopped, tossed with olive oil and Greek seasoning, put in a steamer basket and grilled—absolutely divine! Use your imagination!

1 ½ large onions, thinly sliced	4 zucchini squash, thinly sliced
4 Tbsps. olive oil	Salt and pepper, to taste
4 yellow squash, thinly sliced	1 cup shredded Mozzarella cheese
2 large tomatoes, thinly sliced	1 cup grated Parmesan cheese

Sauté onions in olive oil; set aside. Layer one-half of the veggies in a greased 13x9x2-inch baking dish as follows: yellow squash, tomatoes, zucchini, and onions. Sprinkle with salt and pepper, one-half Mozzarella and Parmesan. Repeat layers. Bake in a 350-degree oven for 45 minutes.

Yield: 6 servings

FRIED EGGPLANT PATTIES

1 large eggplant	1 egg, lightly beaten
Salt and pepper, to taste	1 tube buttery crackers, crushed
1/2 onion, grated	Cooking oil

Peel and boil eggplant; mash. Blend together all ingredients. Heat oil in deep pot and fry patties until golden brown. Serve immediately.

*When eggplant is roasted, pureed, and mixed
with chopped tomato, onion, olive oil, and Greek seasoning,
it is often referred to as "poor man's caviar." It is delicious served
cold as a dip with assorted breads or crackers.*

EGGPLANT CASSEROLE
This casserole is so wonderful, everyone will be begging for seconds.

1 large or 2 small eggplants
Salted water for soaking
Olive oil
1 ½ lbs. ground chuck
2 onions, sliced
2 bell peppers, chopped

2 fresh ripe tomatoes, sliced
Salt, black pepper, red pepper,
    garlic powder, to taste
1–1 ½ lbs. sharp Cheddar cheese,
    grated
1/2 stick butter, cut in slices

Peel and slice eggplant into 1-inch thick slices; soak in salted water for 30 minutes; drain. Simmer slices in a little olive oil until slightly tender. Layer the bottom of a 3-quart baking dish with one-half of the eggplant slices. Brown and drain the ground chuck. On top of eggplant slices, layer one-half of the ground chuck, onions, green pepper, and tomatoes. Season with salt, pepper, red pepper, and garlic powder. Top with one-half the grated cheese. Repeat layers with remaining ingredients; top with grated cheese and dot with butter. Cover and cook in a 350-degree oven for 1 hour. Uncover the last 15 minutes to brown top.
Yield: 6 servings

CHINESE BEETS
You don't have to be a beet lover to enjoy my friend Mollie Weldon's Chinese beets. The medley of ketchup, vanilla, and cloves, blended with the beets makes for a deliciously cool side dish.

3 jars tiny beets
1 cup sugar
2 tsp. cornstarch
1 cup vinegar
3 Tbsps. cooking oil

3 Tbsps. ketchup
Dash of salt
1 tsp. vanilla
24 whole cloves

Drain beets, reserving 1 ½ cups juice. In a saucepan, bring to a boil sugar, cornstarch and vinegar. Add oil, ketchup, salt and vanilla; stir in 1 ½ cups juice from beets and cloves. Add beets and simmer 10 minutes; chill.
Yield: 1 qt.

STEWED OKRA

On our frequent trips to Baton Rouge, we love to stop at Lea's Restaurant in Lecompte, Louisiana. The folks at Lea's are known for their fabulous ham sandwiches, mile-high homemade pies and country-style plate lunches. Their fabulous stewed okra has always held a special place in my heart. This version is a little different—it contains no tomatoes.

1/2 lb. bacon, diced
4 cups sliced okra
1 cup onions, chopped
1/2 cup bell pepper, chopped
1 tsp. garlic, minced

1/4 cup parsley, chopped
Salt, to taste
1 Tbsp. soy sauce
1 Tbsp. Louisiana Hot Sauce
Pinch of sugar

Fry bacon; drain all but 2 tablespoons drippings. Add okra, onions, bell pepper, and garlic; simmer 10 minutes, stirring often. Add remaining ingredients; cover and cook until okra is tender, stirring often.
Yield: 6 servings

HOLIDAY BROCCOLI CASSEROLE

This delicious broccoli dish is an up-scaled version of a simple vegetable.

2 (10-oz.) pkgs. frozen
   broccoli spears
1 cup (4 oz.) shredded
   cheddar cheese
2 eggs, lightly beaten

1 can cream of mushroom soup
1/2 cup Hellmann's mayonnaise
1 small onion, finely chopped
2 tubes buttery crackers, crushed
1 stick butter, melted

Prepare broccoli according to package directions—do not overcook. Drain well. Arrange broccoli spears in a sprayed 13x9x2-inch baking dish. Sprinkle with cheese; set aside. Combine eggs and next 3 ingredients; spread carefully over cheese. Combine crushed crackers with melted butter, tossing well; sprinkle over casserole. Bake uncovered in a 350-degree oven for 30-40 minutes, or until hot and bubbly.
Yield: 8 servings

MUSHROOM FLORENTINE

This is a great company dish—rich and luscious. It's from the kitchen of my friend and chief "cookbook proofer" Bev Pierce.

2 pkgs. frozen chopped spinach
1 lb. fresh mushrooms
1 ¼ sticks butter, melted, divided
4 Tbsps. dry sherry
Juice of 1/2 lemon

1 tsp. salt
1/4 cup chopped onion
1 cup grated Cheddar, divided
Garlic salt, to taste

Thaw spinach and drain well, squeezing out excess moisture; set aside. Separate mushroom caps from stems; slice stems. Sauté mushroom stems and caps, cap side down, in 1 stick butter, until brown. Drizzle sherry and lemon over mushrooms and remove from pan. Season spinach with salt, onion, and remaining ¼ stick melted butter; arrange in the bottom of a lightly buttered 11x9x2-inch baking dish. Sprinkle with one-half cup of the grated Cheddar cheese. Arrange sliced stems and then caps on top of cheese. Add garlic salt and sprinkle remaining cheese on top. Bake uncovered in a 350-degree oven for 20 minutes.

TOMATO PIE

This luscious pie is a perfect example of pure-country comfort food. It's at its best during the summer months when fresh tomatoes are in season.

4 ripe tomatoes
1 (10-count) roll refrigerated
   biscuits
1 medium onion, chopped

1/3 cup bell pepper, chopped
3 Tbsps. butter
1 cup Hellmann's mayonnaise
1 cup grated Mozzarella cheese

Peel and slice the tomatoes. Place biscuits in the bottom of a 9x9-inch pan, sides touching. Place tomatoes on top of biscuits. Sauté onion and green pepper in butter; sprinkle on top of tomatoes. Mix mayonnaise and cheese together and spread on top. Bake in a 350-degree oven for 40 minutes.
Yield: 6 servings

TOMATO STUFFED CAULIFLOWER

This dish was shared by my cousin from Baton Rouge, Deryl Hamilton.
It is beautiful served for a holiday dinner.

1 large head cauliflower
1 lb. Roma tomatoes, peeled
  and cut into ½-inch wedges
Salt and pepper, to taste

6 Tbsps. melted butter, divided
1/3 cup bread crumbs
1/2 cup grated Monterrey Jack
  or Swiss cheese

Remove leaves from cauliflower. Boil whole in salted water until just tender—do not overcook. Remove from water and place in a greased 2-quart round baking dish. Place tomato wedges between the florets of cauliflower; salt and pepper. Drizzle ¼ cup butter over cauliflower and tomatoes. Mix bread crumbs and cheese. Pack into the spaces around the cauliflower and tomatoes. Pour remaining ¼ cup butter over the bread crumbs. Bake in a 375-degree oven for 30 minutes or until golden brown.
Yield: 8-10 servings

CORN AND SHRIMP CASSEROLE

What better duo than corn and shrimp? It's like wine and cheese or
peanut butter and jelly.

1 ½ sticks butter, divided
1 medium onion, chopped
1 small bell pepper, chopped
1 clove garlic, minced
3 medium fresh tomatoes, chopped

1/2 lb. shrimp, peeled and deveined
1 (15-oz.) can whole-kernel corn
1 (15-oz.) can cream-style corn
Salt and pepper, to taste
Cracker crumbs

Melt 1 stick butter in large skillet; sauté onion, bell pepper, and garlic until tender. Add chopped tomato and continue to cook five minutes. Stir in shrimp, whole kernel corn (drained), cream style corn, and salt and pepper. Place in a sprayed 2-quart baking dish; cover with cracker crumbs and dot with remaining butter. Bake uncovered in a 350-degree oven for 30 minutes.
Yield: 6 servings

SCALLOPED CORN

1/2 small onion, chopped	1 cup cracker crumbs
3 Tbsps. butter	1 cup milk
1 (17-oz.) can cream-style corn	2 eggs, slightly beaten
1 (7-oz.) can whole-kernel corn,	1 tsp. salt
drained	1/2 tsp. pepper

Sauté onion in butter until tender; stir in remaining ingredients. Place mixture in a lightly greased 1 1/2-quart baking dish. Bake in a 350-degree oven, uncovered, for 1 hour and 10 minutes.
Yield: 6 servings

SHOE PEG CORN CASSEROLE

Shoe peg is tiny white corn—normally more tender and sweet than its counterpart, the yellow (Golden Bantam) corn. This little dish has the zip of green chilies to enhance its flavor.

5-6 ears shoe peg corn, or	1 stick butter, divided
2 cans shoe peg corn, drained	1 small sweet onion, chopped
1 (8 oz.) pkg. cream cheese	1 can chopped green chilies
1/4 cup half-and-half or cream	1/2 cup breadcrumbs

Shuck corn and cut kernels off cob. In a 2-qt. saucepan, heat cream cheese and half & half until cream cheese melts; set aside. In a skillet, melt ½ stick butter and sauté onion and corn; simmer about 15 minutes. Fold in cream cheese/half & half mixture; blend in chilies and mix well. Pour into a greased baking dish and top with breadcrumbs; dot with remaining butter. Bake uncovered in a 325-degree oven about 30 minutes, until hot and bubbly.
Yield: 4-6 servings

It is important to buy corn as soon after it's picked as possible. It is best cooked the same day. Strip off husks and silk just before cooking.

LISA'S SIMPLE CORN CASSEROLE

This recipe is from the kitchen of my friend Lisa Gray. It is a creamy blend that lends itself to any menu. Kids love it!

1 can whole-kernel corn, drained   1 egg, slightly beaten
1 can cream-style corn   1 box (sweet) corn bread mix
16 oz. sour cream   1 stick butter (cut into pats)

Mix first 5 ingredients together; pour into greased baking dish and top with butter pats. Bake uncovered in a 325-degree oven for 45 minutes, or until top is golden brown.
Yield: 6-8 servings

NINA'S VEGGIE CASSEROLE

This delicious dish is from the kitchen of my godchild Nina Barnett Marceaux from Lake Charles. Nina is mother to four precious children. She's a dynamic cook and homemaker who always has time for the quality moments that ensure happiness and well being in her home. This nutritious casserole is so tasty, the kids will never know it's good for them, but will probably think it's dessert!

2 (11-oz.) cans Mexi-Corn, drained   1 (8 oz.) pkg. shredded Velveeta
2 (15 oz.) cans Veg-All, drained   1 roll Ritz Crackers, crushed
1/2 onion, chopped   1 stick butter
3/4 cup Hellmann's mayonnaise

Mix corn, Veg-All, onion and mayonnaise together in a greased baking dish. Cover with a layer of cheese, followed by a crushed cracker layer. Cut butter into slices and put on top. Bake in a 350-degree oven for 30 minutes or until bubbly.
Yield: 10 servings

Sweet fresh corn doesn't need enhancements—a little butter, salt and pepper are all it takes. When it is in season, Olathe corn from Colorado is my number one choice.

ORANGE-GLAZED CARROTS

3 Tbsps. butter   1/3 cup frozen orange juice
4 cups sliced carrots   concentrate, thawed
1/3 cup brown sugar   4 Tbsps. dry sherry (optional)

Melt butter in heavy skillet; sauté carrots until crisp-tender, stirring often.   Add brown sugar, orange juice concentrate and sherry.   Let simmer about 10 minutes; serve hot.
4-6 servings

CARROT FRITTERS

A little unorthodox, but who ever said fritters have to be made with corn or salmon? Carrots provide a delightful sweetness to these little patties. The batter may need a little adjustment to get the desired consistency to form into patties.

1 egg, lightly beaten   1/4 tsp. pepper
1/4 cup Hellmann's mayonnaise   2 ½ cups cooked, mashed carrots
1/2 cup finely chopped onion   3 ½ cups soft bread crumbs
2 Tbsps. vegetable oil   2 Tbsps. cream (if needed)
1/2 tsp. salt   2 cups crushed cornflakes

Blend together first 7 ingredients.   Add the bread crumbs and mix thoroughly. (If mixture is dry, add cream, a little at a time, until desired consistency to form a patty.) Shape into 10-12 patties; coat with crushed cornflakes. Place on a greased baking sheet. Bake in a 375-degree oven for 25 minutes.
Yield: 6-8 servings
Note: These fritters can be fried in cooking oil in a skillet if desired.

*Not only are carrots healthy for us, they are available
year round. They also keep well in the refrigerator.
If they become limp, recrisp them in a bowl of ice
water. The same rule applies to celery.*

ED'S BRAISED CABBAGE

Forget boiled cabbage—this kicked up version is absolutely delicious! The cabbage, cooked with bacon, onion and peppercorns, has a roasted taste. Whenever we serve this dish to company, it draws raves. Make it a part of your menu on New Year's Day.

4-5 slices lean bacon	1 medium onion, chopped
1 medium head cabbage,	Black peppercorns, to taste
cut into 5-6 chunks	Salt, to taste

In heavy (cast-iron) Dutch oven or skillet, fry bacon slices; remove bacon, drain and crumble. To bacon drippings, add chopped onion and simmer on low heat about 5 minutes. Remove onion from skillet and lay chunks of cabbage, cut-side down in bacon and onion drippings. Sprinkle onions and crumbled bacon on top of cabbage; add salt and peppercorns. Cover tightly, turn heat down and simmer on low heat until tender.
Yield: 4-6 servings

CABBAGE CASSEROLE

5 slices bacon	1 medium bell pepper, chopped
1 large cabbage, chopped	1 can Ro-Tel tomatoes
1 large onion, chopped	1 minced jalapeno pepper, optional

Fry bacon, drain and crumble. In bacon drippings, cook cabbage, onion and bell pepper about 10 minutes. Add tomatoes and jalapeno pepper. Cover and simmer about 30 minutes, stirring often. To serve, sprinkle cabbage with crumbled bacon pieces.
Yield: 6 servings
Note: This is delicious with smoked sausage cut into rounds in place of the bacon. Brown sausage and add remainder of ingredients to cook.

ORIENTAL CABBAGE

I first sampled this Oriental Cabbage on Christmas Day in 1992 when we joined my son-in-law Lee's family for their annual celebration. This delicious dish is a creation of Lee's sister, Linda Primeaux.

1 lb. bacon
1 large cabbage, chopped
2 bunches green onions, chopped

4 cups cooked long-grain rice
1/4 cup soy sauce

Fry bacon in a large skillet; drain on paper towels. To bacon grease, add cabbage and green onion; cook covered until tender, about 40 minutes, stirring often. Crumble bacon and add to mixture; add cooked rice and soy sauce. (Taste before adding any salt because soy sauce is salty.) Keep warm until ready to serve.

BAKED BEANS—THE REAL THING!

Most folks opt for using quick-fix canned pork and beans when preparing baked beans. As a rule, my husband Ed chooses a simple method, and his rendition is divine, but when the kids come, he prepares them from scratch, using dried beans. These beans are superb!

1 lb. pkg. dried navy beans
1/2 lb. lean salt pork
1/2 cup dark molasses
1/2 cup ketchup
3 Tbsps. sugar

1 ½ Tbsps. Worcestershire sauce
1 ½ Tbsps. dry mustard
1 tsp. salt
1 tsp. pepper
1 medium onion, chopped

Sort and rinse beans; place in a large pot. Cover with water about 2 inches above beans; cover and refrigerate overnight. Drain. Cut salt pork into three pieces; place with navy beans in a large heavy Dutch oven. Add water about 2 ½ inches above beans. Bring to a boil; cover and reduce heat and simmer 30 minutes. Drain, reserving 2 cups liquid. Combine all remaining ingredients; stir well. Blend molasses mixture into beans, salt pork and reserved liquid. Pour mixture into a 3-qt. baking dish; cover and bake at 250-degrees for 6 hours. Uncover and bake an additional 45 minutes.
Yield: 12 to 15 servings

ED'S QUICKIE BAKED BEANS

This is my hubby Ed's easy way to bake beans—simple to prepare, with scrumptious flavors.

1 (16-20 oz.) can pork and beans   1/4 cup ketchup
1/4 cup brown sugar   5 lean bacon slices

Mix beans, brown sugar and ketchup. Place in a 1 ½-quart greased baking dish. Cover with bacon slices. Bake uncovered in a 275-degree oven for 1 ½-2 hours, until beans are tender.
Yield: 4 servings

BAKED ONIONS

This side dish will kick up any entree, but is especially enticing served with char-grilled steaks. The crunch of the potato chips paired up with the creaminess of the soup and cheese is what makes it so captivating. It is a lovely company dish.

10 medium onions   2 cans cream of mushroom soup
1 (14-oz.) bag plain potato chips,   1/2 cup homogenized milk
  crushed   or 2/3 cup half-and-half cream
1/2 lb. mild Cheddar cheese, grated   1/4 tsp. cayenne pepper

In a 13x9x2-inch buttered baking dish, place alternate layers of thinly sliced onions, crushed potato chips and grated cheese. Mix mushroom soup and milk and pour over the top of the onion mixture, making little spaces with a spoon to help juices go all the way down. Sprinkle cayenne pepper over the top and bake 1 hour at 350 degrees.
Yield: 6-8 servings

Chopping onions can turn you into a cry-baby!
I've tried everything—biting on a toothpick...running water...
goggles. I shed the fewest tears having a lit candle in the room.
It also makes the kitchen smell good!

GRANDMA'S ONION PIE

When my maternal grandmother made this onion pie, she always made two because we made total pigs of ourselves. I never got the recipe, but this one is a close second..I hope!

1 pie shell
3 cups thinly sliced sweet onions
3 Tbsps. melted butter
1/2 cup homogenized milk
1 ½ cups sour cream, divided

1 ½ tsps. salt
2 eggs, well-beaten
3 Tbsps. flour
3 bacon slices, fried crisp and
    crumbled

Bake pie shell in a 400-degree oven for 10 minutes or until golden. Cook onions in butter until lightly browned. Spoon into pie shell. Add milk, 1 ¼ cup sour cream and salt to beaten eggs. Blend flour with remaining ¼ cup sour cream. Combine with egg mixture; pour over onion mixture. Bake in a 325-degree oven for 30 minutes or until center is firm. Garnish with crumbled bacon.
Yield: 8 servings

CHARBROILED SWEET ONIONS

What's more delicious when grilling a steak than to include some onions seasoned and wrapped with foil?

6 large sweet onions
1 stick butter, cut in pats

Salt and pepper, to taste
Creole seasoning, to taste

Place onions individually on foil, top with pats of butter and sprinkle with Creole seasoning, salt and pepper. Sprinkle lightly with paprika, if desired. Seal foil, place on grill and charbroil until onions are tender.
Yield: 6 servings

The onion, a member of the lily family, has played a major role in seasoning the cuisines of the world for centuries. The Vidalia is the first sweet onion to be promoted and distributed nationally.

PLAIN OLD MASHED POTATOES

My husband Ed's mashed potatoes are the creamiest and the best. His secret is lots of butter, and not to over beat them. As potatoes cook, the starch granules inside them swell. Too much beating after cooking can rupture the granules, resulting in a gluey mess.

4-5 medium red potatoes	2-3 Tbsps. milk or cream
1 stick butter	Salt and pepper, to taste

Peel and quarter potatoes; place in 3-qt. saucepan and cover with water that has been salted. Bring to a boil. When potatoes are tender, drain well and return to pot they were boiled in; add 1 stick butter, salt and pepper. Beat with electric mixer on low speed until lumps are out—do not over beat. If needed, add a little milk. Serve immediately.
Yield: 4 servings
Note: If there are leftover mashed potatoes, refrigerate them for another meal. When ready to prepare, add one beaten egg to potatoes, blending well. Form into patties and sauté in butter in a skillet. Delicious served for breakfast!

SIMPLE ROASTED POTATOES

I love the "dirty" taste of new potatoes. It's in the springtime that new potatoes are at their peak, and the simpler the preparation, the better. Try this delicious rendition of our Louisiana spud.

8 cups small red potatoes, washed and halved	Freshly ground black pepper
1/2 cup extra virgin olive oil	1/2 stick butter, melted
Salt, to taste	Fresh chopped parsley, to taste

Toss the potatoes, olive oil, salt and pepper in a large-sized roasting pan. Roast for 45 minutes in a 350-degree oven, stirring occasionally. Drizzle butter over potatoes, tossing well; return to the oven for 10 minutes. Toss again, sprinkle parsley on top, and serve.
Yield: 8-10 servings

NEW POTATO CASSEROLE

This heavenly dish gets an A+ served with baked ham and a green veggie. It's an old family favorite of Sue Calhoun and her family.

12 new potatoes	1 jar Hormel Bacon Pieces
1 cup grated sharp Cheddar	1 stick butter

Boil new potatoes in their skins. Grease a 13x9x2-inch baking dish. Cut potatoes in half—do not peel. Layer potatoes, grated cheese, and bacon pieces. Melt butter and drizzle on top. Bake in a 350-degree oven until cheese melts and casserole is hot and bubbly—about 20 minutes.
Yield: 6-8 servings

HELEN'S SWEET POTATO DESSERT CASSEROLE

This magnificent casserole graces the table each year when Helen and Harold Turner invite kith and ken for a Thanksgiving celebration. Traditionally, our family shares this holiday with them and we wouldn't miss it for the world! Helen's serving table is always laden with the most luscious dishes imaginable. The only thing better than the food is the gracious hospitality.

4 cups cooked sweet potatoes	2 eggs, beaten
1/2 cup sugar	1 tsp. vanilla
1/2 cup butter, cut up	1/3 cup milk

Mash potatoes until there are no lumps; add sugar, butter, eggs, vanilla and milk. Mix until well blended. Pour mixture into a sprayed 13x9x2-inch baking dish; set aside. Prepare topping.

Topping:

1/3 cup butter, melted	1/2 cup flour
1 cup brown sugar	1 cup chopped pecans

In a heavy saucepan, melt butter; add remaining ingredients, blending well. Cook on low heat, stirring constantly, about 15 minutes. Remove from heat and let cool for a few minutes, then sprinkle on top of sweet potatoes, using as much or as little of the pecan topping as desired. Bake in a 350-degree oven for 25 minutes.

DOTTIE'S YAMS

Dottie Hogg is much in demand each year when the Shreveport Power Squadron holds its annual Pig Roast, for her yams are legendary.

8-10 medium sweet potatoes
1/2 stick butter
1 cup orange marmalade
1/2 cup light brown sugar
1/4 cup honey
1 Tbsp. lemon juice
1 Tbsp. (frozen) orange
   juice concentrate

3 Tbsps. cane syrup or
   dark brown sugar
1/2 tsp. cinnamon
1/4 to 1/3 cup brandy
2 cups fresh cranberries
1/4 to 1/3 cup pecans

Boil sweet potatoes until just tender; drain and cool. Peel and slice ½ to ¾-inch thick. Arrange in a large greased baking dish. Make a syrup of butter, orange marmalade, brown sugar, honey, lemon juice, orange juice concentrate, cane syrup and cinnamon. Heat and stir until the butter melts; remove from heat and add brandy. Sprinkle cranberries and nuts over sweet potatoes and pour syrup mixture over all. Bake in a 350-degree oven for 30 minutes.
Yield: 12 servings
Note: This dish can be prepared days ahead and frozen; allow it to thaw before baking. If dish is cold, add 10 minutes to baking time.

BAKED APRICOTS

My friend Mary Rademacher shared this recipe with me, and Doris Wedgeworth created it. I applaud both of them, for this is a treasure.

4 cans apricot halves, drained
1 cup light brown sugar
1 ¼ sticks butter, melted

2 sleeves buttery crackers,
   crumbled

Place drained apricots on bottom of a greased 13x9x2-inch baking dish. Sprinkle with brown sugar. Mix butter and Ritz cracker crumbs and sprinkle on top of brown sugar. Bake uncovered in a 325 degree oven for 45 minutes to one hour.
Yield: 6-8 servings

RIVERS' MACARONI AND CHEESE

Who doesn't love macaroni and cheese. Both young and old, we love it because it's a reminder of home and safety and love. It represents cooking from the heart. When my daughter Donna was little, she ate two things: macaroni and cheese and bologna. The kid knew good comfort food when she tasted it! This recipe for Rivers Wallace's classic macaroni and cheese is hard to beat. It is the original—torn from a magazine in the 1940's and is still the one Rivers uses. Some things cannot be improved on.

2 cups elbow macaroni
1 small onion, minced
3 Tbsps. margarine or butter
1 Tbsp. all-purpose flour
3/4 tsp. salt
1/2 tsp. dry mustard

1/2 tsp. ground pepper
2 cups milk
1/2 lb. Velveeta cheese,
   shredded
3/4 cup fresh bread crumbs

Prepare macaroni as label directs. Over medium heat, cook onions in 2 tablespoons butter until tender. Stir in flour, salt, dry mustard, and pepper; cook one minute. Slowly add milk, cooking and stirring until smooth. Add about 3/4 of the cheese, stirring until melted. Turn cooked, drained macaroni into a greased 1 ½ quart baking dish. Pour cheese sauce over, tossing with a fork to coat all macaroni well. Top with remainder of cheese. Melt remaining 1 tablespoon butter; stir in bread crumbs and sprinkle over cheese layer. Bake uncovered in a preheated 400-degree oven for 20 minutes.
Yield: 6 servings

*Elbow macaroni, a short curved tube, is the
most popular for making macaroni and cheese.
When boiling macaroni, be sure to have ample water,
because most macaroni will double in size during cooking.*

WANDA'S PINEAPPLE CASSEROLE

This delicious casserole lends itself beautifully to luncheons, brunches or dinner—with ham, pork, or chicken. My cousin, Wanda Annison from Jackson, Mississippi claims this as an old family favorite.

1 (20-oz.) can pineapple chunks	1 cup shredded Cheddar cheese
1/2 cup sugar	1 cup crushed butter crackers
3 Tbsps. flour	1/4 cup melted butter

Drain pineapple liquid into a large bowl, reserving 3 tablespoons in a small container. To pineapple liquid, add sugar and flour; mix well. Add cheese and pineapple chunks. Place in a greased 13x9x2-inch baking dish. Top with crushed crackers. Drizzle melted butter over all. Sprinkle reserved pineapple juice over butter. Bake in a 350-degree oven for 45 minutes until hot and bubbly.
Yield: 4-6 servings

ELEANOR'S DEVILED EGGS

When my friend Eleanor Higgs places a tray of her special deviled eggs on a buffet table, it's interesting to watch them disappear. I try to hold back and remember I'm a lady, but what I really want to do is pick up the tray and scarf them down. There are many varieties of these little gems--these are delightfully different.

12 hard-cooked eggs	1/2 tsp. dill weed
1/2 cup Hellmann's mayonnaise	1/4 tsp. salt
2 Tbsps. milk	1/4 tsp. paprika
1 tsp. diced parsley flakes	1/8 tsp. white pepper
1/2 tsp. diced chives	1/8 tsp. garlic powder
1/2 tsp. ground mustard	Parsley, paprika for garnish

Cut hard-cooked eggs in half and carefully remove yolks, being careful not to tear up the white. Mash egg yolks well and blend in the remaining ingredients, except parsley and paprika (for garnish). Pipe or spoon filling into egg whites and garnish tops. Refrigerate until serving.
Yield: 24 deviled eggs

LEMON RICE

This simple, yet sublime rice dish has been a favorite in our home for thirty-five years. With its own delicate flavor, it lends itself to any meat on the menu, adding its own special lightness to rich, heavy dishes. This is a very healthy dish for those of you watching your calories and fats.

3 Tbsps. butter or margarine	3/4 tsp. salt
3 stalks green onion tops, chopped	1 tsp. white pepper
1 cup long-grain raw rice	Grated peel of 1 lemon
1/4 cup dry vermouth	2 Tbsps. dried parsley flakes
1 ¾ cups chicken broth	or 1/4 cup fresh chopped parsley

Melt butter in a 2-quart saucepan that has been sprayed with cooking spray. Add rice and stir until coated (1-2 minutes). Add green onion tops; simmer a few seconds. Blend in vermouth, broth, and seasonings. Bring to a boil; cover and lower heat. Simmer 20 minutes or until liquid is absorbed. Toss with lemon peel and parsley; serve.

Yield: 4 cups

Note: For a main entrée, sauté 1 lb. peeled shrimp in butter before adding the other ingredients. Delicious!

RICE AND ARTICHOKE DISH

1 pkg. Chicken Rice-a-Roni	1/4 tsp. curry
1 (6-oz.) jar marinated artichokes	4 green onions, chopped
hearts, reserve liquid	1/2 cup stuffed salad olives
1/3 cup Hellmann's mayonnaise	

Prepare Rice Mix by package directions. Drain artichoke hearts, reserving liquid. Chop artichokes into quarters and mix with prepared Rice-a-Roni. For dressing: mix remaining ingredients, adding juice from artichokes. Toss together dressing, Rice-a-Roni and artichokes. Place in a 2-quart greased baking dish; cover and bake in a 350-degree oven for about 20 minutes—just until hot. Also delicious served cold as a salad.

Yield: 4-6 servings

FRENCH BREAD CASSEROLE

Once I sampled this moist and cheesy dish, I was hooked. My friend of many years, LaMuriel Poulsen served this one night at a dinner party. Accompanying this glorious dish were broiled red snapper, asparagus, and a Caesar Salad. This sensational side dish adds class to any menu.

2 large yellow onions,
  sliced in 1-inch rounds
4 Tbsps. butter
1/2 lb. shredded Swiss cheese
1 can cream of chicken soup

1/2 cup half-and-half
Cracked black pepper
4 leaves fresh sweet basil, chopped
1-3 cups coarsely crumbled crusty
  French bread

Sauté sliced onions in butter until tender. Place in a 13x9x2-inch baking dish; cover with shredded Swiss cheese. In the skillet onions were sautéed in, place chicken soup, half and half, cracked black pepper, and sweet basil. Mix well and heat. Place crumbled French bread over Swiss cheese in baking dish. Pour soup mix over bread; poke with a knife to allow juices to go through layers. Bake, uncovered, in a 375-degree oven for 45 minutes.
Yield: 6 servings

CROCKPOT DRESSING

If you're looking for a new slant on an old dish, try this flavorful dish that "cooks itself." My friend, Margaret Robinette, shared this recipe.

1 (8-inch) pan cornbread,
  crumbled
8 slices white bread, torn in pieces
4 eggs
1 medium onion, chopped
1/2 cup chopped celery

1 ½ tsps. sage
1 tsp. salt
1/2 tsp. black pepper
2 cans cream of chicken soup
2 (14-oz.) cans chicken broth
2 Tbsps. butter

Grease crock pot with buttery flavored cooking spray. In a large mixing bowl, combine crumbled cornbread with next 9 ingredients; mix well. Pour into the crock pot. Dot top with butter. Cover crock pot and cook on high for 2 hours, or on low for about 3 ½ hours. (If desired, pour in a greased baking dish and bake in 350-degree oven for 1 hour.)

CHAVANNE FAMILY DRESSING

This old family recipe dates back to Charles Chavanne's grandmother. I have had the privilege of sampling it, as well as helping my best friend, Nel Chavanne, make it on many occasions. This wonderful person passed away in 1996, so you can imagine what these memories mean to me. We loved cooking together and the month of December held many adventures in the kitchen—chopping, deboning, crumbling..and much laughter. Shelley Braswell, Nel's daughter, shared an old handwritten copy dating back to a holiday when she watched Nel make it and recorded every step. The Chavannes are excellent cooks—Charles, Sr., Shelley, Tom and Charles, Jr. and they are keeping all the treasured family traditions.

Turkey neck
Chicken livers
Salt and pepper
4 large onions, chopped, divided
8 stalks celery, chopped, divided
Water for boiling
1 stick butter

1/2 green bell pepper, chopped
1 double recipe of cornbread,
   baked and crumbled
7-8 slices white bread
1 bunch green onions, chopped
1 cup chopped fresh parsley

Boil turkey neck, chicken livers, salt, pepper, 2 onions, 4 stalks celery until tender—about one hour. Reserve broth. Remove meat from turkey neck and chop livers very fine. Melt butter in a skillet and sauté remaining onion, celery, and bell pepper until tender. Place crumbled cornbread in a large bowl; add sautéed veggies, turkey and livers. Drop bread in broth, saturating it; then remove bread from chicken broth and add to cornbread mixture. Add green onions, parsley, salt and pepper. If too dry, add a little of the broth. Place in a greased 15x10x3-inch baking dish or small roaster and bake in a 350-degree oven for one hour. Make gravy from turkey drippings to serve with dressing.
Note: When Nel made this dressing with pork loin, she would fold in some of the gravy from the pork—talk about delicious!
Yield: 12-14 servings

Sara Grace Daniel

Breakfast

Brunch

Breads

Brunch as a theme for entertaining is a lifestyle that the South has traditionally embraced with gusto. Whether it's to celebrate a bride, a brand new baby, a graduate or a horserace at the fairgrounds, it is a memorable culinary experience.

The historic city of New Orleans is credited with introducing the brunch. In 1884, it all started at a popular Crescent City breakfast restaurant called Madame Begue's. After many requests by both locals and tourists for a more substantial midmorning meal, Madame Begue introduced the "late breakfast", a hearty meal of many courses that caught on immediately. She soon brought this mid-morning repast to a high art— the meal we now refer to as brunch.

Then along came the Brennan family who turned brunch into a celebration at Commander's Palace with the New Orleans Jazz Brunch. It soon became a number-one choice of places to kick off the day; and who can forget the famous Breakfast at Brennan's?   From the eye-opener Bloody Mary to the luscious Bananas Foster, it's a culinary experience.

Today's brunches are so much more than bacon and eggs, and have become quite popular, both for home and restaurant gatherings. A combination of breakfast and lunch, brunch is usually eaten sometime between 11 a.m. and 2 p.m.   This leisurely late morning meal is a delightful and economical way to entertain!

What could be more inviting than a table laden with slabs of ham, sausage, crisp lean bacon, quiches, omelets, fluffy biscuits, hot steaming grits, a tureen filled with steaming bisque, and a lavish array of fresh fruit on a beautiful tray. For a smashing New Orleans themed brunch, prepare the famous Grillades and Grits, Pain Pardu and Coconut Rum Fruit Salad (See Index).

Let's raise our glass and propose a toast to that magnificent old city that is steeped in tradition—New Orleans!

EGG CASSEROLE

I sampled this hearty egg dish at a bridal shower hosted by my friends Amy Prather and Phyllis Graham. Accompanying dishes were: Crab Casserole (recipe follows), cheese grits, fresh fruit bowl, miniature muffins and biscuits, jellies and preserves.

1 lb. pork sausage,
  cooked and drained
1 (8 oz.) pkg. Monterrey Jack
  cheese, shredded
1 (8 oz.) pkg. sharp Cheddar,
  shredded

2 (4-oz.) cans chopped green
  chilies, drained
1 bunch green onions, chopped
12 eggs
3 Tbsps. sour cream
1 large tomato, thinly sliced

Combine sausage with cheeses, chilies, and onions. Place in a greased 13x9x2-inch baking dish. Combine eggs and sour cream; beat well. Pour mixture over sausage/cheese mixture (you may need to shake dish gently to distribute egg mixture) refrigerate overnight. **To bake**: Place baking dish in cold oven and set temperature at 350 degrees – bake 20 minutes. Remove from oven and add tomato slices to top for garnish. Return to oven and cook until done – a minimum of 20 minutes, until center is set.

BREAKFAST CRAB CASSEROLE

8 thick slices whole wheat bread
1 ½ cups water
1 tablespoon butter, melted
1 onion, chopped
2 cloves garlic, chopped
1/2 cup bell pepper, chopped
1/2 cup chopped celery

8 ozs. sharp Cheddar, shredded
8 ozs. sliced water chestnuts
1 lb. lump crabmeat
3 eggs
1/2 cup Hellmann's mayonnaise
Salt & pepper, to taste
Tabasco, to taste

Soak bread in water about 15 minutes. Melt butter and sauté onions, garlic, bell pepper, and celery until tender. Add cheese to bread and water mixture. Add vegetable mixture, drained water chestnuts, and crabmeat. Blend eggs, mayonnaise and seasonings; add to crabmeat mixture. Place in a 2-quart baking dish; bake in a 350-degree oven (uncovered) for 40 minutes.

CRABMEAT QUICHE

1 (10-in.) pastry shell
4 Tbsps. butter
1/2 cup green onions, chopped
1/2 cup chopped fresh mushrooms
3 large eggs
1 cup heavy cream

1 Tbsp. tomato paste
1 tsp. salt
1/2 tsp. red pepper
1 cup fresh crabmeat
2 Tbsps. vermouth
1/2 cup grated Cheddar cheese

Preheat oven to 425 degrees. Bake pricked pastry shell approximately 12 minutes. Remove pastry shell and reduce oven to 375 degrees. Melt butter; sauté onions and mushrooms 5-10 minutes. In a bowl, beat eggs and cream; add tomato paste, salt and pepper; mix well. Stir crabmeat and vermouth into mushroom mixture and cook over low heat about 5 minutes. Pour crabmeat mixture into eggs and cream; stir until combined. Pour mixed ingredients into pastry shell and bake. After 30 minutes, sprinkle with cheese and return to oven until knife inserted in center comes out clean, approximately 10 minutes.
Yield: 6 servings

COUNTRY POTATO DISH

This is a hearty meal-in-a-skillet eye-opener—men love it!

8 bacon slices
6 cups frozen cubed or shredded
   hash browns
3/4 cup chopped bell pepper
1 small onion, chopped

1 tsp. salt
1/2 tsp. pepper
6 eggs
1/2 cup shredded Cheddar cheese

In a large heavy skillet, fry bacon until crisp; remove and crumble. Reserve 3 tablespoons bacon drippings in skillet; add potatoes, bell pepper, onion, salt and pepper and cook, stirring for 5 minutes. Cover and cook, stirring occasionally until potatoes are tender and browned, about 15 minutes. Make six indentions in the potato mixture and break one egg into each one. Cover and cook on low heat for 15 minutes or until eggs are completely set. Sprinkle with cheese and bacon and serve.
Yield: 6 servings

HAM QUICHE

You do not get any easier than this! The blend of mayonnaise and cheese lends flavor and creaminess to the quiche. This quiche is so delicious served with grits and homemade biscuits!

4 beaten eggs
1 cup Hellmann's mayonnaise
1 cup milk
4 Tbsps. flour
16 ozs. sharp Cheddar, grated

2/3 cup chopped green onions
1 cup small cubes of ham
1 cup sliced mushrooms
2 deep-dish frozen pie crusts
   (Pet Ritz or Mrs. Smith)

Mix all ingredients. Pour into 2 deep-dish pie crusts. Bake in a 350-degree oven for 45-50 minutes. Let stand 10 minutes before cutting.
Note: All ingredients can be mixed the day before. You can also substitute 1 lb. regular sausage browned and drain for the ham and mushrooms. Freezes well after cooking.
Yield: 8 (2 slice) servings

CHILIE EGGS

How about a little zip at breakfast? This South of the Border casserole, is guaranteed to wake up your taste buds.

4 slices bread, cubed
1/4 stick butter, melted
1 cup grated sharp Cheddar
1 can diced green chilies

4 eggs, beaten
1 Tbsp. milk
Salt and pepper, to taste
Dash of Tabasco

Toss bread cubes in butter and place in a 9-inch greased baking dish. Layer cheese, then chilies on top of bread cubes. Blend eggs with remaining ingredients and pour over chilies. Chill several hours. Bake in a 350-degree oven for 20 minutes, or until firm in center.
Yield: 4 servings

LIL'S BREAKFAST CASSEROLE

My friend Lil Appel is a laid-back, at ease hostess. She can whip up a gourmet brunch with little or no effort in the time it takes most of us to set the table. This breakfast casserole is simple, yet sublime. Serve it with the Coconut Rum Fruit Salad (recipe follows).

1 lb. hot bulk pork sausage
3 cups frozen shredded hash-
  brown potatoes
1/2 tsp. salt
1/2 cup chopped onion
2 small cans diced green chilies

6 sliced mushrooms
12 ozs. Cheddar cheese, shredded
1/2 cup chopped green bell pepper
12 eggs, beaten
1 cup milk

Cook sausage in a skillet until browned, stirring to crumble; drain well. Place hash browns in a lightly greased 13x9x2-inch baking dish; sprinkle with salt. On top of hash-browns, layer onion, sausage, green chilies, mushrooms, cheese and green bell pepper. Combine eggs and milk, stirring well; pour over bell pepper layer. Bake in a 350-degree oven for 50 minutes until set and nicely browned.
Yield: 6 servings

LIL'S COCONUT RUM FRUIT SALAD

Another of Lil Appel's creations, this salad makes a dazzling presentation. Best of all, it will set your tastebuds to singing. Serve it with the breakfast casserole (above recipe) for a memorable breakfast or company brunch.

4 cups nectarines, sliced
2 cups strawberries, sliced
Juice of one lemon
1/4 cup sugar

1 cup blueberries
1/4 cup coconut rum
1 Tbsp. Raspberry Schnapps

Mix nectarines and strawberries together with the juice of the lemon. Sprinkle 1/4 cup sugar over nectarines and strawberries; mix well. Let mixture sit for a few minutes for fruit to absorb sugar. Add blueberries, coconut rum and Raspberry Schnapps to nectarine and strawberry mixture; mix well. Refrigerate for an hour or overnight.

LIZ'S POTATO AND ARTICHOKE FRITTATA

In Fredericksburg located in the Texas Hill country, The Inn on the Creek Bed and Breakfast pampers guests each morning with divine breakfast dishes. Manager Liz Wilkerson's robust Potato and Artichoke Frittata is downright irresistible. Liz paired this with slab bacon.

8 ozs. artichoke heart quarters,   1/8 to 1/4 cup chopped onion
   frozen or canned in water   1 tsp. Italian seasoning
3 oz. fresh mushrooms, sliced   2 tsps. olive oil
3-4 red new potatoes, sliced thin   8 eggs
1 tsp. minced garlic   1 cup sour cream

In a heavy skillet with oven proof handle, sauté artichokes, mushrooms, potatoes, garlic, onion, and Italian seasoning in olive oil. While veggies are cooking, mix eggs and sour cream until well blended. When veggies are tender, pour egg mixture over veggies. Bake in a 350-degree oven for 45-60 minutes until set and slightly browned on top.
Yield: 8-10 servings

APRICOT CREAM CHEESE MUFFINS

At The Inn on the Creek, these absolutely divine muffins are the creation of Chef Deb Phillips. This talented lady is in the process of writing a breakfast/brunch cookbook—my order has already been placed!

3/4 cup butter, softened   3 cups flour
1 (8 oz.) cream cheese, softened   1/2 tsp. baking powder
2 cups sugar   1/2 tsp. salt
2 large eggs   1/2 tsp. baking soda
1 tsp. vanilla extract   1 can apricots, drained and
1 tsp. almond extract   chopped

Blend butter and cream cheese until smooth; add sugar. Add eggs one at a time. Add extracts. Mix all dry ingredients together and add to cream cheese mixture. Gently fold in apricots; do not over mix. Scoop into muffin tins and bake in a 350-degree oven for 25 minutes, or until golden brown. (Can substitute bananas and pecans for the apricots.)
Yield: 24 muffins

ASPARAGUS STRATA

10 slices white bread,
  crusts removed,
1/2 stick butter, softened
1 lb. fresh asparagus, trimmed
  and cut into 1-inch pieces
8 bacon slices, cooked
  and crumbled
3 eggs

1 ½ cups half-and-half cream
1 cup grated Parmesan cheese
  divided
3 Tbsp. sliced green onions
1 tsp. sugar
1/2 tsp. salt
1/4 tsp. pepper
Pinch ground nutmeg

Spread butter on one side of bread slices. Place bread buttered side up in a greased 13x9x2-inch baking dish, sides touching. Cook asparagus in a little water until crisp-tender, about 4 minutes; drain well. Arrange the bacon and asparagus on top of bread slices. In a bowl, beat eggs; add cream, ½ cup cheese, onions, sugar, salt, pepper and nutmeg. Pour over asparagus/bacon layer and sprinkle with remaining cheese. Bake in a 400-degree oven for 10 minutes. Reduce heat to 350 and bake 25 minutes longer or until a knife inserted in center comes out clean. Cut in squares to serve. For bread to absorb liquid well, make the night before and refrigerate. Let come to room temperature before baking.
Yield: 6-8 servings

BREAKFAST ORANGE FRUIT
This is a classy side dish to a breakfast strata or quiche.

Fruit: Pineapple, peaches, pears, apricots, cherries.
Sauce:
1/3 cup sugar
2 Tbsps. cornstarch
1/4 tsp. salt

1 cup orange juice
2 Tbsps. orange rind
1/2 cup light corn syrup

Drain fruit well; arrange in a sprayed 13x9x2-inch baking dish, placing cherries in hollows of fruit; set aside. Combine all sauce ingredients; heat to a boil in a heavy saucepan. Remove from heat and pour sauce over fruit. Bake in a 350-degree oven for 30 minutes.
Yield: 12 servings

NEW ORLEANS GRILLADES AND GRITS

I cannot write a Southern cookbook without including my New Orleans cousin, MiMi Nothacker. The story of how we met is worth sharing. When my first cookbook came out, MiMi received a copy as a gift. As she thumbed through the "Memories" chapter, she was amazed to discover we shared the same great-grandfather, General Allen Jumel! She tracked me down, which culminated in an unforgettable weekend visit to her home in New Orleans. MiMi, husband Greg, and daughter Alice, were the ultimate hosts. MiMi and Alice gave a brunch so I could meet their aunt, Dr. Mignon Jumel, who is also my mother's first cousin. As Aunt Mignon kept us enthralled with stories of Jumel history, we feasted on a medley of Creole dishes: Grillades and Grits, baked bananas, and icy cold ambrosia. In place of biscuits or toast, MiMi served hot, crusty New Orleans French bread. The meal was perfect, and the table was breathtaking—fine linen, exquisite china, sparkling crystal, and the Madame Jumel sterling. This silver pattern was named to honor an ancestor of ours who lived in the late 1700's. This reunion was a step back in time that left me with cherished family memories...

2 lbs. veal or beef round steak	1 ½ tsps. Canola oil
2 teaspoons salt	1 cup onion, chopped
1 teaspoon black pepper	1 large tomato, coarsely chopped
1/8 teaspoon cayenne pepper	1 cup water
1 tablespoon garlic, finely minced	2 ½ to 3 cups cooked grits
2 tablespoons flour	(more, if needed)

Trim off all fat from meat and remove any bones. Cut into pieces about 2-inch square, and pound out with a mallet to about 4-inches square. Rub salt, black pepper, cayenne and garlic into pieces of meat on both sides. Rub in the flour. In a large heavy bottomed skillet or sauté pan, melt oil over medium heat and brown grillades well on both sides. Lower heat, add onion, tomato and water. Bring to a simmer, cover loosely, and cook over low heat for 30 minutes, uncovering to turn meat over every 10 minutes. A rich brown gravy will form when meat is cooked. Remove meat to heated platter and place in preheated 200 degree oven to keep warm. Prepare grits, according to package directions. Serve meat. Gravy should be served on grits.
Yield: 4 servings (MiMi doubled the recipe—seconds for everyone!)

CHEESY GRITS PIE

I have adjusted this old recipe many times and it just seems to get better and better. This appealing dish makes a nice offering for a morning brunch or a family breakfast. In the winter, hot curried fruit adds taste and color, and in summer, fresh melon and berries add brilliance. The presentation of this brunch dish can be very attractive, garnished with sprigs of bay leaf or parsley and cherry tomatoes.

Crust:
1 ½ cups water   1/2 cup quick grits (not instant)
1/2 tsp. garlic powder   1/2 cup shredded Cheddar cheese
1/2 tsp. salt   1/4 cup flour
Red pepper, to taste   1 egg, beaten

Filling:
6 eggs   1/2 lb. ground pork sausage,cooked
1/2 tsp. dry mustard   drained and crumbled
1/8 tsp. nutmeg   1 cup (4 ozs.) shredded Cheddar
1/2 tsp. salt   Dash of Worcestershire
1/4 tsp. ground black pepper   4 green onions, chopped

For crust: combine water and garlic powder, salt, and red pepper in a medium saucepan; bring to a boil. Stir in grits and bring back to a boil. Reduce heat to medium-low, cover and cook 5-6 minutes or until thick, stirring often; set aside. In a small bowl, combine cheese, flour and egg. Stir cheese mixture into grits. Firmly press grits mixture in the bottom and up sides of a greased 9-inch spring form pan. For filling: Whisk eggs, dry mustard, nutmeg, salt and pepper in a large bowl. Stir in crumbled sausage, cheese, Worcestershire, and onions. Pour into crust. Bake 50 minutes or until a knife inserted in center comes out clean. Serve piping hot. This dish can be frozen and reheated in a 350-degree oven until hot.
Yield: 8 servings

CREOLE GRITS

If you've never been a big fan of grits in the past, you just haven't had them cooked properly. Being from South Louisiana, I have loved grits all my life, in any way, shape or form, but I couldn't entice my children to eat it until I began "enhancing" it. They love this kicked up French version, as well as my cheese grits. This is great with poached eggs.

4-6 slices bacon
2 Tbsps. flour
1/2 small onion, chopped
1/2 small bell pepper, chopped

3 fresh tomatoes, peeled and
  chopped
1 cup Quick Grits (not instant)
1 cup finely chopped cooked ham

In a heavy skillet, fry bacon slices; retain 2 tablespoons bacon drippings. Drain and crumble bacon; set aside. To the bacon drippings, add flour, stirring constantly, to make a light brown roux. Add onion and bell pepper; cook 5-8 minutes. Stir in chopped tomatoes and sauté 5 minutes. Cook grits according to package directions and blend into roux. Add ham; sprinkle with bacon and serve immediately.
Yield: 6 servings

PERFECT POACHED EGGS

A poached egg should be big and round with a runny yolk—all the better to serve with the creamy Creole Grits. Poached eggs are also used for Eggs Benedict, a popular gourmet breakfast dish. The whites of a poached egg should be firm, never runny—the secret is in the vinegar…

2 qts. water
2 Tbsps. white vinegar

8 fresh large eggs
Salt and pepper, to taste

Combine the water and vinegar in a large shallow pan; bring to a simmer over medium heat. One at a time, break each egg into a small cup—do not break yolk. Gently slide each egg into the slowly simmering water and cook 3-4 minutes—until set, but not hard. Carefully remove eggs from water with a slotted spoon. Gently pat dry with a towel; serve immediately.

APPLE AND SAUSAGE BAKE

This is a great little dish when a light breakfast is desired. It can be prepared ahead and popped into oven when ready to serve. I've been known to heat it up the following morning for a quick breakfast.

1 (8-oz.) Little Sizzlers sausage	1 tsp. sugar
1 cup pancake mix	1/2 cup milk
(complete, buttermilk or light)	1 egg
1/4 tsp. cinnamon	1/2-3/4 cup peeled, chopped apple
1/4 tsp. nutmeg	Maple syrup for drizzling

Spray a 9-inch round cake pan. Fry sausages—do not overcook. In a medium bowl, blend pancake mix, cinnamon, nutmeg, sugar, milk and egg at medium speed with an electric mixer; about one minute. Stir in chopped apple. Pour mixture into greased cake pan. Arrange sausage links on top in a pinwheel fashion. Bake in a 375-degree oven for 20-25 minutes or until deep golden brown. Serve piping hot with maple syrup.
Yield: 4-6 servings

STUFFED FRENCH TOAST

8 thick slices French bread	2 eggs
2 Tbsps. butter, softened	1/2 cup milk
1/2 lb. pork sausage, cooked	1 ½ tsps. sugar
crumbled and drained	1/4 tsp. ground cinnamon
1 cup shredded Swiss cheese	4 Tbsp. butter

Cut a pocket in the crust of each slice of bread; butter the inside of pocket. Mix cooled sausage with shredded cheese. Stuff mixture into pockets. In a shallow bowl, beat eggs, milk, sugar and cinnamon; dip both sides of bread. Melt 4 tablespoons of butter in a large skillet and cook French toast until golden brown on both sides. Serve with maple syrup if desired.
Yield: 4 servings

CINNAMON APPLE TREATS

This apple mixture is marvelous to have on hand for a quick breakfast, a snack, or a dessert. When I'm trying to cut back on fats and calories, this is a healthy lifesaver for those weak moments when I crave sweets.

2/3 cup sugar or sweetener
2 Tbsps. cinnamon
1/2 stick butter or margarine
  (can use light)

5-6 large hard apples, peeled and
  thinly sliced
1/4 cup water (approx.)

Mix sugar or sweetener and cinnamon; set aside. Melt butter or light margarine in a large skillet; add apple slices and sprinkle cinnamon mixture over apples. Simmer slowly, adding water a little at a time as needed. When apples are tender, cool and place in a covered container. This mixture will keep in refrigerator for a week to ten days, if it lasts that long.

For breakfast: Place two slices bread on a cookie sheet and toast one side under broiler. Turn bread over and spread about 4 tablespoons lo-fat Ricotta cheese on the unbroiled side. Top with about ½ cup apple mixture and place under broiler until hot and bubbly. Tastes like a cheese Danish!

For a snack or dessert: Heat about ½ cup apple/cinnamon mixture in the microwave for about 20 seconds, just to warm. Stuff into pita bread or spread it on a flour tortilla and roll up. Pop into microwave for about 14 seconds, just until warm. Do not over-microwave as bread will become tough.

Note: If you're lean and your cholesterol levels are low, try this warm apple/cinnamon mixture on vanilla ice cream. For another treat, cut golden pound cake into thick slices, smear one side with butter, and pop under the broiler for a few seconds. Serve topped with the warm apple/cinnamon mixture. Divine!

ORANGE FRENCH TOAST

This French toast is absolutely divine! Great company brunch dish! I sampled this recipe at a bed and breakfast in Jefferson, Texas, formerly owned by my friends Mary K. and Ray Rex. I have taken a few liberties with the original recipe.

1 small jar orange marmalade
1 (8-oz.) pkg. cream cheese,
   softened

1 loaf French bread, sliced
   diagonally ½-in. thick

Mix marmalade, and cream cheese until well blended. Spread mixture on one side of each slice of French Bread. Put two pieces of bread together like a sandwich. Place in a shallow baking dish; pour sauce (recipe follows) over bread. When it has absorbed, pick up each "sandwich" and flip on other side. Cover with foil and refrigerate for several hours or overnight. When ready to bake, remove from refrigerator and flip again—if there is any excess liquid, drain it off. Bake in a 400-degree oven for 25-30 minutes

Sauce
5 eggs
1/4 cup sugar
1/4 cup half-and-half
2/3 cup orange juice

4 Tbsps. Grand Marnier liqueur
1/4 tsp. nutmeg
1/4 tsp. cinnamon
1/2 tsp. vanilla

With a mixer, beat above ingredients until well blended. Pour over bread. Follow above instructions.

In France, French Toast is called pain perdu (pan pair DOO) or lost bread. It is a great way to use up day-old bread. The more stale the bread, the better the French toast.

MARK'S PAIN PERDU

This New Orleans style Pain Perdu is from the files of Mark and Kelly Schexnaildre of Baton Rouge. Mark and Kelly's welcome mat is always out..their door is always open..and their pot is always full! Mark says this is great as a midnight snack right out of the refrigerator cold!

3 eggs, well beaten
1 cup milk
1/2 cup sugar
1 tsp. cinnamon
1/2 tsp. nutmeg

1 tsp. vanilla
12 slices stale French bread, sliced
   about 1 inch thick
Peanut or other cooking oil
Powdered sugar or syrup

In a large bowl, mix the eggs, milk, sugar, cinnamon, nutmeg and vanilla. Beat well with a wire whisk for about one minute. Place each slice of bread in the mixture and soak each side well. Heat oil in a heavy frying pan or skillet, using approximately one-half inch oil in the pan. Once oil is hot, fry each piece of bread until it has browned on each side. Serve warm with powdered sugar sprinkled liberally on it, or drizzle with syrup.

HONEY CHEDDAR BISCUITS

This recipe came off a box of baking mix many years ago—these biscuits are still among my favorites.

3 cups Bisquick baking mix
1 cup milk
1 tsp. honey

1/2 stick butter, melted
8 ozs. Cheddar cheese, grated

Preheat oven to 450-degrees. Combine Bisquick, milk, honey, and butter; let stand for 5 minutes. Add cheese to mixture and blend well. Turn out dough onto a floured board and knead several times. Roll dough to ½-inch thickness and cut out with round biscuit cutters. Place on lightly-greased baking sheet and bake for 10-12 minutes.

COUNTRY MUFFINS

These are great for mornings when the kids are making a dash for school and have no time for a bona fide breakfast. They freeze well.

1 egg
2 cups baking mix
2/3 cup milk
2 Tbsps. vegetable oil

2 Tbsps. honey mustard
1/4 lb. Canadian bacon or ham, chopped, or crisp, crumbled bacon

Put cooking spray on bottom only of 12 medium muffin cups (2 ½-inch), or line with paper baking cups. Beat egg and stir in baking mix, milk, oil and mustard just until moist. Fold in ham or bacon. Divide batter evenly among muffin cups. Bake in 400-degree oven for 18-20 minutes or until golden brown on top. Remove immediately from pan. Wrap and refrigerate any remaining muffins.
Yield: 12 muffins

BRAN MUFFINS

This is another freeze-well muffin. They taste so good, you don't even think of them as healthy!

1 cup bran flakes
1 cup buttermilk
1 egg
1/4 cup vegetable oil
1 cup flour

1/3 cup light brown sugar
1 tsp. baking powder
1 tsp. baking soda
1/2 tsp. salt

In a mixing bowl, stir together bran flakes and buttermilk. Let stand three minutes. Beat in egg and oil. Sift together flour, brown sugar, baking powder, baking soda and salt. Add to bran mixture. Mix well, but do not over mix. Spray Pam on medium size muffin tins. Fill ¾ full with batter and bake in 350-degree oven for 15 to 20 minutes.
Yield: 1 dozen
Note: Chopped apple, dates, nuts, or raisins may be added for added flavor.

BILL'S BRUNCH BREAD

Another of Bill Berger's classic recipes, this sausage and cheese-filled bread is a scrumptious addition to a brunch buffet table. If there are any leftovers, this bread can be cut into thick slices, wrapped tightly and frozen. For a quick breakfast, simply thaw slices a few seconds in the microwave, slather with butter and place under the broiler until it is hot.

1 pkg. frozen bread dough
  (3 to a pkg—each 1 ft. long)
2 lbs. hot Jimmie Dean sausage

2 cups grated Parmesan cheese
4 eggs, lightly beaten

Thaw dough at room temperature. Grease three 9-inch bread pans. Spread dough on floured board like a pizza. Brown sausage; drain, reserving a little drippings to brush on top of bread. Mix together Parmesan cheese, egg, and sausage. Spread mixture down the middle of bread dough. Fold dough in from each side and ends; seal well. Brush with reserved sausage drippings. Place in greased bread pans; cover each with a dish towel and let rise to the top of the pan. Bake in a 350-degree oven for 30 minutes or until golden brown.

ONION SQUARES

4 bacon strips, diced
3 large onions, finely chopped
3 Tbsps. butter
1/2 cup sour cream
1 Tbsp. flour

1/2 tsp. salt
3 eggs, beaten
1 (8-oz.) tube refrigerated crescent
  rolls

In a skillet, cook bacon until crisp; drain and discard drippings. In the same skillet, sauté onions in butter until tender; cool. In a mixing bowl, combine sour cream, flour and salt; blend in eggs. Stir in bacon and onions; set aside. Separate crescent dough into four rectangles. Pat dough into the bottom and 1-inch up sides of a 9-inch square baking pan. Pinch edges together to seal. Pour onion mixture over dough. Bake in a 375-degree oven for 30 minutes or until set and crust is golden. Cool slightly and cut into small squares.
Yield: 16-18 servings

CHEESE BREAD

My friend Dr. Jim Boyd's culinary claim to fame is his incredible Cheese Bread. It is the creation of A.E. and Olive Brink. The Brinks made—and shared—this bread for friends and church members for many years. Olive Brink personally taught Jim to make this succulent bread and it fast became a classic among family and friends. When his children, Lesley and Baylor, were young, Dad's bread was their favorite after-school snack. Now that they're grown, Jim bakes cheese bread often on Sundays after church. He and wife, Laura, invite friends over where everyone gathers in the kitchen to feast on cheese bread, smoked sausage, smoked oysters, and Norwegian sardines. No one ever sits down—they simply stand around eating, drinking wine, and enjoying each other's company." This is what "breaking bread" truly means— love, friends and sharing. A perfect recipe for life!

2/3 cup sugar   2/3 cup oil
2 Tbsps. salt   4 lbs. Pillsbury or Gold Medal All
3 pkgs. dry yeast   Purpose flour (approximately)
1 qt. water (105 to 110 degrees F.)

In a large warm bowl, add sugar, salt, and yeast to water and mix well. When mixed, add oil, then flour, stirring vigorously. When you think you have added enough flour, add a little more. Dump dough onto a floured towel and knead. Dough should still feel a little warm to the touch. When kneaded, place dough back into the bowl and cover with a little cooking oil. Let rise in a warm place until doubled (about 1 and ½ hours). An oven that has been slightly warmed ahead of time is a good place to let the dough rise. When doubled, knead again until the air has been expressed from the dough. Then, cut and shape into 5 or 6 loaves. Place loaves into warmed and oiled bread pans. Let rise in a warm place until dough fills the pan (about 1 and ½ hours). Bake 30-40 minutes at 350 degrees in a preheated oven. When baked, remove from pans and let cool on a rack or turned crossways on the bread pan.

Modification for Cheese Bread: After the first rising, divide dough into fifths or sixths and roll each portion flat with a rolling pin (one at a time). Spread grated cheddar cheese over dough and sprinkle with cayenne pepper. Roll up and gently shape each portion into a loaf. Resume with instructions for second rising as for plain bread (above).

SAMMY'S CHEESE BREAD

This is my buddy Sammy Pedro's famous Cheese Bread. The recipe was not easy to come by, for Sammy's cooking is a "little of this", a "little of that" so he seldom uses recipes. With help from his wife, Linda, we came up with exact measurements. Sammy owned Pedro's Restaurant, a popular eatery in Shreveport for more than 25 years. To say Sammy "knows his way around a chopping block" would be an understatement—he is a master!

1 loaf French bread	1 Tbsp. basil
1/2 stick butter	1/2 tsp. seasoned salt
3/4 cup extra virgin olive oil	1/2 tsp. cayenne pepper
3-4 pods or crushed garlic	4 Tbsps. Parmesan cheese
1 Tbsp. chopped parsley	6-8 slices Provolone or
2 Tbsps. crushed dried	mozzarella cheese
oregano leaves, divided	

Cut a loaf of French bread in half lengthwise. Mix together the butter, olive oil, and garlic in a microwave safe container. Microwave in 20-30 second increments only until butter is melted. Add parsley, 1 tablespoon oregano leaves, basil, seasoned salt and cayenne pepper. Mix well. Using ½ of this mixture, brush on each side of French bread. Sprinkle each side of bread with Parmesan cheese; then drizzle remainder of butter/oil mixture. Lay slices of Provolone or mozzarella cheese overall. Sprinkle remaining tablespoon of oregano on top. Bake uncovered on foil in a 375 degree oven until bread is hot and cheese is melted.
Remove from oven and slice diagonally in 1-1/2 inch slices.

BEER BREAD

3 Tbsps. sugar	1 can Lite beer (room temperature)
3 cups self-rising flour	2 Tbsps. butter, softened

Mix together all ingredients and pour into a greased 9-inch bread baking pan. Bake bread in a 350-degree oven for one hour. Remove from oven and spread with softened butter; return to oven for 15 minutes and serve.

MELT-IN-YOUR-MOUTH CORNBREAD

This is a sweet, buttery version of a classic. It never fails to get rave reviews. If you like a "cakey" cornbread, you'll love this one.

2/3 cup butter, softened   2 1/3 cups flour
1 cup sugar   1 cup cornmeal
3 eggs   4 ½ tsps. baking powder
1 2/3 cups milk   1 tsp. salt

In a mixing bowl, cream butter and sugar. Combine eggs and milk. Combine flour, cornmeal, baking powder and salt; add to creamed mixture alternately with egg mixture. Pour into a greased 13x9x2-inch baking pan. Bake in a 400-degree oven for 25 minutes, or until a toothpick inserted near center comes out clean. Cut into squares and serve piping hot.
Yield: 12 servings

QUICK AND EASY CORNBREAD MUFFINS

This is more of a "mealy" cornbread than the previous one. It is one I have used for many years, and my husband's favorite.

2 cups yellow cornmeal   1 pkg. dry yeast
1/2 cup flour   1 cup onion, diced
1 Tbsp. baking powder   2 large eggs
1 tsp. salt   2 cups buttermilk
1/2 tsp. baking soda   1/2 cup bacon drippings
3 ½ Tbsps. sugar

Mix together first 8 ingredients. In a separate bowl, mix eggs, buttermilk, and bacon drippings; add to dry ingredients, stirring just until moistened. Spoon into greased muffin tins, filling half full. Bake in a 400-degree oven for 15 minutes or until golden brown.
Yield: 24 muffins

BROCCOLI CORNBREAD

This vegetable-filled cornbread needs no menu—it's a meal in itself. It is moist, delicious, healthy and spicy! Be sure to have a spoon handy, for you may not be able to pick it up.

3 boxes Jiffy cornbread mix	1 large onion, chopped
12 ozs. small curd cottage cheese	2 pkgs. frozen chopped broccoli
1 ½ sticks butter	1 jalapeno pepper, chopped fine
3/4 cup milk	2 Tbsps. pimiento, chopped
4 eggs, beaten	2 cups grated Cheddar cheese

Mix together all ingredients except cheese. Pour one-half the batter into a greased 13x9x2-inch baking dish. Spread cheese over batter; spread remaining batter on top of cheese. Bake in a 375-degree oven for approximately 45 minutes, until done.

MEXICAN CORNBREAD

There are many Mexican cornbread mixes on the grocery shelves. They just are not the same—this one's my favorite.

2 eggs, beaten	1 tsp. salt
1 cup sour cream	3 jalapeno peppers,
1 cup cream-style corn	deseeded and chopped fine
1/2 cup oil	2 Tbsps. pimiento, chopped
1 ½ cups cornmeal	1 ½ cups sharp Cheddar cheese,
1 Tbsp. baking powder	grated

Mix together all ingredients, except cheese, in the order given. Pour half of the mixture into a hot, well-greased iron skillet. Sprinkle half the cheese over the batter. Add remaining cornmeal batter. Bake in a 375-degree oven for 30-40 minutes. Remove from oven, sprinkle remainder of cheese on top, and return to oven until cheese melts.
Yield: 8 servings

DYLAN'S CRAWFISH CORNBREAD

Crawfish Cornbread is a unique rendition of an old favorite. Credit for this delicious dish goes to Dylan Fausto, son of Pete and Dawn Fausto. A teenager now, Dylan was a fourth grader when he entered this specialty in a 4-H cooking contest where it took fourth place. The first time I served Dylan's mouth-watering dish, there was not a crumb left. This cornbread lends itself to any southern dish, such as black-eyed peas, red beans and rice, shrimp Creole.. or all by itself.

1 stick butter
2 tsps. Old Bay seasoning
  or dry Crab Boil seasoning
1 medium onion, chopped
3 stalks celery, chopped
1-2 medium zucchini, chopped fine

1 lb. frozen, peeled crawfish tails,
  thawed and drained
2 pkgs. cornbread mix
2 tsps. Creole seasoning
1 ¾ cups grated Cheddar cheese.
  divided

Preheat oven to 425 degrees. In a large saucepan, melt stick of butter; stir in Old Bay seasoning. Add onion, celery, and zucchini; sauté. Add crawfish tails, stir in well, and heat thoroughly; set aside. In a medium mixing bowl, combine 2 packages cornbread mix with Creole seasoning; blend in milk and eggs, according to cornbread mix package directions. Add ¾ cup grated cheese and stir well. Pour heated crawfish mixture into cornbread mixture and blend well. Pour the combined mixture into a 13x9x2-inch baking dish. Sprinkle remaining 1 cup grated cheese on top of batter. Bake at 425 degrees for 30-40 minutes, until cornbread is golden brown and cheese topping is melted.
Yield: 8 servings (approximately)
Note: For contest, Dylan used Corn-Kits Mix, but also uses Jiffy for a sweeter version.

When cooking with frozen cooked crawfish,
drain well in a colander and flush out juices with water.
This will prevent having a fishy taste in the dish you're preparing.

Danny Allen (Tripp) Daniel, III

Beyond Our
Borders

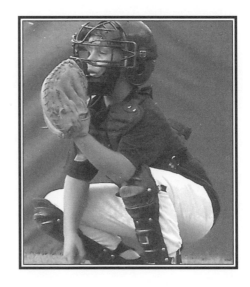

This chapter is a hodge-podge of foods from other countries. I have included my favorite "beyond our borders" fare.

I begin with Italian for that is my #1 favorite. When I was little I would ask, "What's for supper tonight, Mama?" On the nights when her reply was, "We're dining Italian tonight," my little heart would jump for joy! Those words are still popular in my home. My mind tells me I am French, but my heart says, "Italian", for I love all Italian fare, from hearty lasagna to light pasta primavera.

Then there's Mexican...another winner. When we think of Mexican fare, it's chili or hot tamales that come to mind. My husband Ed's prize-winning chili is right up there with the best of them, as is my classic tamale recipe. Each year Americans savor and celebrate Mexico's commemoration of its victory over French-led insurgents at the Battle of Puebla in 1862 with a Cinco de Mayo Festival. It has become a custom in our home to host our own little Cinco de Mayo, complete with festive decorations and an authentic Mexican menu.

I am also enamored with anything that has to do with Greece—the hospitality of the people, the traditions and rituals, the celebrations, and best of all, some of the greatest food in the world. The Greeks truly appreciate the simple and healthy way of life—perfectly ripe fruit, home baked coarse bread, fish fresh from the sea, bathed in olive oil and herbs and grilled to perfection... I love it all!

If you're a fan of Oriental cuisine, you will not be able to resist my Best Egg Rolls in the South (See Index) These crispy egg rolls are filled with crab meat, shrimp and pork, as well as tasty Chinese vegetables.

Whether it's Italian, South of the Border, Greek or Oriental food, you can't go wrong with the delectable dishes offered in this chapter. Make a big batch, call me, and I'll come to dinner...

SAMMY'S LASAGNA

My good buddy, Sammy Pedro is famous for his magnificent lasagna. Only problem is Sammy never measures—he just puts things together and turns up with classic dishes. I requested the recipe, so Sammy made a batch while his wife, Linda got the procedure down on paper. They delivered a casserole of this luscious lasagna right to our front door. I don't know when we've enjoyed such a feast! This recipe was not easy to record, and it takes a little time, but it's well worth the effort—especially since the it makes two large pans of lasagna. Serve one tonight and freeze one for another meal.

1/2 onion, chopped
2-3 Tbsps. olive oil
2 or garlic pods, minced
1 lb. ground turkey or beef
  and/or pork, or mixture
Salt and pepper, to taste
Oregano and basil, to taste
5 eggs, slightly beaten
36 oz. Ricotta cheese

4 cups shredded mixed cheeses
  Mozzarella, Provolone, Romano,
  Parmesan, etc.
16 oz. frozen chopped spinach
1 large eggplant
3 cups tomato sauce, homemade
  or Prego
2 boxes no-boil lasagna noodles

Sauté onion in 2-3 tablespoons olive oil, add minced garlic and sauté another 2-3 minutes. Add ground meat and season with salt, pepper, oregano and basil. Mix eggs, Ricotta and other cheeses in a bowl; set aside. Cook spinach and drain thoroughly. Peel eggplant, if desired, and slice in ¼-inch rounds. Season eggplant with salt and pepper and grill or bake for about 10-15 minutes. Remove from oven; set aside. Spray two 13x9x2-inch pans with olive oil spray. Layer in the following order:

　　　Tomato sauce (thin layer)
　　　½ No-boil lasagna noodles
　　　½ Meat/onion mixture (spread half)
　　　½ Spinach (small dollops)
　　　½ Grilled (or baked) eggplant
　　　½ Cheese/egg mixture (in dollops, not a solid layer)

Repeat layers, ending with cheese/egg mixture on top. Bake, foil covered, at 350 degrees for approximately 30-35 minutes, or until edges are bubbly; remove foil, bake another 10 minutes. Let set for 10 min. before serving.

ITALIAN SHELL CASSEROLE

2 lbs. ground beef
Italian seasoning, to taste
Salt and pepper, to taste
3 Tbsps. olive oil
1 medium onion, chopped
1 bell pepper, chopped
1/2 lb. mushrooms, sliced

3 Tbsps. minced garlic
2 qts. Bertolli Olive oil & Garlic
  Spaghetti Sauce
1 ½ bags medium-sized shell pasta
1 cup grated Parmesan cheese
1 cup shredded Mozzarella cheese
Parsley, to taste

Sprinkle ground meat with seasonings. In a Dutch oven, sauté ground meat in olive oil until brown; add onion, bell pepper, mushrooms, and garlic; simmer for about 15 minutes. Add spaghetti sauce, blending well; adjust seasonings. Let cook slowly about 20 minutes. Boil shells until al dente; drain well and fold into sauce. Fold in Parmesan cheese. If serving immediately, serve piping hot from the pot. If serving later, place in a 15x10x3-inch baking dish that has been coated with cooking spray. Cover with shredded Mozzarella and top with more Parmesan. Bake in a 350-degree oven about 20 minutes, just until hot and bubbly.
Yield: 12 servings

STUFFED SHELLS

1 lb. Italian Sausage, cut in short
  links
1 box frozen, chopped spinach
1 qt. jar spaghetti sauce

1/2 lb. grated mozzarella cheese
1 bag large pasta shells, cooked
3/4 cup grated Parmesan cheese

Sauté sausage, removing skins as they separate from meat. Thaw spinach, drain completely and chop. Put a small amount of spaghetti sauce into bottom of a 13x9x2-inch sprayed baking dish. Combine spinach, sausage and one-half of the mozzarella; fill cooked shells with this mixture. Place stuffed shells in baking dish; cover with remainder of sauce. Sprinkle with remaining mozzarella and Parmesan. Bake in a 350-degree oven for 45 minutes.
Yield: 6 servings

MARLYN'S CHICKEN SPAGHETTI

This is another recipe calling for bottled spaghetti sauce. There are many brands on the grocery shelves, and after much trying and testing, I found this blend of olive oil and garlic. It is the very best, and the addition of tomato sauce and wine makes it even more flavorful. I serve this dish with an Italian salad and crispy garlic bread. This is probably one of our most popular Italian dishes—I like to think of it as "from scratch" with a little help.

6 boneless skinless
   chicken breasts
Garlic powder, to taste
Salt and pepper, to taste
4 Tbsps. olive oil
1 medium onion, chopped
1/2 medium bell pepper, chopped
1 can drained mushrooms
4-5 peeled garlic cloves

1 qt. Bertolli Olive oil and Garlic
   Spaghetti Sauce
1 small can tomato sauce
1/2 cup red wine (Merlot)
Pinch of sugar
1/2 tsp. crushed red peppers
1/2 tsp. dried basil
1 lb. spaghetti or vermacelli
Freshly grated Romano cheese

Season chicken with garlic powder, salt and pepper; sauté in a heavy Dutch oven (black iron preferably) in olive oil until golden brown. Add onion, bell pepper, and mushrooms. Simmer about 8 minutes and stir in garlic cloves, spaghetti sauce, tomato sauce and wine. Add a pinch of sugar, crushed red peppers, and basil. Stir well, bring to a simmer, turn heat on low, cover pot and cook about 1 ½ hours. Boil spaghetti in salted water until al denté. Serve chicken and sauce over spaghetti and sprinkle with Romano cheese.

Yield: 4-6 servings

Variations: Ground beef or chunks of pork may be substituted for the chicken breasts. Use 1-1/2 pounds ground beef, and either one pork tenderloin or four pork chops cut into large pieces.

ED'S SHRIMP FETTUCINE

This is my husband Ed's dish. He prepares his fettucine sauce different than most, substituting sour cream for the whipping cream. We often leave out the shrimp and serve the fettucine as a side dish with veal medallions, pork tenderloin or leg of lamb. As an entrée with shrimp, it goes hand in hand with an Italian salad and hearty Italian bread. You may use either fettucine or linguini pasta—we prefer the smaller linguini.

Basic Ingredients:

1 lb. fettucine or linguini pasta	Cayenne pepper, to taste
1 ½ sticks butter	Nutmeg, to taste
1 (8 oz.) sour cream	3/4 cup Romano cheese
2 Tbsps. minced or pureed garlic	Chopped parsley, to taste

Boil pasta al dente; drain and set aside. Melt butter in a heavy saucepan; add sour cream, garlic, pepper and nutmeg. Beat with a whisk until smooth. Add Romano and beat until well blended. Adjust seasonings, if desired. Toss with hot pasta and shrimp (see below) garnish with chopped parsley and serve immediately.

Shrimp Preparation:

1 stick butter	Garlic powder, to taste
1 lb. large raw, deveined shrimp	White and black pepper, to taste
Juice of 1/2 lemon	1/3 cup dry vermouth
Tabasco, 1 squirt	

Melt butter in heavy skillet; add shrimp. Sprinkle with lemon juice, Tabasco, garlic powder, white and black pepper. Cook shrimp, stirring, until it turns pink. Add dry vermouth; bring to a simmer and cook without cover about 5 minutes, until vermouth has cooked down. Toss shrimp with fettucine or linguini pasta; sprinkle with extra Romano cheese and parsley. Serve immediately.

Yield: 6 servings

VEAL PICCATA

Veal Piccata is a light, heart healthy entrée. It is perfect served with fettucine or Lemon Rice (See Index).

1/2 cup flour	2/3 cup chardonnay or Chablis
Salt and pepper, to taste	Juice of 1 freshly squeezed lemon
8 thin veal medallions	2 Tbsps. nonpareilles capers,
scallopini cut	drained
6 Tbsps olive oil	

Combine flour, salt and pepper. Lightly coat veal slices with flour mixture. In a heavy skillet, heat olive oil to medium high heat, add veal and cook about 3 minutes on each side. Remove veal from skillet; set aside. Turn heat up and add wine and lemon juice to skillet drippings. Cook on medium-high heat, scraping drippings from bottom of pan for about 1 minute. Return veal to skillet and coat or deglaze in sauce. Toss in the capers and heat a few seconds. Serve immediately.
Yield: 4 servings

VEAL MARSALA

This divine entrée is from the collection of Cynthia "Magnolia" Jett. It is my husband's #1 favorite Italian dish. I have amended it slightly.

4 Tbsp. butter, divided	1/2 cup flour
1/2 lb. fresh mushrooms, sliced	1/2 tsp. salt
1 ½ Tbsps. fresh lemon juice	1/2 tsp. pepper
8 thin veal medallions	3/4 cup Marsala wine
or 4 pounded veal cutlets	1 tsp. beef bouillon granules

Melt 2 tablespoons butter in a large skillet; add mushrooms and sprinkle with lemon juice. Simmer 5 minutes; remove from skillet. Mix flour with salt and pepper and dust veal lightly. In the same skillet, melt remaining butter; add veal and brown on both sides. Remove veal and keep warm. Add Marsala wine and beef bouillon to skillet; cook rapidly over high heat, stirring constantly and scraping browned particles from bottom of skillet. Return mushrooms and veal to skillet and heat thoroughly. Serve immediately.

VEAL FRANCESCA

4 Tbsps. extra virgin olive oil
4 (8-oz.) veal cutlets
4 slices peeled eggplant
4 Tbsps. olive oil
6-8 ozs. egg noodles
4 Tbsps. tomato sauce

Garlic puree, to taste
4 Tbsps. red wine
1/2 cup grated Parmesan
4 slices mozzarella cheese
Fresh basil strips (optional)

Sauté veal in 4 tablespoons extra virgin olive oil in skillet about 5 minutes each side. Remove from heat; keep warm. Sauté peeled eggplant slices in olive oil for about 4 minutes each side; set aside. Boil noodles until tender; place on the bottom of a 9-inch baking dish. Arrange veal on top of noodles. Mix tomato sauce, wine and garlic puree; spread on veal. Top veal with fried eggplant slices. Sprinkle with Parmesan, cover with mozzarella; place under broiler until cheese melts to a golden brown. Serve with Italian salad and crusty Italian bread.
Yield: 4 servings

FRESH TOMATO BASIL PIZZA

This bold, hearty pizza is from "Hey, Momma! What's For Supper?" cookbook. The author of this delightful family cookbook is my cousin, Jeanne Annison Peat of Jackson, Mississippi.

1 Boboli pizza crust or
  a favorite crust
2 cups grated mozzarella cheese
2 medium tomatoes or
  3-4 Roma tomatoes

1 bunch fresh basil (about ¼ cup)
1/4 cup pine nuts
Olive oil
Black pepper, to taste

Set oven to 375 degrees. Spread grated mozzarella cheese on pizza crust. (Can be baked or unbaked—if you do the unbaked crust, just increase the baking time until the crust is brown). Slice tomatoes very thin and place on top of cheese. Add finely chopped basil and pine nuts. Drizzle a little olive oil on top. Add black pepper to taste. Bake for around 15-20 minutes until cheese is melted and the crust is browned. Note: Black olives are good on this, too. Use your imagination!

LAMURIEL'S SPAGHETTI PIZZA

My friend LaMuriel Poulsen's hearty spaghetti pizza casserole is not only a great family dish, but is perfect to bring to a pot luck dinner or as a company entreé, paired with an Italian salad and hot, crispy garlic bread. It is easy to assemble and can be made a day ahead and baked before serving.

2 eggs
1 cup milk
1 pkg. (16 oz.) spaghetti,
  cooked and drained
1 lb. bulk Owens Italian Sausage,
  crumbled, cooked and drained
28 oz. or more pizza sauce
1 (3 ½-oz.) pkg. sliced pepperoni
1 can sliced mushrooms, drained

1/2 cup chopped onion
1 green bell pepper, chopped
1 red pepper, chopped (optional)
1/2 cup black olives, sliced
1/2 cup green olives with
  pimientos, sliced
Garlic salt, to taste
2 cups (8-oz.) shredded mozzarella
1 cup (4-ozs.) shredded Cheddar

In a large bowl, beat the eggs and milk together. Add cooked spaghetti; toss to coat. Transfer to a greased 13x9x2-inch baking dish. Top with cooked Italian sausage, pizza sauce, pepperoni, mushrooms, onion, bell pepper, black olives and green olives. Sprinkle with garlic salt. Bake, uncovered, at 350 degrees for 20 minutes. Sprinkle with cheeses. Bake 5 minutes longer or until cheese is melted. Let stand 15 minutes before cutting.
Yield: 10-12 servings

Option: For variety, add your own favorite veggies. If you are a vegetarian, leave off the meat and substitute with chunks of eggplant, artichoke hearts, zucchini and fresh tomato. Simply toss these veggies with a little olive oil before layering on the pizza casserole to ensure moisture. Or…split this into two pizzas—one with meat and one without. Use your imagination!

ED'S PRIZE-WINNING CHILI

My husband Ed has a prize-winning chili recipe which took him years to perfect. It is the unofficial chili for our boating friends of the Shreveport Power Squadron. On February 19, 2005, it was officially confirmed to be a Grand Prize Winner at the American Cancer Society Chili Cook-off in Mobile, Alabama, thanks to our friend David Hayden. David's Mobile Gas company team, consisting of "five guys and a girl" (his wife Merle) entered it in the annual fundraiser, of which Mobile Gas is not only a participant, but a sponsor as well. With eighty-four teams competing, Ed's chili won 1st place in the Meat with Beans category, as well as Best Overall Chili! This was a first-time win for Mobile Gas. I wasn't surprised, for it has always been a prizewinner to me!

1 1/2 lbs. ground lean pork	2 large cans whole tomatoes
4 1/2 lbs. ground beef	2 cans jalapeno pinto beans
(ground "chili" meat is best)	5 cans chili beans
3 (10-oz.) pkgs. frozen	3 tsps. cumin
chopped onion	1 heaping Tbsp. molé
1 (10-oz.) pkg. frozen chopped	3 Tbsps. chili powder
bell pepper	2 Tbsps. crushed garlic
1 packet dry chili mix	2 cups chicken broth
1 packet taco seasoning mix	1 Tbsp. chicken bouillon granules
1 packet burrito mix	

Brown meat well, breaking it up as you stir. When browned, add onion and bell pepper. When tender, add packets of mixes (chili, taco & burrito). Mix well and simmer about one hour on low heat, stirring often. Add remaining ingredients, mixing well. Simmer about an hour longer on low heat, stirring often, until all flavors are well blended.
Yield: 30 servings
Note: For flavors to blend well, make a day ahead. Make a large amount, for it freezes well; if you want only 15 servings, it's easy to cut in half. Do not halve the dry seasoning mixes—use the whole packet.

Mole (MOH-lay) is a rich, dark Mexican specialty sauce.
It is a blend of onion, garlic, chiles, and a tad of Mexican chocolate.
The chocolate contributes richness without overt sweetness.

HOT TAMALES

This is a classic recipe, shared by my old friends Jane Barnett and the late Ruth DeBlanc of Lake Charles. The fun in making these is getting a group together, for as Jane put it, "You need many hands, and besides, it makes a great party!" They are not difficult to make, only time consuming. They freeze beautifully, so make plenty to keep on hand. I was in on one of these "tamale parties" and had great fun!

1st step: 3 pkgs. corn shucks—soak overnight in the sink.

Meat Filling:

3 lbs. ground beef	6 Tbsps. Chili Seasoning
1/2 Tbsp. red pepper	1/2 cup water
2 medium onions, chopped	1/2 cup white self-rising cornmeal
1 bell pepper, chopped	1 (6-oz.) can tomato paste
1 ½ Tbsps. salt	1/2 can Rotel Tomatoes
4 cloves garlic, chopped	1 (8 oz.) can tomato sauce
6 Tbsps. chili powder	

Combine all meat filling ingredients well; use food processor if desired for the chopped vegetables. Roll lightly, shaping into 2-inch logs. Roll logs in corn meal mixture (see below). Boil shucks for 10 minutes, leaving in water until soft; drip dry. Place tamale log on one end of shuck and roll. Turn up one end (fold over). Repeat procedure. As these are rolled, stack them with the flap down in a huge pot. Pour sauce over all layers. (see below) Cook on low heat for 2 ½ to 3 hours.
Yield: 12 dozen

Corn Meal Mixture:

3 cups white self-rising cornmeal	1 Tbsp. red pepper
1 Tbsp. salt (or less)	2 Tbsps. chili powder

Combine all ingredients; mix well.

Sauce:

3 cans tomato sauce	3 Tbsps. Chili Seasoning
3 tsps. salt	1 ½ cans Rotel Tomatoes

Combine and simmer a little.

MEXICAN CASSEROLE

This easy layered dish is always a hit in our home. All it needs is a Mexican Salad and cornbread muffins.

1 ½ lb. ground chuck	1 medium onion, chopped
1 pkg. taco seasoning mix	1 can undrained Ranch Style Beans
1 pkg. soft corn tortillas	1 can Golden Mushroom Soup
8 oz. sharp Cheddar	1 can Rotel tomatoes, undrained
cheese, shredded	

Brown meat in a heavy skillet. Drain and add taco seasoning, mixing well. Line a deep greased baking dish with three-four whole tortillas. Layer as follows: Meat, grated cheese, onions, and tortillas (that have been torn apart). Repeat layers until all meat is used. Pour on top in this order without mixing: Ranch Style Beans, mushroom soup, Rotel tomatoes. DO NOT STIR! Bake in a 350-degree oven for 25 minutes, or until bubbly.
Yield: 6 servings

PAULA'S SALSA

Salsa is the simplest Mexican hors d'oeuvre on the planet. It can be made ahead and put on the table with a bowl of chips when guests arrive. For an added bonus, salsas are lo-fat and versatile—great for snacking and as a garnish for Mexican dishes. This recipe, courtesy of my friends Paula and Doug Daniel of Peachtree City, Georgia, is perfect to keep on hand for those snacking moments.

1 (28-oz.) can whole tomatoes	1 Tbsp. Accent
1 bunch green onions, chopped	1 ½ Tbsps. ground cumin
1 or 2 banana peppers, chopped	Pinch of oregano
2 cloves garlic, minced	Ground cayenne pepper, to taste

Mix all ingredients, except red pepper, in a food processor for 2 to 3-second "bursts." When all ingredients are chopped and of a lumpy consistency, stir in red pepper, adding a little at a time until it suits your taste. This salsa is best left in refrigerator to "season" overnight.

CHICKEN OLÉ

6 boneless, skinless chicken
  breasts
Salt, pepper, flour, to taste
1/2 cup butter
1/2 cup chopped onion
1 tablespoon crushed garlic
8 large chopped fresh mushrooms
2 Tbsps. flour

1 tsp. celery salt
1/2 tsp. white pepper
1/2 cup chicken stock
1/2 cup dry white wine
1 mashed avacado
1 ½ cups grated Monterey
  Jack cheese

Place chicken breasts between sheets of waxed paper and pound until thin (¼ inch). Lightly sprinkle with salt and pepper and dust with flour. Melt half of butter in a large skillet and sauté breasts, a few at a time, until tender. Remove breasts and set aside. Melt remaining butter in same skillet and sauté onion, garlic and mushrooms slowly,
until vegetables are soft, but not brown. Stir in flour, celery salt, pepper, chicken stock and wine. Cook over low heat until thickened, about 5 minutes. Blend in mashed avacado and ½ cup grated cheese. Adjust seasonings to taste. To bake, arrange breasts in a 13x9x2-inch baking dish that has been sprayed with Pam. Spoon avocado mixture on each breast; top with remaining grated cheese. Bake in a 350-degree oven for about 20 minutes, until casserole is hot and bubbly.
Yield: 6 servings

WANDA'S MEXICAN RICE

Another classic dish from my cousin Wanda Annison.

4 Tbsps. oil
1 medium onion, chopped
1 medium bell pepper, chopped
1 lb. Mexican Velveeta (mild)

4 cups cooked rice (1 ½ cups raw)
2 cans cream-style corn
1/2-3/4 small jar pimiento
1 deseeded jalapeno, minced

Sauté onion and bell pepper in oil. Add Velveeta and stir until melted. Add cooked rice, corn, pimento, and jalapeno. Place in a 13x9x2-inch baking dish that has been coated with cooking spray. Bake in a 350 degree oven for 30 minutes.

SOUTH OF THE BORDER SHRIMP

This divine Mexican party dish, a creation of Sandy Laramie, is different from your ordinary Mexican fare. Sandy, one of the most talented and inventive chefs I've ever known, worked with me at Occasions Catering. This shrimp/black bean combination is fabulous served in soft tortillas as a dinner party entrée or in a chafer, served with crispy tortilla chips. For my Cinco de Mayo parties, this dish is always on the menu, whether as an entrée or an appetizer.

1 Tbsp. extra virgin olive oil
1/4 cup chopped onion
1 Tbsp. minced garlic
1 (15 oz.) can black beans
1 tsp. ground cumin
1 small can chopped green chilies
1/2 stick butter

2 lbs. medium raw peeled shrimp
1/4 tsp. red pepper
1 small jar picante sauce
1/2 lb.Monterey Jack cheese
 with hot peppers, grated
1/4 cup sour cream
Sliced jalapeno peppers, to taste

Sauté onion and garlic in olive oil in a large skillet, about five minutes. Add black beans, cumin, and chilies; simmer on low heat until mixed well and beans are tender. Remove from skillet. Melt butter in the skillet black beans were cooked in and add shrimp. Season with red pepper and sauté about 3-5 minutes. Add picante sauce and simmer another 3-5 minutes, stirring well. Return black bean mixture to skillet; blend well with shrimp mixture. Simmer five minutes until all flavors merge. Spoon mixture onto four individual serving plates and garnish with grated cheese, sour cream and jalapenos. Serve hot accompanied with hot flour tortillas and butter.

Yield: 6 servings

Note: To serve individual plates for a sit-down dinner, this mixture can be placed in flour tortillas, sprinkled with cheese, and rolled up. Top with cheese, sour cream and jalapenos for garnish. Serve with a Mexican salad and margaritas. Ole!

Mexican Trivia:
Astronaut Bill Lenoir carried a bag of
fresh jalapenos aboard the space shuttle Columbia
during a November 1982 flight—it was a first for "peppers in orbit".

QUICKIE LAYERED MEX CASSEROLE

If you're planning a night on the town, prepare this for the kids and the sitter. All they'll have to do is pop it in the oven. I promise the kids will love this dish so much, they will be wearing sombreros and shouting Viva Zapata!

4 large flour tortillas or coarsely crumbled corn chips
1 large can tamales, broken in pieces
1 large can good brand chili

1 (8-oz.) sour cream
1/2 lb. sharp Cheddar, grated
Garnish: chopped fresh tomato, guacamole dip, sliced black olives, shredded lettuce

Line bottom of a 13x9x2-inch baking dish with flour tortillas or crumbled chips. Layer with tamales, chili, sour cream, and top with cheese. Bake in a 350-degree oven for approximately 40 minutes.
Yield: 4-6 servings

FRUIT ENCHILADAS

I have served many baked fruit recipes through the years—this one is a special favorite, for a family or a company dessert. It is great served as a dessert for a Mexican dinner. This is from the kitchen of Beth Keese of Denison, Texas. Beth said, "These keep well in refrigerator—just take out what is needed and put in microwave for a minute or so. That is, if any are left!"

1 doz. medium flour tortillas
2 sticks butter
2 ½ cups sugar, divided
1/2 cup chopped pecans

2 (14-oz.) cans pie filling strawberry, apple or cherry
1 ½ cups water
1 tsp. cinnamon

Put 2 tablespoons pie filling into each tortilla; roll up tight. Line rollups in a 13x9x2-inch casserole dish. Melt butter in a saucepan; add water and 2 cups sugar and cook until sugar dissolves. Pour mixture over tortillas and let stand over night—do not refrigerate. When ready to serve, bake 30 minutes uncovered in a 350-degree oven. Mix ½ cup sugar, cinnamon and nuts. Sprinkle on top and bake another 15 minutes. Delicious served hot with whipped cream or ice cream on top.

BEST EGG ROLLS IN THE SOUTH

The name of this recipe is no exaggeration—these egg rolls are the best in the South! In the sixties, my Lake Charles friend, Jane Barnett, and I would get together with another buddy and each prepare a batch, sipping on wine, exchanging confidences, and altogether "passing" a good time, as they say in South Louisiana. To facilitate preparation, each of us would have our pork and shrimp cooked and cut up, and our crabmeat picked over for shell before we got started. That evening we would gather together with our families and have an Oriental feast. Those were some of my life's "moments to remember".

2 cups well-seasoned cooked pork	3 Tbsps. cooking oil
2 ½ cups cooked shrimp	4 ½ tsps. salt
2 ½ cups white crabmeat	4 ½ tsps. sugar
9 green onion tops, chopped	3 Tbsps. soy sauce
4 ½ ribs celery, chopped	60 egg roll wrappers
1 can bean sprouts	1 bottle peanut oil
2 cans chopped water chestnuts	1 egg, beaten

Chop cooked pork and shrimp into small pieces in food processor—DO NOT PULVARIZE! Chop all vegetables in food processor. Mix together all ingredients and place on egg roll wrappers. Seal edges of wrapper with beaten egg and fry in deep peanut oil. All ingredients are already cooked, so it doesn't take long to fry—just until golden. Drain completely; serve with hot mustard, sweet and sour sauce, or Jezabel Sauce (recipe below). To freeze: After frying lightly and draining well, flash freeze on cookie sheets and place in sealed container. To serve: drop in hot peanut oil and fry a little or bake in oven on a cookie sheet. The quick refrying method is best for flavor.
Yield: 60 egg roll wrappers or 150 small wonton squares for appetizers.

Jezabel Sauce:

1 (16-oz.) jar pineapple preserves	1 (5-oz.) jar horseradish
1 (16-oz.) jar apple jelly	Salt and pepper, to taste
1 (1 ½ oz.) can dry mustard	

Combine all ingredients; refrigerate. Will keep for two months.

PEPPER STEAK

This was a favorite of my precious friend, the late Nel Chavanne.

1 (1/4-in.thick) sirloin steak
1/2 cup flour
Salt and pepper, to taste
2 Tbsps. oil
Water, to cover
1 cup soy sauce
Worcestershire sauce, to taste

1/4 cup cornstarch
1/4 to 1/2 cup water
3 stalks green onion, cut in strips
1 small bell pepper, cut in strips
8 mushrooms, sliced
2 tomatoes, quartered

Slice steak in 2-inch strips; flour, salt and pepper it. Brown in 2 tablespoons oil and cover with water; add soy sauce and Worcestershire sauce. Do not add salt. Cook steak one hour or so, then add mixture of cornstarch and water to thicken. Add green onion and bell pepper; cook for 10 minutes. Add sliced mushrooms and quartered tomatoes; cook about 8-10 minutes longer. Serve with fluffy rice.
Yield: 6 servings

SWEET AND SOUR PORK

1 ½ lb. pork tenderloin, cut up
3 Tbsps. cooking oil
1 cup beef bouillon
2 ½ cups pineapple chunks
1/4 cup brown sugar
3 Tbsps. cornstarch

1/4 cup vinegar
2 to 3 Tbsps. soy sauce
1/2 tsp. salt
1 bell pepper, cut in strips
1/2 small onion, thinly sliced

Brown pork chunks in oil; add beef bouillon, cover and simmer on low heat for one hour. Drain pineapple, reserving syrup. Combine sugar and cornstarch; add pineapple syrup, vinegar, soy sauce, and salt. Add to pork; cook and stir until gravy thickens. Add pineapple, green pepper, and onion. Cook an additional 10 minutes and serve over rice.
Yield: 4 servings

STUFFED GRAPE LEAVES
(Dolmathes Avogolemono)

Any Greek dishes I can prepare are due to the tutelage of my Greek friend, Fran Lorant Moore. When I moved to Shreveport in 1980, Fran began teaching me how to make some of her family specialties. I learned to make Greek salad, stuffed grape leaves, rice pilaf with raisins and nuts, and various lamb and chicken dishes. I even learned how to "burn" butter—no kidding! These grape leaves are the best!

2 lbs. lean ground beef or lamb
2 large onions, grated
1/2 cup minced parsley
2 Tbsps. dill
1 ½ cups long-grain rice
2 Tbsps. lemon juice

2 egg whites (reserve yolks)
2 Tbsps. fresh mint leaves,
   or 2 tsps. dried mint
Salt and pepper, to taste
1 (2-lb.) jar grape leaves
2-3 qts. chicken broth

Combine all ingredients except grape leaves and broth in a bowl; mix well and set aside. Rinse, drain and separate grape leaves. Cover bottom of a 4-qt. saucepan with 4-5 grape leaves. Prepare rolls by placing one heaping teaspoon filling on the bottom of each leaf. Fold over, fold in sides and roll up. Place closely together in even layers in saucepan on top of grape leaves. Add enough broth to cover rolls. Place a small plate directly over rolls to weigh them down. Cover and simmer for 1 hour; remove rolls to a serving bowl. Serve drizzled with Lemon Sauce (recipe follows).

Lemon Sauce for Grape Leaves:
2-3 cups chicken broth
2 eggs
2 egg yolks
1/3 cup lemon juice
2 Tbsps. cornstarch

In a small saucepan, boil broth. In a blender, combine eggs, yolks, lemon juice and cornstarch. With machine running, slowly add hot broth. Return contents of blender to saucepan. Stir over low heat until thickened. Pour sauce over rolls.
Yield: 6-8 servings

YA YA'S GREEK SPAGHETTI

Another of Fran Lorant Moore's specialties, Ya Ya's Greek Spaghetti, is a divine dish that is baked in a casserole. It is an original—not seen in any Greek cookbook. The recipe (origin 1910) was handed down from Fran's grandmother, Frangoula "YaYa" Lorant. This matriarch of the family never learned to speak English, and none of her superb recipes were ever recorded. Fran acquired these treasures by observing, tasting, and adapting other Greek recipes until they tasted like her grandmother's. This Greek Spaghetti is marvelous!

2 lbs. lean ground beef	1 heaping tsp. parsley
1 large onion, chopped	1 tsp. salt
3 pods garlic, minced	1/2 tsp. pepper
2 (16 oz.) cans stewed tomatoes	1 tsp. sugar
1 (8 oz.) can tomato sauce	1 lb. spaghetti
1 can mushrooms with juice	1 cup Parmesan cheese
1 heaping tsp. oregano	3/4 stick butter (do not substitute)
1 heaping tsp. sweet basil	

Brown beef, add onions and garlic and cook till glassy; drain. Place in a tall saucepan and add next nine ingredients. Bring to a boil, then simmer for at least 2 ½ to 3 hours. Boil spaghetti, al dente; drain and rinse. In a greased 13x9x2-inch baking dish, layer as follows: one-half Parmesan cheese, one-half spaghetti, one-half meat sauce; repeat layers, ending with meat sauce. In a saucepan, melt butter over medium heat, stirring constantly until it is golden brown. (This is what the Greeks called "burning" the butter). Insert spoon about every 3 inches into top of spaghetti to bottom of casserole; drizzle burned butter over top. Cover with foil and bake in a 325-degree oven for 40-45 minutes. Cut into squares to serve.
Yield: 8-10 servings

Note: For those of you on a low-carb diet, you can substitute eggplant for the spaghetti layers of the recipe. Slice eggplant, sauté in olive oil and drain well before layering.

GREEK MEATBALLS
(KEFTEDAKIA)

For delicious hamburger patties, try YaYa's Keftedakia. Fran doubles this recipe, because "one is never enough." You will note on the recipe it calls for "Krinos Kefalotyri cheese" – that's Parmesan to us!

4 slices whole wheat bread
1 lb. lean ground beef
1 onion, grated
1/4 cup dry wine
1 egg
1 clove garlic, minced
3 Tbsps. minced parsley

3 Tbsps. minced fresh mint, or
  1 tsp. dried mint
1 Tbsp. grated Krinos Kefalotyri
  cheese (Parmesan)
1/2 tsp. oregano
Salt and pepper, to taste

Moisten bread with water, then squeeze dry. Combine with remaining ingredients and blend. Shape into patties ¾ the size of the palm of your hand. Dredge in flour and fry in olive oil and butter until browned. Serve hot or cold with lemon squeezed on patties.

GREEK PUDDING
(RIZOGALO)

This pudding is to-die-for delicious!

8 cups homogenized milk
1 cup white rice,
  rinsed and drained
1 ½ cups sugar
1 lemon rind, grated

2 egg yolks
2 Tbsps. cold milk
1 Tbsp. cornstarch
1 Tbsp. ground cinnamon

Put milk on to boil, stirring constantly to prevent sticking; add rice. Bring to a boil, reduce heat and simmer for about 30 minutes, stirring occasionally. Add sugar and lemon rind; simmer 8-10 minutes longer. In a heavy saucepan, mix egg yolks with cold milk and cornstarch. Whisking vigorously, blend in 1 ½ cups of the hot milk and rice mixture. When it's incorporated, add remaining hot milk mixture; let simmer a few minutes until thickened. Serve in dessert bowls, sprinkle with cinnamon. Refrigerate.

Carol Ann & Sara

Jillian

Sweets

Justin & Adam

Alec & Tripp

Courtney

"Animal crackers, and cocoa to drink,
That is the finest of suppers, I think;
When I am grown up and can have what I please
I think I shall always insist upon these.
--Christopher Morley

Childhood memories of the cookies my mother baked are so etched in my mind that I can close my eyes and see them...and smell them.
My favorites were teacakes and peanut butter cookies. When I was a child, my mom's idea of pampering was often a teacake or cookie and hot cocoa at bedtime.

Then there were the "fudge" days when Mom got out the big heavy pot that was her mother's and went to work stirring and beating... Mom always had lots of "helping hands", especially when it came to licking the pot. Those were especially happy days in our kitchen.

A beautiful dessert embellishes a meal. It's like a still life ready to be painted. Desserts are not just about beauty – they are comforting and soothing. In the television series, "The Golden Girls," the "girls" pulled out the old cheesecake every time one of them was stressed out. Many confidences were exchanged as they ate their way thru a whole cheese cake at a time! It's true that a little sugar confection can be a calming sedative in times of anxiety.

Wouldn't Grandma be shocked today if she could come back and see the huge variety of convenience products we enjoy? When I was small, there was one cake mix on the market—Dromodary. It came in white, yellow and devil's food. I'd better stop right here, for I am definitely telling my age!

These "sweets for the sweet" offer an eclectic blend of both elegant desserts for entertaining, as well as simple and memorable family favorites. There is something here for everyone. Enjoy!

RASPBERRY-PEACH TRIFLE

I have been serving this captivating fruit trifle for thirty years. I serve it for dinner parties, feature it in cooking classes and have demonstrated it on television cooking segments. It matters not where I introduce it—it draws rave reviews.

1 (11-oz.) frozen Sara Lee
  pound cake, thawed
1/3 cup Amaretto liqueur
2/3 cup raspberry preserves
1 (3-1/2 oz.) pkg. vanilla instant
  pudding

1 (12-oz.) Cool-Whip, thawed
2/3 cup chopped almonds, toasted
1 (16-oz.) pkg. frozen peach slices,
  thawed and drained well
Extra almonds for topping
  (optional)

Slice cake in half <u>lengthwise</u>. Reserving 1 tablespoon liqueur, sprinkle remaining liqueur over cake. Spread with preserves. Cut each half into eighths; set aside. Prepare pudding mix as directed on package, except use only 1 ½ cups milk. Fold in 2 cups whipped topping and the almonds. In a 2-quart glass bowl, layer 1/3 cake slices, 1/3 whipped topping mixture and 1/3 peaches. Repeat layers, ending with cake. Add reserved liqueur to the remaining whipped topping; spread over cake layer. Top with additional almonds. Chill overnight or several hours.
Yield: 10-12 servings

DEATH BY CHOCOLATE

2 (6-oz) pkgs. instant
  chocolate pudding
1 pan baked brownies, crumbled
1/2 cup Kahlua liqueur

1/2 (16-oz.) raspberry preserves
1 (12-oz.) Cool Whip, thawed
1/2 bag Brickle (crushed toffee)
  reserve some for topping

Make chocolate pudding according to package directions, but do not chill; set aside. Sprinkle crumbled brownies with Kahlua liqueur; spread with raspberry preserves. In a glass trifle bowl, layer ingredients as follows: 1/2 crumbled brownies, 1/2 pudding, 1/2 whipped topping, 1/2 brickle. Repeat layers, ending with whipped topping and brickle. Garnish with fresh raspberries and mint, if desired.
Yield: 18-20 servings

NEL'S CHOCOLATE TORTE

This was a favorite of my dear friend, Nel Chavanne—she and I made it for numerous dinner parties. It boasts light meringue layers with a profusion of rich creamy chocolate in between. Preparation of this delicacy takes time, but the good news is that it can be made ahead and frozen. This is decadent dining at its best!

3 egg whites	2 cups heavy whipping cream
1/2 tsp. cream of tarter	2 Tbsps. granulated sugar
3/4 cup granulated sugar	3/4 cup Hershey's chocolate syrup
3/4 cup finely ground pecans	1 tsp. vanilla

To prepare meringue: Place foil on two cookie sheets. With an 8-inch round cake pan, draw a circle on each cookie sheet; set aside. In a large bowl, beat egg whites with cream of tarter until foamy. Beat in 4/5 cup sugar, one tablespoon at a time, beating 2 or 3 minutes after each tablespoon until very stiff and glossy. Gently fold in pecans. Place 1/2 of the batter onto each foil circle; take a flat knife and spread to fit the circle, smoothing tops and edges. Each circle of meringue batter will be about 1/8-inch thick. Bake in a 275-degree (preheated) oven for 45 minutes. Turn oven off after 45 minutes of baking, but **do not remove**—leave in oven for another 45 minutes. While meringue is cooling, proceed with the filling: (Before making filling, place large clean glass bowl and mixer beaters in the freezer for 10 minutes; put whipping cream in freezer for 5 minutes.) Beat whipping cream until very stiff in the cold glass bowl. (When beating cream a good rule is to beat, stopping about one minute between intervals—cream does better when not beaten continuously.) When cream is very stiff, add 2 tablespoons sugar and fold in chocolate syrup and vanilla; set mixture aside. Gently loosen meringue, tearing off foil. Place one layer on serving plate. Pile one-half cream mixture on top; add second layer and cover with remaining cream. Place in freezer and freeze uncovered until set; when set, cover well. To serve: Remove from freezer about 20 minutes before serving—cut into wedges. Garnish with chocolate curls. Yield: 8 servings (approximate)

CHOCOLATE TREAT

This is a simple layered dessert that will appeal to everyone who has a yen for chocolate. Very luscious—very delicious!

1 ½ cups coconut
1 cup chopped pecans
1 German Chocolate Cake Mix

1 stick butter
1 (8-oz.) cream cheese
1 lb. box confectioners' sugar

Spray a 13x9x2-inch baking dish; sprinkle with coconut and chopped pecans. Prepare cake mix according to package directions; pour over coconut and nuts. Melt butter and cream cheese together and beat in confectioner's sugar. Drizzle over cake mix. Bake in a 350-degree oven for 45-50 minutes.
Note: This dessert is best if made the day before serving.

TIRAMISU

The word Tiramisu means "carry me up". Tiramisu, an Italian dish, is comprised of a rich custard, layered with cake or ladyfingers that have been soaked with a good liqueur. There are hundreds of versions of Tiramisu—all delicious. This especially wonderful rendition was dreamed up by my precious friend, Linda Pedro. It is a true masterpiece!

1 pt. heavy whipping cream
8 ozs. mascarpone cheese or
   mixture of 4 ozs. cream cheese
   and 4 ozs. sour cream
1 cup strong coffee

1/2 cup Kahlua liqueur or brandy
4 Tbsps. cocoa powder
4 Tbsps. powdered sugar
1 pkg. split ladyfingers

Beat whipping cream on high to form soft peaks. Beat (on low speed) mascarpone cheese (or mixture of cream cheese and sour cream). Gently fold in whipped cream with cheese mixture. Mix together coffee and Kahlua; set aside. Mix together cocoa and powdered sugar; set aside. To layer: Place split ladyfingers in bottom of a 15x10x3-inch baking dish. Drizzle this layer with one-half coffee/liqueur mixture. Layer one-half cheese mixture, spreading to edges. Sprinkle with cocoa/sugar mixture. Repeat layers and chill.
Yield: 20 servings (approximate)

HELEN'S CLASSIC BREAD PUDDING

I named this recipe "classic" because that is what it is—a classic. This old favorite embraces tradition and familiar comfort, offering soothing food at its best. Helen Calhoun Turner, a talented hostess, has been pleasing family and friends with this down-home bread pudding for as long as I have known her. For years, she and I have playfully competed as to whose bread pudding is better—hers or mine! I featured my version in book #1, so it's time I shared a taste of Helen's—or heaven (as Helen puts it). Don't let the length of the recipe deceive you—it is quite simple to put together, and well worth the effort.

2 loaves French bread, torn into small pieces	1 ½ cups chopped pecans
	1 ½ cup raisins

Place French bread pieces into a 15x10x3-inch greased baking dish. Cover with dish cloth; let sit overnight to stale. Sprinkle pecans and raisins over stale bread and mix together with hands until blended all through the bread.

Sauce Ingredients:

6 eggs	4 tsps. vanilla
2 cups sugar	4 tsps. cinnamon
2 pints whipping cream	3 tsps. nutmeg
4 cups whole milk	1 stick butter, melted

Beat eggs with an electric mixer for two minutes; beat in sugar and whipping cream. When well-blended, add milk, vanilla, cinnamon and nutmeg. Once mixed well, add butter. Continue beating until well-blended. Pour this mixture over the bread, pecans and raisins. Again, mix all together in dish so that everything is blended together. Let it sit for 1 hour, stirring occasionally. Put oven rack on middle to low setting and preheat the oven at 350 degrees. When ready to bake, turn oven to 300 degrees and bake for 1 hour. After time is up, turn the oven to 400 degrees and bake about 10 minutes longer. It will puff up so keep an eye on it.

During the last 20 minutes of the bread pudding baking, start Whiskey Sauce.

Helen's Classic Bread Pudding (Continued)

Whiskey Sauce
1 cup sugar	1/2 tsp. cornstarch
1 cup heavy whipping cream	1/4 cup water
Dash of cinnamon	1 tsp. vanilla
1 Tbsp. butter	1 Tbsp. bourbon

In a heavy saucepan combine sugar, cream, cinnamon and butter. Bring mixture to a boil. Keep an eye on it because it will begin to boil suddenly, and may boil over. Mix together cornstarch and water in a separate cup. Pour into sugar and cream mixture. Cook, stirring until sauce is slightly clear. Remove from heat and add vanilla and bourbon. Stir until blended.

Once your bread pudding is done and the bread has gone down from its puffy stage, pour 1 cup sauce over the bread pudding to let it soak into the bread. This pudding is best when served warm. Cut or scoop out each portion of bread pudding and drizzle warm whiskey sauce over it. Then, sit back and enjoy a little taste of heaven.

STEVE'S APPLE COBBLER

My friend Steve Aymond, a very talented cook, shared this recipe with me several years ago. The first time I made it and brought it to a church gathering, everyone went wild! It's no wonder, for it is a delicious dessert—especially for holiday meals.

2 cans Comstock Apple Pie filling	1 cup sugar
1 lb. Velveeta cheese (regular)	1 ½ sticks butter
1 cup self-rising flour	

In a 13x9x2-inch sprayed baking dish, place apple pie filling. Cut Velveeta into slices and place a layer on top of pie filling. Mix flour and sugar together and sprinkle over Velveeta. Cut butter into pats; place on top, covering the entire flour/sugar layer. Bake uncovered in a 350-degree oven for 45 minutes. Serve with a dollop of vanilla ice cream. Yield: 8-10 servings

BLUEBERRY BREAD PUDDING

If you're looking for something different and dynamic, just put this bread pudding on the buffet table and watch it disappear. We can always count on our talented, yet unassuming friend, Lil Appel, to come up with a crowd pleaser—every time. The delicate blueberries combined with the flavors of Amaretto, maple syrup and hearty sour dough bread will make you come back for more—again and again. It can be prepared the day before, chilled, then baked when ready to serve.

1 (16 oz.) French sour dough
   bread loaf, cubed
1 (8-oz.) pkg. cream cheese,
   cut into small pieces
3 ½ cups fresh or frozen
   blueberries, divided
6 large eggs

4 cups milk
1/2 cup sugar
1/4 cup butter or margarine, melted
1/4 cup maple syrup
1 (10-oz.) jar blueberry preserves
1/4 to 1/2 cup Amaretto liqueur
   (or more)

Arrange half of bread cubes in a lightly greased 13x9x2-inch pan. Sprinkle evenly with cream cheese and 1 ½ cups blueberries; top with remaining bread cubes. Whisk together eggs, milk, sugar, butter, and maple syrup. Pour over bread mixture, pressing bread cubes to absorb egg mixture. Cover and chill for 8 hours. Bake, covered in a 350-degree oven for 30 minutes. Uncover and bake 30 more minutes or until lightly browned and set. Let stand 5 minutes before serving.

For Sauce: Stir together remaining 2 cups blueberries and blueberry preserves in a saucepan over low heat until warm. Remove from heat and stir in 1/4 to 1/2 cup Amaretto liqueur. Serve blueberry mixture over bread pudding.

Note: This is best when pudding and sauce are served warm. It reheats well. Earth Grain pre-sliced sour dough bread works great in this recipe.

For a captivating treat, slice fresh peaches into a glass of sparkling wine with a splash of peach schnapps. This makes a great poolside refresher!

BANANA LIQUEUR CAKE

What can I say about this family favorite? I can tell you the original recipe hails from my cousin, Wanda Annison, of Jackson, Mississippi. She brought it to a family reunion about 20 years ago and it's been a favorite every since—of family, friends and our Occasion's Catering customers. It has even been used as a groom's cake! This elegant cake is marvelous served warm as a brunch dessert..for a baby's christening party..a formal dinner dessert... I can also tell you that this is probably the first time I've shared the recipe. The only change I have made to Wanda's original recipe is to substitute one small jar of baby food bananas for the mashed ripe bananas. We could not always count on bananas being good and ripe. Enjoy!

1 Duncan Hines Butter Golden Cake Mix (do not substitute)	1/4 cup Crisco oil
	1 small jar baby food bananas
1 small vanilla instant pudding	4 eggs
1/2 cup water	1 cup finely chopped pecans

Glaze:
1 stick margarine	1/2 cup water
1 cup sugar	1/2 cup banana liqueur

Liberally spray Bundt or angel food pan with cooking spray; sprinkle pecans in the bottom. Mix all cake ingredients and bake in a 350-degree oven for 50-55 minutes, until cake pulls away from sides and center is firm.

Glaze: About 30 minutes before cake is done, melt margarine in a heavy saucepan; blend in sugar. Add water and mix well. Bring mixture to a boil and cook 5-10 minutes, until it begins to thicken, stirring often. Add banana liqueur and cook until reduced and thickened. Caution: If glaze is boiled to long, it can turn sugary. Keep warm until cake is done.

When cake is done, remove from oven and drizzle one-half of the glaze on top as soon as it comes out of the oven. Let cool 10 minutes and invert on a plate. Drizzle remainder of glaze on cake, letting it drip down the sides.

LEMON SUPREME CAKE

This delicious lemon cake is an all-time favorite of my Mom.

1 Duncan Hines Lemon Supreme   1/2 cup Crisco oil
  Cake Mix   1 cup water
1 (3.5 oz) pkg. vanilla   4 eggs
  instant pudding
Glaze: 1 cup powdered sugar and 3 Tbsps. lemon juice

Blend all cake ingredients in a large bowl with electric mixer on medium speed for 2 minutes. Do not overbeat. Bake in a greased 10-inch tube pan or Bundt pan for 45-55 minutes, until center springs back when touched lightly. Remove from pan after 10 minutes. When cake is removed from oven blend powdered sugar and lemon juice until it is thickened; drizzle on hot cake.

RUM CAKE

This cake is from the kitchen of my cooking partner and sous chef, Sylvia Norton. Sylvia and I do cooking demos together and, if I may brag, we make a perfect team! Sylvia's hot glazed cake is divine!

1 box yellow cake mix   1/2 cup water
1 small pkg. instant French   1/2 cup oil
  vanilla pudding   1/4 cup dark rum
4 eggs   1/4 cup chopped pecans

Mix all ingredients except pecans. Grease and sprinkle a little sugar in a tube pan. Sprinkle nuts in bottom of pan and pour in batter. Bake in a 325-degree oven for 1 hour, or until done when tested with a toothpick.

Glaze:
1/4 cup water   3/4 stick butter
3/4 cup sugar   1/4 cup rum

Heat water, sugar, and butter. Stir until sugar dissolves; remove from heat and add rum. Punch holes in hot cake; pour over warm glaze. Let cake sit in pan until cold and remove from pan.

ANN'S CARROT CAKE

This simple recipe for a classic—Carrot Cake—is a joy to make! No grating carrots! It was shared by my friend, Ann May. Ann could be my dessert chef any old day, for she has a way with cakes and pastries. Better still, she loves to share with friends.

2 cups sugar
4 eggs
1 ½ cups Wesson oil
1 tsp. vanilla

2 cups self-rising flour
1 ½ tsps. soda
2 tsps. cinnamon
2 jars junior size baby food carrots

Cream together sugar, eggs, oil and vanilla. Sift flour, soda and cinnamon and add to sugar mixture. Beat well and fold in jars of carrots. Grease and flour three 9-inch layer pans; bake in a 350-degree oven for 30 minutes. Ice cake with Cream Cheese Frosting (recipe below)

Cream Cheese Frosting:
1 (8-oz.) pkg. cream cheese
   softened
1 stick butter, softened

1 (16-oz.) box powdered sugar
1 tsp. vanilla
1/2 cup chopped pecans (optional)

Beat cream cheese and butter; add powdered sugar and vanilla. Continue to beat until fluffy. Add nuts and spread frosting between layers and over entire cake.

PINEAPPLE CAKE

1 Lb. Sara Lee Pound Cake,
   sliced in 3 layers
1 (20-oz.) can crushed pineapple,
   drained

16 ozs. sour cream
3/4 cup powdered sugar
1 cup chopped pecans
1 (8-oz.) Cool Whip, thawed

Mix pineapple, sour cream, sugar and pecans. Put between layers and top of cake. Ice the sides with Cool Whip; refrigerate. Slice to serve.

HONEY BUN CAKE

This is a wonderful cake, compliments of Kristin Meaux, wife of my buddy and fellow chef, Tommy Meaux. Tommy hails from Lafayette, Louisiana where he grew up cooking and enjoying great southern fare.

1 box yellow cake mix	3 tsps. cinnamon
3/4 cup oil	Chopped nuts, optional
1 cup buttermilk	Icing:
1/2 cup sugar	1 cup powdered sugar
4 eggs	1 tsp. vanilla
1 cup brown sugar	3 Tbsps. milk

With an electric mixer, combine first 5 ingredients. In a separate bowl, mix brown sugar, cinnamon, and nuts. Pour this into the batter and stir with a spoon—do not use mixer. Pour into a sprayed 13x9x2-inch pan and bake in a 350-degree oven for 40 minutes. While cake is baking, mix icing ingredients until smooth. When cake is removed from oven, pour icing over it immediately.

CHOCOLATE CHIP CAKE

This is my son Danny's favorite cake. I taught his daughters, Sara and Carol Ann, to make it and they bake one for him every year on his birthday. The original version calls for a yellow cake mix. For a richer cake, I make it with a chocolate cake mix.

1 box Duncan Hines Swiss or Chocolate Fudge Cake Mix	1/2 cup water
	4 eggs
1 (6-oz.) box chocolate instant pudding	1 (8-oz.) carton sour cream
	1 (6-oz.) pkg. semi-sweet chocolate chips
1/2 cup oil	

Mix first 6 ingredients; beat for 2 minutes at medium speed of mixer, scraping sides of bowl often. Stir in chocolate chips. Place in a sprayed Bundt pan and bake in a 350-degree oven for 50 minutes. Let sit 10 minutes before removing from pan. Drizzle hot cake with melted chocolate chips or powdered sugar mixed with a little milk. Delicious!

GEAN FORD'S FAMOUS GROOM'S CAKE

This dream of a cake is my favorite chocolate cake of all time. When I was in the catering business, I often worked closely with Gean Ford, owner of Gean's Cake Decorating (she has now retired). There may have been Groom's Cakes more elaborate, but there were never any more heavenly in flavor. I always made it a point to confiscate a hunk of this delicacy every time we catered together. Gean and husband Henry were familiar figures at weddings, and will long be remembered. And, best of all, this luscious cake is simple, simple, simple to make! This rich cake is reminiscent of the old Cajun Sheet Cake, but much better. It is a tradition to serve this cake at our Christmas gatherings, garnished with bright red cherries. I'm so happy that Gean agreed to share this culinary secret with us. Thanks Gean!

3/4 cup shortening
2 cups sugar
2 eggs
1/2 cup buttermilk
2 cups all purpose Gold Medal flour

1/2 tsp. salt
1 tsp. soda
6 Tbsps. cocoa
1 cup boiling water

Mix together first 4 ingredients, blending well; set aside. Mix together flour, salt, soda and cocoa; blend into first mixture. Last, add boiling water and blend. Place in greased pans—either three 8-inch pans or a 15x10x3-inch sheet pan. Bake in a 350-degree oven until done (about 45 minutes). Cake will pull away from sides when done.
Note: I prefer baking this luscious cake in a sheet cake pan.

Icing:
1/4 lb. margarine (1 stick)
2 ½ Tbsps. cocoa or
   1 square baking chocolate
6 Tbsps. evaporated milk

1 lb. box powdered sugar
1 tsp. vanilla
1 cup chopped nuts (optional)

Melt margarine, cocoa and milk in saucepan—do not boil! Add powdered sugar, vanilla and nuts. Spread hot icing on cake.

CHOCOLATE KAHLUA CAKE

This is rich and decadent! It's not something you'd serve at a child's birthday party, considering the amount of Kahlua, but I can assure you it will score high points at any other occasion.

1 box Duncan Hines Swiss	4 eggs
Chocolate Cake Mix	3/4 cup Kahlua liqueur
1/2 cup Crisco oil	1/2 cup water
1 (6-oz.) pkg. instant chocolate	6 Tbsps. Kahlua liqueur
pudding mix	1 cup confectioner's sugar

Combine first 6 ingredients; blend on medium speed of mixer for 2 minutes. Pour into a 9 ½-inch Bundt pan that has been sprayed with Pam. Bake for 45-50 minutes or until cake springs back when lightly touched. For glaze: combine 6 tablespoons Kahlua and confectioners sugar. While cake is hot in Bundt pan, drizzle slowly one-half of the glaze over it. Allow cake to cool for 10 minutes, remove from pan and drizzle remainder of glaze over the top.

FUZZY NAVEL CAKE

This flavorful creation from the kitchen of Lil Appel will make your mouth water. It gets better every day, if you can keep it that long.

1 box yellow cake mix	1/2 tsp. orange extract
1/2 cup vegetable oil	
1 (6-oz.) pkg. instant vanilla	Glaze ingredients:
pudding mix	4 Tbsps. peach schnapps
4 eggs	2 Tbsps. orange juice
3/4 cup peach schnapps	1 cup confectioner's sugar, sifted
1/2 cup orange juice	

Preheat oven to 350 degrees. Combine first 7 ingredients in mixing bowl and blend well. Pour into a greased and lightly floured 9 ½-inch Bundt pan. Bake 45 to 50 minutes or until cake springs back when lightly touched. For glaze: combine all glaze ingredients. While cake is still warm in pan, poke holes in cake, and pour glaze mixture over cake. Allow cake to cool in pan at least 2 hours before removing from pan.

PRALINE PECAN LIQUEUR CAKE

I got the recipe for this sinful cake from my friend and neighbor, Lillian Kendrick. To give credit where credit is due, Lillian says, "this recipe is the fault of my dear friend, Louise Kelly." It seems Louise gave Lillian a bottle of Praline Pecan Liqueur for her birthday and told her it was "good on everything". Lillian, in turn, got out her old rum cake recipe and "worked on it." It matters not who is responsible—this cake is absolutely addictive. Lillian took this to a charity auction recently and it sold for $30.00—not bad!

1 cup finely chopped,
  toasted pecans
1 pkg. Duncan Hines Butter
  Recipe Golden Cake mix
1 (3.4-oz.) pkg. instant vanilla
  pudding mix

1/4 cup water
1/2 cup canola oil
3/4 cup Praline Pecan Liqueur
4 eggs

Grease well a 12-cup Bundt pan. Sprinkle ½ nuts on bottom of pan, and a little way up the sides. In a large mixing bowl, mix remaining ingredients on medium speed for 2 minutes. Carefully spoon one-half batter into the pan. Sprinkle remaining nuts on batter and add remaining batter to the pan. Bake in a preheated 325-degree oven for 65-70 minutes. Test center of cake for doneness. If cake begins to pull away from sides of pan, it is ready. Remove from oven and cool for 10 minutes in pan; remove from pan and cool completely.
Note: When completely cooled, store cake in a covered container; the flavors get better daily.

With the advent of Bundt cakes, and the ease in preparing them, cooks today don't make many old fashioned layered cakes. Does anyone remember the 1910's Lady Baltimore Cake, or everyone's favorite from the Roaring Twenties— the Pineapple Upside-Down cake?

JANE'S FIG PRESERVE CAKE

I met my new friend, Jane Edmonds, of Homer, Louisiana, at a garden club luncheon and auction. Her divine fig cake brought in $50 in the auction that day. When I featured this cake in my food column, I was amazed at the letters, e-mails and calls I received from people who "hated" figs, but this cake was "the best thing" they ever tasted. The captivating buttermilk glaze is a good one to have in your recipe files, for it lends flavor to other cakes as well.

1 ½ cups sugar	1 cup vegetable oil
2 cups all-purpose flour	3 eggs
1 tsp. soda	1 cup buttermilk
1 tsp. salt	1 Tbsp. vanilla
1 tsp. ground nutmeg	1 cup fig preserves, chopped
1 tsp. ground cinnamon	1/2 cup chopped pecans or walnuts
1/2 tsp. ground allspice	Buttermilk glaze (recipe follows)
1/2 tsp. ground cloves	

Combine dry ingredients in a large mixing bowl; add oil, beating well. Add eggs and beat well. Add buttermilk and vanilla, mixing thoroughly. Stir in preserves and pecans. Pour batter into a greased and floured 10-inch tube pan; bake at 350 degrees for 1 hour and 15 minutes. Let cool 10 minutes; remove from pan. Pour warm buttermilk glaze (recipe follows) over warm cake.

Buttermilk Glaze:

1/4 cup buttermilk	1 ½ tsp. cornstarch
1/2 cup sugar	1/4 cup margarine
1/4 tsp. soda	1 ½ tsps. vanilla

Combine first 5 ingredients in a saucepan. Bring to a boil and remove from heat. Cool slightly and stir in vanilla.
Note: Praline Liqueur may be substituted for vanilla.

HONEY'S CHEESE CAKE

This fabulous cheesecake is from a tattered old handwritten cookbook belonging to my daughter-in-law, Carol Daniel. It is a reminder of her maternal grandmother, Honey. Carol says it's the best! I agree!

1 small pkg. lemon gelatin	3/4 cup sugar
1 cup hot water	1 large can evaporated milk,
1 (8-oz.) pkg. cream cheese,	well chilled
softened	1 prepared graham cracker crust
1 (3-oz.) pkg. cream cheese,	Crushed graham cracker crumbs,
softened	for topping

Mix gelatin and hot water; let congeal to consistency of egg white. Combine cream cheese and sugar; fold in partially congealed gelatin. Whip cold evaporated milk into cream cheese mixture. Pour into prepared graham cracker crust. Sprinkle crushed graham crackers on the top; chill until ready to serve.

LEMON PIE

This pie was another in the old family files of my daughter-in-law Carol. When I asked her for a favorite for my new cookbook, she replied, "My favorites are in your original cookbook." I love that girl!!

1 pie shell	2 Tbsps. butter
3 eggs	2 Tbsps. flour
1 cup + 4 Tbsps. sugar, divided	Grated rind and juice of 1 lemon
1 cup milk or cream	

Bake pie shell; cool. Beat lightly 3 egg yolks and one egg white, leaving 2 egg whites for meringue. Mix 1 cup sugar and flour together, then add to eggs; add milk and butter. Put in a double boiler and heat thoroughly; stir in lemon juice and rind. Continue stirring until thick; remove from heat and cool. Place pie filling in baked pie shell. Beat remaining egg whites and 4 tablespoons sugar until stiff peaks form. Pile lightly over pie filling, sealing meringue to pastry edge. Bake in a 350-degree oven for 15 minutes, or until meringue is delicately browned. Cool.

BUTTERMILK PIE

This is a rich creamy pie—comfort food at its best. It's been in my family for decades—every reunion we could count on buttermilk pie.

1 ½ cups sugar
3 tablespoons flour
1 cup buttermilk
2 eggs, slightly beaten

2 tsps. vanilla
1 scant tsp. lemon extract
1 stick butter, melted
1 unbaked pie shell

Mix sugar and flour; add buttermilk, and next four ingredients, blending well. Pour into unbaked pie shell. Bake in a 450-degree oven for 10 minutes. Reduce temperature to 350 degrees and continue baking for 40 minutes longer. Lightly cover with foil if pie begins to get too brown. Chill; serve with a dollop of whipped cream.

LEMONADE PIE

1 can Eagle Brand Condensed milk
1 can frozen pink lemonade
   concentrate, thawed

1 (8-oz.) container Cool Whip
1 drop red food coloring, optional
1 graham cracker crumb crust

Mix all of the above ingredients together and pour into a prepared graham cracker crumb crust; chill and serve.

CHESS PIE

Chess pie is memorable for its simplicity. This is an old Baton Rouge recipe, courtesy of my cousin, Deryl Hamilton.

1 ½ cups sugar
3 eggs
1 tsp. white vinegar
1/4 tsp. vanilla

1 heaping Tbsp. yellow
   cornmeal
3/4 stick butter, melted
1 prepared pie shell

Stir (do not beat) together first 6 ingredients; pour into pie shell. Bake in a 350-degree oven for 45 to 50 minutes.

SANDY'S MARGARITA PIE

This delicious pie adds a cool ending to a meal. The recipe was shared by my friend, Sandy Toney. I served Sandy's pie for a Cinco de Mayo dinner party one evening and every guest asked for the recipe! The pretzel based crust is a perfect accompaniment to the creamy filling.

Crust:

1/2 cup butter, melted   2 Tbsps. sugar
1 ¼ cups pretzels, crushed
Combine ingredients and press in a pie plate; freeze.

Filling:

1 (14 oz.) condensed milk   1/4 cup fresh lime juice
1 ½ ozs. Triple Sec   1 pt. heavy whipping cream,
1 ½ ozs. Tequila   whipped
Combine all ingredients and place in frozen crust. Freeze for 4-5 hours. Garnish with lime slices to serve.

DODIE'S KEY LIME MERINGUE PIE

For a luscious dessert, our friend Dodie Edwards Smith can be counted on to bring her divine key lime pie whenever I'm having a dinner party. To make it even "sweeter", Dodie brings not one, but two pies—one for my husband Ed (it's his favorite) and one for the party.

1 (10-in.) prepared graham   1 (6-oz.) bottle Key Lime Juice
   cracker crust   6 egg whites
6 egg yolks   1/8 tsp. cream of tartar
2 (14 oz.) cans condensed milk   6 Tbsps. sugar

Bake crust at 400 degrees for 9 minutes; cool completely. For filling: Beat egg yolks lightly; add condensed milk. Stir in Key Lime Juice. Pour into cooled crust. For meringue: Place egg whites in mixer bowl with cream of tartar. Beat until thick and glossy (not dry). Add sugar one tablespoon at a time, beating well after each addition. Put meringue on pie filling, sealing edges well. Bake at 325 degrees for 15 minutes.

HOLIDAY BLENDER PECAN PIE

This pie is another that requires almost no effort, yet is very delicious. I make it every year for Thanksgiving. This pie freezes well.

2 eggs
2/3 cup sugar
1/2 tsp. salt
1/2 cup light corn syrup
2 Tbsps. butter, melted

1 tsp. vanilla
1 ½ cups pecans
1 unbaked 8-in. pie shell
15-20 pecan halves, for top

Place first 6 ingredients in an electric blender; blend well. Add 1 ½ cups pecans; blend just enough to chop nuts coarsely. Pour into pie shell. Place pecan halves on top. Bake in a preheated 425-degree oven for 15 minutes; reduce heat to 350 degrees and continue baking until the top is lightly browned—about 30 minutes.

MARGARET'S LIGHT LEMON PIE

My slim, trim friend, Margaret Buccola, has been making this health-conscious pie for many years. The first time I tasted it, I was bowled over by the rich flavor. What a surprise when I found out this pie is low-fat and low-sugar!

2 small boxes sugar-free
  instant lemon pudding
2 ½ cups skim milk
1 (16-oz.) Cool Whip Light

Crystal Light Lemonade Mix
  or sugar-free
  (1 tub inside the tubular pkg.)
2 graham cracker crusts

With electric mixer on low speed, blend pudding and milk; add Cool Whip and 1 tube of Crystal Light; mix only long enough to combine. Place filling in two graham cracker crusts; refrigerate.
Note: This pie can be made with other flavored puddings; if using other flavored pudding, do not use Crystal Light Lemonade Mix.

LOUISIANA PRALINES

It doesn't matter how you pronounce it—PRAH-leen or PRAY-leen—these gems are to-die-for-delicious! When I think of pralines, I think of New Orleans—the home of pralines.

2 cups sugar	1/4 stick butter
1 can condensed milk	1 tsp. vanilla
1 small can evaporated milk	2 cups pecan halves

Bring sugar, condensed milk, evaporated milk and butter to a boil. Add vanilla and cook until juice darkens to a caramel color. Fold in pecans and cook until mixture thickens. Remove from heat and beat with a heavy whisk until creamy and thick. Drop on waxed paper and cool. Store in an airtight container.

OLD TIME CHOCOLATE FUDGE

As a child, I loved to watch Mom make chocolate fudge. It was comforting to watch her stir, and test for the "hard boil stage" She knew the precise moment to add the butter, marshmallow cream and pecans. She would beat the fudge in a sink one-half full of water before pouring it into my grandmother's old platter. The best part arrived when it was time for my brother Scotty and I to "lick the pot". This is one of the well-loved recipes from my childhood that conjures up the happy innocent moments when all was right with the world.

4 cups sugar	1/2 stick butter
4 Tbsps. cocoa (approx.)	1 tsp. vanilla
1 large can evaporated milk	2-3 Tbsps. marshmallow cream
1/2 cup water	1 cup coarsely chopped pecans

Mix sugar and cocoa (add more cocoa if you want a darker fudge) in a large heavy saucepan. Add evaporated milk to dampen sugar and stir in water to make it juicier. Cook to the soft ball stage. Add butter, vanilla and marshmallow cream. Place pot in a sink that is halfway full of cool water. Beat fudge until thickened; add pecans and blend quickly. Place in a buttered pan. Cool and cut.

Note: The milk and water amounts are guessed at—Mom just "poured".

PEANUT BUTTER FUDGE

I got this recipe from my daughter Debbie. Deb cut the recipe from a magazine years ago, but has changed the ingredients to suit her taste. It is delicious!

1 ½ cups chocolate chips
3 ½ cups sugar
1 ½ cups (12 oz.) evaporated milk
1/2 cup butter
2 Tbsps. light corn syrup

1 Tbsp. white vinegar
2 ½ cups creamy or crunchy peanut butter
1 (7-oz.) jar marshmallow cream

Line 13x9x2-inch baking dish with foil. Place 1 cup chocolate chips in a large heatproof bowl; set aside. In a heavy 4-quart saucepan, combine next 5 ingredients. Cook over medium heat, stirring constantly until mixture comes to a full rolling boil. Boil and stir for 5 minutes; remove from heat. Add peanut butter and marshmallow crème; stir until smooth. Pour one half of peanut butter mixture over chocolate chips; stir until smooth. Pour chocolate mixture into prepared pan; top with remaining peanut butter mixture. Immediately sprinkle remaining ½ cup chips over surface. With knife or spatula, gently swirl chips for a marbled effect.
Yield: 8 dozen pieces (approximately)

BOURBON BALLS

These old-fashioned bourbon balls are the product of my baby sitter, Grandma Gussie, from Lake Charles. She took loving care of my children when they were small. Gussie always declared that no liquor had ever "passed her lips", but she could whip up a batch of these delicacies before you could blink an eye!

3 cups finely crushed vanilla
   wafers
1 cup powdered sugar
2 Tbsps. cocoa

1 cup finely chopped walnuts
3 Tbsps. corn syrup
1/2 cup bourbon
Powdered sugar for rolling balls

Mix together first 6 ingredients; shape into 1-inch balls; roll in powdered sugar. Store in an airtight container.
Yield: 40-45 balls

PEANUT PATTIES

Do you remember the pink peanut patties we used to buy in the movie theatre? I don't know if they still sell them, but I do know how we can make them! These gems are a great addition to a holiday gift basket. Wrap goodies individually in cellophane and tie with pretty ribbons—don't forget to include the recipe.

2 cups raw peanuts	2/3 cup evaporated milk
or raw pecans	1/2 stick margarine
2 cups sugar	1 tsp. vanilla
4 Tbsps. corn syrup	1 drop red food coloring

Cook peanuts, sugar, syrup and milk to the hard-ball stage (250-to-260 degrees F with candy thermometer)—about 15 to 20 minutes after mixture begins to boil, stirring constantly. Remove from heat and add margarine, vanilla, food coloring; blend well. Pour into buttered muffin pans and cool, or drop on a buttered surface as you would pralines.

WANDA'S PEANUT DROPS

When I receive a recipe from my cousin Wanda Annison of Jackson, Mississippi, I can count on its being something new and innovative. These peanut drops are great. One year at Christmas, I made six batches, packaged them in festive bags and gave them to friends.

2 cups Captain Crunch	2 cups roasted salted peanuts
Peanut Butter Cereal	20 ozs. white bark (no nuts)
2 cups Rice Krispies	melted

Combine cereal and nuts in a large bowl, mixing well. Pour melted bark over all and stir until well coated. Drop by teaspoonful on waxed paper. If batter begins to harden, zap it in the microwave for a few seconds to soften bark or sit bowl in hot water in the sink for a few minutes.
Note: To melt bark, break it up and place in a microwave safe container. Melt on high 1 minute. Stir well. Return to micro and heat at 15-second intervals, stirring after each until melted and smooth. It takes about 1 minute and 30 seconds total time.

PECAN TASSIES

Every cookbook worth its salt needs to have a good recipe for Pecan Tassies for there are hundreds of things we can do with them. They masquerade well as both hors'doeurves filled with seafood or meat fillings, or as fabulous desserts filled with puddings, custards, or nut mixtures. As an appetizer or dessert, these filled pastries are perfect for cocktail parties where non-messy finger foods are always welcome.

1 (8-oz.) cream cheese	1 cup light brown sugar
2 sticks butter	2 eggs, lightly beaten
2 cups flour	2 Tbsps. softened butter
1 ¾ cups chopped pecans	2 Tbsps. vanilla

Crust: Place cream cheese and butter in a bowl and let soften. With hands, work flour into this mixture until completely blended. Chill for at least one hour. When chilled, shape into small one-inch balls of dough, then press each into ungreased miniature muffin tins, shaping with fingers.

Filling: Mix together remaining ingredients and fill each crust with mixture. Bake in a 350-degree oven for 25 minutes. Cool five minutes before removing from pans.
Yield: 48 tassies

HONEY BARS

1 stick margarine, melted	1 cup self-rising flour
1/2 cup packed brown sugar	1 cup chopped pecans or walnuts
1/2 cup sugar	1 tsp. vanilla
1 egg, beaten	

Blend melted margarine with sugars; beat well. Let cool and add egg. Blend in flour, nuts, and vanilla. Place in a greased 8-inch baking dish and bake in a 300-degree oven for 35 minutes. Cut into squares to serve.

MY KAHLUA BROWNIES

These are the best! Catering sweet trays for cocktail parties could become difficult because finger foods are required. We would pair these luscious brownies with lemon squares, meringue kisses and pecan tassies for a beautiful tray. Be careful not to overcook, for brownies begin to dry shortly after baking.

1 Duncan Hines Dark Chocolate
  Fudge Brownie Mix
2 eggs
1/3 cup total liquid:
  Equal parts Kahlua and water

1/3 cup Crisco oil
1 cup semi-sweet chocolate chips,
  divided
1/2 cup finely chopped pecans
1 drop Crisco oil for glaze

With a spoon, mix dry brownie mix with eggs, Kahlua liqueur and water mixture, 1/3 cup oil, 1/3 cup chocolate chips and pecans. Grease bottom only of a 13x9x2-inch baking pan and pour in mixture, spreading evenly. Bake in a 350-degree oven for 25 minutes; check for doneness. If wet in center, bake another 4-5 minutes, but do not over bake. While brownies are baking, melt remaining 2/3 cup chocolate chips and 1 drop oil in microwave—do not cover while melting. This chocolate will burn easily, so stir midway of melting. When brownies come out of the oven, immediately spread melted chocolate over them in a thin layer. Score top with a sharp knife before chocolate hardens for ease in cutting into squares. Cool, cut and serve.

Yield: 48 small brownies (approximate)
Note: Never use chocolate flavored chips—only the real thing!

CHEWY BROWNIES

1 1/3 cups graham cracker crumbs
2 Tbsps. cocoa
1 ½ sticks butter

1 cup chopped pecans
1 bag Almond Joy bits
1 can sweetened condensed milk

Mix graham cracker crumbs, cocoa and butter; pat in a greased 9-inch baking dish. Sprinkle pecans over bottom layer. Follow up that layer with Almond Joy bits. Pour condensed milk on top and bake in a 350-degree oven for about 30 minutes.

MISSISSIPPI LEMON SQUARES

There are many ways to make lemon squares. I tried so many recipes, many of which were wet and messy. It took lots of searching to find the perfect ones. Lo and behold! There it was in the files of one of my best friends, Ann May.

1 ½ cups flour	4 eggs
1/2 cup soft butter	2 cups sugar
1/2 cup powdered sugar	Rind and juice of two lemons
1/8 tsp. salt	Powdered sugar for topping

Mix together first 4 ingredients; press into a greased 13x9x2-inch baking pan. Bake in a 350-degree oven for 20 minutes; set aside. For topping: mix eggs, sugar, rind and juice of lemons and blend together with mixer. Pour mixture on top of baked crust that has cooled slightly. Bake an additional 20 minutes in a 350-degree oven. Cool and sprinkle powdered sugar on top. (Freeze to cut, if necessary.)

TEACAKES

This is an old family recipe of Charlotte Peters' mother-in-law. Charlotte graciously agreed to share it with us. Charlotte loves to make these teacakes because you mix the batter by hand, which makes it quick and easy! I can vouch for these—they are wonderful.

1 cup shortening	3 tsps. baking powder
1 cup + 2 Tbsps. sugar	1/4 tsp. salt
2 eggs, beaten	1 tsp. vanilla
2 cups all-purpose flour	

Use a metal bowl and mix by hand; do not use electric mixer. Cream shortening with sugar and beaten eggs. Add flour, baking powder, salt, and vanilla; mix well. Coating your hands with flour, pinch off dough just like you were making biscuits. Place on lightly greased cookie sheet and bake in a 350-degree oven for approximately 20 minutes.

FRUIT COOKIES

One week after we moved into our new home, my next door neighbor, Nell Kyle, dropped by with a plateful of melt-in-your-mouth fruit cookies. It didn't take us long to gobble up these irresistible goodies. They keep beautifully in an airtight container.

3 eggs	1/8 lb. candied cherries
1 ¼ cups sugar	1/2 tsp. baking soda
1 qt. nuts, coarsely chopped	1 oz. pure lemon extract
1 ½ boxes dates, chopped	1/2 lb. butter or margarine,
2 cups flour, divided	melted

Mix eggs and sugar; add nuts and fruits that have been dredged in ½ cup flour. Add remaining 1 ½ cup flour, soda and lemon flavoring; blend well. Add melted butter and drop by teaspoonful on lightly greased cookie sheet. Bake in a 250-degree oven for 30-40 minutes.

OLD FASHIONED BUTTER COOKIES

These creamy cookies are from the files of Irma Holcomb Pope, who lives at the Glen Retirement Village with my mom. She and Mother don't bake anymore, but thoughtful family members often whip up a batch and share. Jo Evans, Mrs. Pope's daughter, gave me this recipe.

1 stick butter, softened	2 tsps. soda
1 stick margarine, softened	2 tsps. cream of tarter
1 cup vegetable oil	2 tsps. vanilla
2 cups sugar	1 tsp. lemon flavoring
1/2 tsp. salt	4 ½ cups flour—do not sift
2 eggs	

Beat butter with next four ingredients. Add eggs, soda, cream of tartar, vanilla and lemon flavoring; mix well. Add flour, one cup at a time; mix well. Chill dough for several hours. To bake: Pinch off a small amount about the size of a marble. Roll and press flat with a floured fork. Bake in a 350-degree oven for about 10 minutes, until lightly browned. (When oven becomes very hot, it may take a little less time to bake.) Dough can be kept in refrigerator and cookies baked as needed.

GINGER SNAPS

Who doesn't love ginger snaps? My friend Shannon Dean shared this fabulous recipe. Shannon is the manager of St. Paul's Episcopal Gift Shop and brings them for special occasions, such as the holiday open house. I am so happy Shannon agreed to share her secrets with us.

3/4 cup shortening   1/4 tsp. salt
1 cup sugar   3 tsps. soda
4 Tbsps. molasses   1 tsp. cinnamon
1 egg   1 tsp. ginger
2 cups flour   1/2 tsp. ground cloves

Cream shortening, sugar, molasses, and egg; add remaining ingredients. Roll into small balls, then roll in additional sugar. Bake in a 350-degree oven for 9 to 11 minutes. They will be soft, but have cracks on top. Yield: 4 dozen cookies

DECADENT CHOCOLATE COOKIE

This moist chocolate cookie represents comfort to me, for my Mom made a similar version when I was small. I did not drink milk, and I envied my brother, as I watched him dunk that delectable morsel into his ice cold milk. These are every bit as rich as brownies, but keep longer when properly stored.

2 pkgs. (16 squares) semi-sweet   1 tsp. vanilla
  baking chocolate, divided   1/2 cup flour
3/4 cup firmly packed brown sugar   1/4 tsp. baking powder
1/4 cup butter   2 cups chopped pecans or walnuts,
2 eggs   optional

Coarsely chop 8 squares chocolate; set aside. Microwave remaining 8 squares chocolate in a large microwavable bowl on high for 1-2 minutes. Stir until chocolate is melted and smooth. Add sugar, butter, eggs and vanilla. Stir in flour and baking powder. Add reserved chopped chocolate and nuts. Drop by 1/4 cupfuls onto a lightly sprayed cookie sheet. Bake in a 350-degree oven for 12-13 minutes or until cookies are puffed and set. Transfer to a wire rack to cool completely.

AFTER SCHOOL COOKIES

My friend, Martie Powell, has many special memories of her mother's gentle influence. One special memory was when Martie had an especially great day, her Mom would say, "You are having a three-cookie day". Her dear mother passed on some great old family cookie recipes, two of which Martie has graciously shared.

1 cup granulated sugar	1 tsp. baking soda
1 cup dark brown sugar	1/2 tsp. ginger
1 cup shortening	1 tsp. cinnamon
1 tsp. vanilla	one pinch nutmeg
2 eggs, well beaten	3 cups oatmeal
1 ½ cups flour	3/4 cup chopped raisins
1 tsp. salt	1/2 cup chopped pecans

Cream together granulated sugar, dark brown sugar and shortening; add vanilla and eggs and set aside. Sift together flour, salt, soda, ginger, cinnamon and nutmeg; add to creamed mixture. Blend in oatmeal, raisins and pecans. Using a teaspoon, drop dough on an ungreased baking sheet. Bake in a 350-degree oven for 10-15 minutes.

PEANUT BUTTER COOKIES

1 cup crunchy peanut butter	2 eggs
1 cup butter or margarine	1 tsp. vanilla
1 cup granulated sugar	2 cups sifted flour
1 cup firmly packed light	1 tsp. baking soda
brown sugar	

Cream together peanut butter and butter; add granulated sugar and brown sugar. Beat eggs and add vanilla. Add to creamed mixture and beat until light and fluffy. Sift flour and soda; gradually add to creamed mixture. Form into 1-inch balls. Place 2 inches apart on an ungreased cookie sheet. With fork, make a criss-cross design to flatten cookies. Bake in a 350-degree oven for 18-20 minutes or until light brown around the edges.

SARA'S MERINGUE KISSES

These melt-in-your-mouth kisses are a repeat from my first cookbook by popular demand—from my granddaughter Sara Grace. I taught Sara to make these when she was about nine years old and she became a master at it right away. There's something I must explain: these light and airy little puffs are not the most cooperative sweets to prepare, for they are temperamental when it comes to damp weather. They simply don't want to "stand up" and become kisses! Well, it seems Sara Grace has had no such problems, because she has had success in every kind of weather, and under all circumstances. For a class project, Sara recently held a cooking class on Meringue Kisses for five classmates while her mother videotaped it. What a precious little cook she is—professional all the way! Next thing I know, the kid is going to have her own cooking show on television. She could handle it.

2 egg whites	1 tsp. vanilla
1/4 tsp. salt	1 cup chocolate chips
1 cup sugar	1 cup finely chopped pecans

Preheat oven to 350 degrees. Beat egg whites with salt until stiff. Slowly beat in sugar. Continue beating until very stiff; fold in vanilla, chocolate chips and nuts. With a teaspoon, drop batter on lightly greased cookie sheets in small amounts. When ready to put in the oven, turn oven off. Place cookie sheets in oven, close oven door, and leave in oven overnight or for at least 6-8 hours. Remove from cookie sheet and store in airtight container.
Yield: 4-5 dozen

Tip: Sara often puts a drop of food coloring to add color to the kisses. If you are making these kisses for gifts or party trays and want them snowy white, use white vanilla; also be sure that oven burner is off when you put them in. They brown very easily if oven is too hot. I once had to sacrifice and eat all the brown ones that could not be used for party trays. It was a tough job, but someone had to do it!

Tip: Meringue Kisses are also delicious with butterscotch substituted for chocolate. They make beautiful party trays when you want dessert that is not messy.

Memories

Continuing with the focus on tradition, I am again sharing special memories with pictures of the people I hold most dear—both family and friends.

When I wrote my original cookbook, my intent was to share all the noteworthy recipes I had accumulated through the years. The memory chapter was included for the enjoyment of my family and friends. Never in my wildest dreams did I imagine that others would also take pleasure in my walk down memory lane.

What can I say about my wonderful family? They are responsible adults with incredible children of their own. Our eight grandchildren are a source of pride every time they excel in their own special endeavors, whether in sports, cheerleading, music or simply preparing a family meal. They are beloved everyday of their lives.

I'm proud the grandkids are showing an interest in cooking. Seventeen-year-old Jill has loved the kitchen ever since she "bellied up" to the chopping board at Occasions Catering. She's famous for her innovative salads. When Carol Ann and Sara visit each summer, they prepare a special birthday dinner for Papaw's birthday, complete with decadent chocolate chip cake. Sara is a "hands-on" cook who has no problem stuffing the roast with garlic, a feat which Carol Ann finds "disgusting." Courtney, who lives in Seattle, enjoys our traditional South Louisiana cuisine when she visits—she and her Mom cannot get enough of it.

As for the boys, oldest grandson Justin recently prepared a delicious meal of chicken cacciatore, which earned rave reviews. Adam, Alec and Tripp haven't made their debut in the kitchen, however, they love anything made by their Mamaw—especially chicken and dumplings, gumbo and breakfast specialties.

To all my family I would like to say "thank you" for a wealth of memories—both the fun and the serious. You have made me proud every day of my life and I love you.

My Family

Mom & Dad - 1957

Scotty, Dad & Me

Mom - 1995
88-years-old

Dad - 1906-1963

Louise & Ed - 1942

Ed's Memories

John R. Monette
1909-1949

Louise & Ed - 1980

Family

Scotty & Ladye White - Cruise 2000

Cousins: Deryl, Wanda & Me
2004

Johnny Hamilton
1974-1998

The Hamiltons: L'Shele, Johnny
John & Deryl - 1988

The Parkers: Hayley, Billy,
Bill & Bobbi

Mia & Billy Parker

MeMe & Danny - 1986

Mama & Me - 1990

The Merry Widows
Mom & Her Sisters - 1968
Verdith, Lena, Meryl & Mom

Tripp & MeMe - 2002

MeMe with Adam & Deb

Justin & MeMe

MeMe & Family

New Orleans Cousins - Aimee, Greg, Alice,
Mignon (MiMi) and William Nothacker

MeMe & Me with
Donna, Lee & Jill - 2004

Danny & Family with MeMe
Easter 2005

Dr. Mignon Jumel, Alice Nothacker
& MiMi Jumel Nothacker

MeMe & Scotty - 2000

Me, Donna, MeMe & Aunt Vu

Kids & Grandkids

Partying ... Ed & Me

Kids ... Deb, Danny & Donna

LSU Tailgating ... Ed & Danny

My girls & me - 2004

LSU festivities
Ed & Me

Seattle ... Ed, Susan & Courtney

Kids & Grandkids

Justin, Carol Ann & Adam

Our 25th Anniversary Celebration

Jill & Papaw - 2005

Papaw & Jill - 1990

Sara, Randy & Adam

Courtney in Concert

Kids & Grandkids

Mamaw & Adam - 18 mos.

Jill's Homecoming - 2005

Tripp & Nanny

Alec & Dad - Easter 2005

Justin & Carol Ann

Carol Ann, Alec & Mom
Bacchus '05

Kids & Grandkids

Carol Ann, Sara & Mamaw - 2004

Courtney & Mamaw
Making handprint cookies

Tripp - 2005 Slugger

Sara & Tripp in Colorado

Jill & Alec - 1990

Jill & Alec - 2005

Fralix Family

Adam & Justin "Cool Dudes!"

Randy & Deb - Holland '05

Adam & Justin
Graduation '04

Randy, Adam, Justin & Deb
Adam's Graduation '04
Bangkok, Thailand

Justin & Adam in Koh Samui,
Thailand

Justin - 5 years old
Adam - 2 years old

Duplichan Family

Lee, Jill, Donna - Homecoming 2005

Jill
Homecoming Queen 2005

Jill - Kindergarten

Happy Baby!

Donna, Jill & Lee

Dancer Jill

Daniel Family

Danny & Carol Bacchus 2005

Carol, Sara & Margie Sutton
"Granny"

Carol Ann & Alec

Carol Ann & Alec

Sara & Tripp

Tripp & Sara

Czarnecki Family

Michael & Susan - 1987

Courtney - France 2005

*Our Fairy Courtney
3 years old*

*The Czarnecki's
Australian Outback 2005*

Susan & Courtney - 18 mos.

Family dining in Australia

Friends: New & Old

Sylvia Norton, Sous Chef
Enjoying a cooking class

My "Lil Sis" Susan Nance
Occasions Catering

Longtime buddies
Me, Ann May & Margaret Buccola

Mary Rademacher
Queen of book signings

Mark & Kelly Schnaildre
Best crawfish cooks in Louisiana!

My cooking friend
Irma Bunkem
Occasions Catering

Friends

Ed, Sarah & Dick Harrison ...
We stirred many a pot!

Bob & Mary Rademacher
Me & Ed Partying!

Doug Daniel, Debbie & Flo
Daniel Aiken ... Old ties!

Sue & Fielder Calhoun ...
Enjoying brunch

La Muriel & Henry Paulsen
The best of friends

Jerry & Nadine Arbaugh
... old times!

Friends: New & Old

A circle of friends ...
Mary Rademacher, Shannon Dean, Me, Dot
Hensley, Beverly Pierce & Fran McRae.

Making memories with Myrna
Cooper

Gary & Dodie Smith
enjoying Mardi Gras

Jane Barnett & Me
Memories of South Louisiana!

Very special folks ...
Linda & Sammy Pedro

Ann & J.T. May enjoying brunch

Friends: New & Old

Friends forever ... Sylvia Bergeron

Dawn Wallwork cooking with Ed

*The Turners - Harold & Helen
Thanksgiving*

Our Nel Chavanne

*We were special ...
Nadine Arbaugh- me-Ann Worley*

*Doris Young
Hostess with the "Mostest"*

*Margaret & Emile Buccola ...
bountiful memories*

Visions of Sugar Plums...

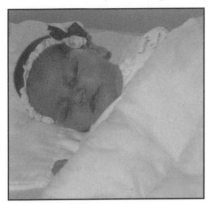

Courtney ... our angel!

Adam & Uncle Lee ... pooped out!

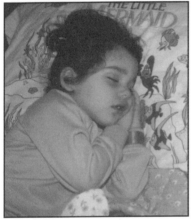

Jill ... all snuggled

Deb & Justin ... Heaven!

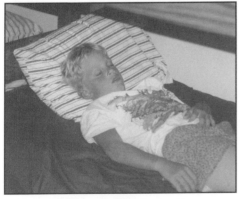

Alec ... all fished out!

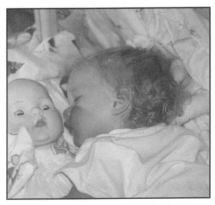

Carol Ann and her baby!

Alec & Sara ... new baby sister

Carol & Carol Ann ... a day of fishing

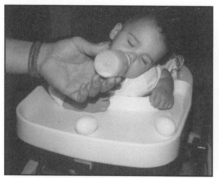

Jill ... a little help

*Sara & Tripp —
It was a big day!*

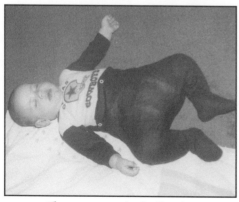

Justin ... our little Cowboy

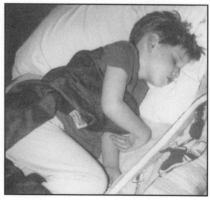

Adam ... All tuckered out

A very special wedding ...
Tom & Paula Chavanne
June 26, 2004

Tom & Paula

Caitlin, Tom, Colby, Paula
& Drake

Front Row: Carly Braswell, Caitlin Chavanne, Taylor Chavanne
Back Row: Robert, Alexa & Shelley Braswell; Tom, Charlie &
Danna Chavanne

Index

Appetizers

Soups

Salads

Meats

Seafood

Veggies/Sides

Breakfast/Brunch/Breads

Beyond Our Borders

Sweets

ORDER BLANK

To Order "So Good...Make You Slap Your Mama — **Volume I**
Please fill out the form below and return it with your check to:

Marlyn Monette — 165 Vidor Lane — Shreveport, LA 71105

Please send _____ copies . . . . @ $16.95 each _____

($4.00 for 1 book; add $2.00 for each additional book)   Shipping _____

(Louisiana 8.6%)   Sales Tax _____

Total _____

Ship to: _____

Your Name: _____

Address: _____

City: _____ State: _____ Zip: _____

Make Checks payable to: Marlyn Monette
Telephone: 318-868-5804 — email: marlynm4@comcast.net

For personalization: Please print name of recipient _____

ORDER BLANK

To Order "So Good...Make You Slap Your Mama — **Volume II**
Please fill out the form below and return it with your check to:

Marlyn Monette — 165 Vidor Lane — Shreveport, LA 71105

Please send _____ copies . . . . @ $19.95 each _____

($4.50 for 1 book; add $2.00 for each additional book)   Shipping _____

(Louisiana 8.6%)   Sales Tax _____

Total _____

Ship to: _____

Your Name: _____

Address: _____

City: _____ State: _____ Zip:_____

Make Checks payable to: Marlyn Monette
Telephone: 318-868-5804 — email: marlynm4@comcast.net

For personalization: Please print name of recipient _____